French verse-art ·

French verse-art
A study

CLIVE SCOTT

CAMBRIDGE UNIVERSITY PRESS

CAMBRIDGE

LONDON   NEW YORK   NEW ROCHELLE

MELBOURNE   SYDNEY

Published by the Press Syndicate of the University of Cambridge
The Pitt Building, Trumpington Street, Cambridge CB2 1RP
32 East 57th Street, New York, NY 10022, USA
296 Beaconsfield Parade, Middle Park, Melbourne 3206, Australia

© Cambridge University Press 1980

First published 1980

Phototypeset in V.I.P. Bembo by
Western Printing Services Ltd, Bristol

Printed in Great Britain
at the University Press, Cambridge

Library of Congress Cataloguing in Publication Data

Scott, Clive, 1943–
French verse-art.

Bibliography: p.
1. French language – Versification. 2. English
language – Versification. I. Title.
PC2511.S3   426   79–50508

ISBN 0 521 22689 9

CONTENTS

PREFATORY REMARKS

This book is something of a strange beast. It is a compound of manual-like information and of critical analysis which often shades into the fanciful; it proposes to arrive at a trustworthy and unambiguous terminology and yet assumes that metaphor is essential to the interpretative application of that terminology; it invites belief in its reliability as a source of one kind of knowledge (the mechanics of prosody) and yet as the source of another kind of knowledge (the understanding of any poetic instance), it calls for scepticism.

This is perhaps not so surprising. We need a terminology, and a pretty complex one at that, if our attention is ever to be directed to the 'sensitive' verse-details, and if we are ever to understand the poem as a *total* system of formal demands – it is not far-fetched to suggest that a poem *can* only be rationalised and explained in terms of the formal demands it makes upon itself. But even though the identification of verse-detail can become a disciplined act, there is no procedural structure for the transformation of verse-detail into meaning. The magician's wand remains the only resource, a magician's wand of intuition, ingenuity, constructive metaphorical thinking.

But if interpretation is still a leap in the dark, that leap cannot be made without the springboard of a steady, fully articulated body of descriptive terms. And it is in this area that English discourse on French verse has too often been misleading. The continuing cardinal sin is the application of the terminology of English scansion (usually classical foot-prosody) to a verse-system which the terminology can only disfigure. In his *French for Sixth Forms: An Introduction*

to *Advanced Level Studies* (1960), for example, F. W. Moss
asserts: 'In French, all feet contain two syllables, theoreti-
cally of equal length' and goes on to say: 'Pentameter is
unusual in French poetry; but hexameter (six feet, twelve
syllables and known as the alexandrine) is common (p. 27).'
The line scanned as an instance of this six-footed hexameter
– 'Jamais nous ne goûtons de parfaite allégresse' – has,
as will become evident in the ensuing pages, only four
measures, which create the syllabic groups 2+4+3+3.

Words such as 'metre' and 'foot', when applied to French
lines, are bound to mislead, since they have their origins in
prosodies – Greek and Latin – which have little relevance to
our grasp of the rhythmic structures of modern languages.
'Metre' is particularly treacherous, because its English
usage is already ambiguous. It describes not only a stress
pattern (iambic, trochaic, etc., that is, the recurrent rhythmic unit); not only different total metric systems (syllabic
metre, pure-stress metre, etc.); but also, and in a syllabically unspecific way, line length (trimeter, pentameter,
etc.). In this last application, '-meter' does not indicate the
underlying rhythmic pulse, but an undefined rhythmic
group, a 'measure', and it is 'measure' that we shall find best
suited to describe the French unit of rhythm. Comments
such as that made by J. A. Hiddleston in his introduction to
Laforgue's *Poems* (1975) – 'Also one is surprised at the
regular Alexandrines and seven, eight and ten metre lines'
(p. 39) – can only beget fundamental misconceptions.

But it is not the English alone who are to blame for the
misapprehensions of the English. The French, too, have
confirmed us in our errors by clinging to the terminology of
the Ancients. Verlaine, for example, writes in one of his
epigrams:

J'ai fait un vers de dix-sept pieds!

He means by 'pieds' 'syllables'; for most English readers, a
foot is a rhythmic unit very rarely involving less than two
syllables.

In order to highlight and explain this need for a radical

differentiation between the terminologies used to describe English verse on the one hand and French verse on the other, and to make allowances for the inbred habits of the English reader, I have used, as my point of departure, the metrical scansion of English verse. It might well be argued that in so doing I am in turn supplying a misleading picture of English scansion. Many would claim that classical foot-prosody is in the process of being superseded by the new orientations of linguistics, which, with the aid of instru-mental data derived from the analysis of recitation and with a concern for the *syntactic* make-up of the verse-line, have directed attention to dynamic features which transcend the foot, namely phrasal stress patterning, variations of pitch and intonation, differing durations and junctures in the larger configurations of utterance. Several French verse-analysts have been exploring similar territory; Henri Morier at Geneva, Monique Parent at Strasbourg, Georges Faure at Aix, have, on the evidence of recitation data, cast doubt on assumptions about the duration of syllables, the nature of ictus (accent), in short, on the regularity of socalled regular verse.

But we should also heed Seymour Chatman's words, in his influential *A Theory of Meter* (1965): 'Actually it is by no means inevitable that the use of linguistic method will disturb all our traditional ideas about English meter; if anything, it strengthens many of them by providing a stronger empirical proof for the judgements of generations of metrists' (pp. 9–10). And we should add the following: there is no evidence that traditional metrical scansion is any less indispensable than it was as one kind, if not the central kind, of prosodic investigation, however much it is com-plemented and qualified by other kinds; and if the notion of a prosodic tradition (which in most instances will be a syllable-stress tradition) is to have any force at all, if we are to benefit from our knowledge that poets have intentionally located themselves in that tradition, then we must keep some faith with it. Many would argue, myself among them, that a fundamental distinction must be made between the informing rhythm (in French verse, the pattern of line-lengths and thus of rhythmic potentialities governing the poem; in English verse, the metre); scansion (the examination of particular lines in the light of the informing rhythm); and recitation (the realisation of particular lines in utterance) – later we shall find ourselves wishing to differentiate also between recitation and pronunciation. They would also point out that such informing rhythms are never more than notional, the lowest common denominator of all possible readings. This line of argument would also draw attention to the many 'paralinguistic' features – features which are not part of the language *system* – which occur in recitation (secondary tonal patterns, speed, emotional colouring) and would suggest that these are irrelevant to scansion. Of all this we shall have more to say, but the general position is concisely formulated by Roger Fowler (1971): 'It seems necessary and practical to assert and preserve the independence of metre from the realization of a poem in oral form' (p. 172).

What I wish to do in this book is to introduce the student of French verse to the fundamental principles and terminology of that verse. Simplification will be inevitable. My treatment of terminology will not be exhaustive – though it should satisfy most practical purposes – nor will it be historical; that is to say, it will not meddle much in the convoluted categories established by Medieval and Renaissance verse-analysts, because this book is not so much concerned to *establish* a terminology as to show how terminology helps in the understanding of poets and movements, poems and genres. Indeed, I shall refer to the early period of French poetry only sparingly, and draw the greater part of my material from later centuries, and from the latter part of the nineteenth century in particular; I must plead that familiarity justifies this partisanship. And having installed English verse in the first chapter, I continue to call on it intermittently thereafter, where it seems appropriate, and return to it at greater length in the final chapter, on free verse.

The plight of French verse in our schools and universities is a sorry one. This may be in part ascribed to a general lack of interest in poetry compared with the large followings commanded by the novel and drama. But it is also to be explained in part, I am sure, by a simple lack of confidence in the handling of the technicalities of verse. It is difficult to perceive, yet alone talk about, a verse-detail you cannot identify; but knowledge of these technicalities is quickly mastered and we are thereby liberated into more satisfying interpretations. Like the writing of verse, the reading of verse is a rigorous *discipline*, and pleasure in the text is proportional to one's willingness to participate in that discipline; verse is verse before it is anything else, and it is important that it should be seen to be so.

Finally, I would like to express my deep gratitude to those who have helped me into the intricacies of verse-structure and poetic language, who have nudged me into a realisation of my errors – some of which, no doubt, stubbornly persist – who have made me think harder and revealed to me subtleties I did not suspect. I think particularly of the exhilarating guidance of Annie Barnes, the ready help and indispensable suggestions of Michael Black, and of absorbing conversations with Malcolm Bowie, Roger Fowler, the late Will Moore, Siegbert Prawer and David Scott.

I

The line (1)

(i) *English metrics and the business of scansion*
(a) *The foot.* In the scansion of English regular verse,
we customarily distinguish between three kinds of metre:
(a) syllabic metre, where the number of syllables in the line
is the principle of regularity and where the number of
stresses per line, though rhythmically important, has no
part in the definition of the metre; (b) pure-stress metre,
which is essentially the reverse of syllabic, in that the
number of stresses per line alone defines the metre, regardless of the number of accompanying unstressed syllables; (c)
syllable-stress metre, in which the metre is defined by the
number of stresses per line and by their ratio and relationship to intervening unstressed syllables. It is the recurrence
of a consistent ratio and relationship which creates the
rhythm of the line, and the ratio and relationship of each
stressed syllable to its adjacent unstressed syllable(s) define
themselves as the foot; the foot is thus a *metrically* (as
opposed to rhythmically) constitutive unit *only* in syllable-
stress metre; we may use foot-references to define the rhythmic composition of lines of syllabic and pure-stress metre,
but they cannot be used to describe the metres themselves.

About these metres, we can make the following loose
generalisations. Syllabic metre, given the as yet uneducated
response of the English ear to the syllable (of which we shall
have more to say) seems to be the least indigenous of the
metres, though it has been practised by many reputable
poets in this century (Marianne Moore, Auden, Thom
Gunn, George MacBeth) and does have the attraction of
rhythmic freedom. Pure-stress metre is the earliest of our
metres and the one to which the language, many would

argue, is best attuned; it is a metre, like the syllabic, which can mould itself to the 'natural' rhythms of ordinary speech, but which, too, allows for syllabic insensitivity; it is the metre of medieval alliterative verse, of Gerard Manley Hopkins, of the later Eliot. But the majority of the verse of the four centuries from the sixteenth to the nineteenth invites a syllable-stress scansion, the most sophisticated of the traditional scansions, the scansion best able to monitor, step by step, the line's intimate rhythmic being. The principal feet are: dissyllabic – iamb (ᴗ /), trochee (/ ᴗ), and the purely substitute feet, spondee (/ /) and pyrrhic (ᴗ ᴗ); trisyllabic – anapaest (ᴗ ᴗ /), dactyl (/ ᴗ ᴗ), amphibrach (ᴗ / ᴗ), amphimacer (/ ᴗ /); tetrasyllabic – ionic (ᴗ ᴗ / /), choriamb (/ ᴗ ᴗ /). If one had to approximate French rhythms to any of the metres mentioned, then it would be to the one which we have called the 'least indigenous', namely syllabic metre.

Philip Larkin's poem about the apprehensions of the sedentary townsman beset by the intrusions and sudden desertions of travellers, 'Arrivals, Departures' (*The Less Deceived*, 1955), plants us, with its first stanza, in the reassuring world of iambic pentameters – lines of five iambs, with or without extra feminine (unstressed) final syllables. No metric world could be more English; it is the world of our dramatic verse, of grand satirical verse, of topographical verse, of epic and narrative verse, and of much else beside. It is not surprising, in a metre so persistent, to find infinite variety; indeed, it is not surprising that persistence should have been made possible by variety. And Larkin's second stanza gives us some notion of the pentameter's resilience, as well as of the waking poet's inner turmoil:

> Ănd wé, bárelў rĕcálled frŏm ṣléep thĕre, sénse
> Ắrrivăls lówĭng ĭn ă dóleful distănce –
> Hórnў dĭlémmăs ăt thĕ gáte ŏnce móre.
> *Cóme ănd chŏose wróng, thĕy crý, cóme ănd chŏose
>   wróng;*
> Ănd só wĕ rise. Ắt night ăgáin thĕy sóund.

The inverted second foot of the first line (/ ᴗ) syncopates the rhythm and brings the jolt of awaking; the third-foot pyrrhic (∪ ∪) of the second line helps to push the alliterating 'doleful distance' into relief, reinforcing and lengthening the stressed syllable of 'doleful'; the inverted first foot and pyrrhic third of the third line suggest, perhaps, first the abrupt inescapability of dilemma, and then the interval as the mind tries to grasp the truth. All these substitutions extend the basic pentameter's expressive range and make the existence of iambic a recurrent act of affirmation, not to be taken for granted, a recurrent resolution of complexity rather than restoration of uniformity. And in the fourth line, the single iambic foot ('thĕy crý') is a kind of irrelevance; the direct-speech challenges belong on their own, as a separate extended foot repeated, a choriamb (/∪ ∪/) if we care to give it a name. The vestigial iambic is recovered unequivocally only in the fifth line.

Two factors here already distinguish English verse from French verse, as will become apparent later in the chapter. First, however often the iambic is interrupted, its basic principle, its driving force, is continuity, repetition in sequence. Secondly, the iambic is established and maintained by the inherent stress-patterns of English words. English words make certain inevitable stress demands. In most monosyllables, stress demand is determined by grammatical status; in dissyllables, by distinctions between radical and prefix or suffix. 'Horny', in any verse context, requires to be, in itself, trochaic (/ ∪); in the Larkin example, it does indeed, as an inverted iamb, constitute a trochee; but it may find itself contributing to any number of different feet:

> thĕ hórnў wárs ŏf bygŏne dáys (iambic)
>
> ăt thĕ hórnў rĕquést ŏf thĕ hórnў búll (anapaestic)
>
> hórnў thĕ béast, hórnў thĕ mán, hórnў thĕ béast ĭn mán (choriambic)

'Horny', while itself remaining firmly trochaic, is transmuted as a *constituent* of different rhythmic continuums.

Many modern verse-analysts would argue that the foot is

an obsolete concept; that it belonged to a Classical quantita-
tive metric which has little to do with modern English; that
feet tend to acquire dangerously independent existences and
are never thought of properly, as related parts of a whole;
that they make a nonsense of the 'natural' linguistic structures – word-groups or speech-units – of which poetry is
made, and poetry is made of language before it is made of
anything else. The foot-boundary which falls within a word
(as in 'Ărrí/văls' or 'dĭlém/măs') is a fruitless fiction,
because it has nothing to do with any real speech division,
pause or juncture. A truer record of the lines by Larkin
might thus read:

> And we,/barely recalled/from sleep there,/sense
> Arrivals lowing/in a doleful distance –
> Horny dilemmas/at the gate/once more.
> *Come and choose wrong,*/they cry,/*come and choose*
> *wrong*;
> And so we rise./At night again/they sound.

Halle and Keyser's (1971) generative metrics arrives at a
description of the iambic pentameter which has no recourse
to foot or iamb, and which treats variations (like the
inverted foot, the pyrrhic and the choriamb of the Larkin
extract), not as deviations from a norm, but as integral,
inherent features of the norm. This allows Halle and Keyser
to make better sense of the differences between iambic and
trochaic verse and to avoid the arbitrariness of lists of allowable licences. But whatever the advantages of such a system,
we must suppose that any sequence of stresses with a degree
of repetition in it will encourage segmentation, if only
because the unit of repetition needs to be identified. And
even though it is better to think of the pentameter as a range
of possibilities rather than as a rigid pattern with licences
thrown in, it *is* necessary to take the comparative frequency
of the various substitutions into account if they are to be of
any expressive consequence at all to the poet and/or reader.
Furthermore, if the pentameter is to be an organisation of
differently sensitive locations – just as, on a larger scale, we

might want to say that the third line of a four-line stanza is sensitive to structural pressures different from those which act on the fourth line of such a stanza, or on the third line of, say, a five-line stanza – then these locations must be categorised (possibly as first foot, second foot, third foot, etc.), though not at the expense of the line's continuity. And many prosodists would still claim that to observe that one foot-boundary falls within a word while another coincides with a major syntactical break is to make a significant and analytically useful distinction.

A foot-analysis of a line of verse by no means precludes analyses of larger units, of word-groups and speech-units. But these larger units are difficult to classify and often attract a descriptive vocabulary very much like that applied to foot-scansion. There is also a dangerous tendency, in the treatment of larger units, to find rhythmically acceptable anything which approximates to normal speech. A corollary, or indeed a cause, of the rejection of foot-scansion might be the principle enunciated by D. W. Harding (1976): 'the established rhythm of the spoken language is basic and inviolable' (p. 35). But this seems to overlook the fact that the metre of a poem, even when denied or obscured by the requirements of normal speech, remains a valid way of *perceiving* the poem. In other words, metre is a way of perceiving verse which frequently coincides with an acceptable way of speaking the verse, but need not. I am not saying that we perceive a line of verse in a way which is prosodically different from the way we speak it aloud, *as we speak it aloud*. But it is true that much of the controversiality surrounding different scansions derives from some peculiar assumption that the scanner is duty bound to push verse towards a single and definitive existence, which is the *recited* existence of verse. On the contrary, we should seek to wrap lines of verse around our consciousness in as many ways as plausibly possible, as things chanted, mumbled, tried out, whispered, and never feel we should deny ourselves any of them.

Harding (1976) quotes a line from Tennyson's 'Ulysses' in which the nominal metre (iambic) is reversed after the caesura; the line in question is the last in Ulysses's description of his dutiful son, Telemachus:

> Most blameless is he, centred in the sphere
> Of common duties, decent not to fail
> In offices of tenderness, and pay
> Meet adoration to my household gods,
> When I am gone. He works his work, I mine.

Harding scans 'Hé works hís work, Í míne', and notes: 'the natural speech phrasing comes as a perfectly acceptable change of rhythm to end what is in effect a verse paragraph' (p. 36). I would not want to disagree with either the reading or the remark. But I would want to add that the *perception* of the whole line as iambic – thus, 'Hĕ wórks hĭs wórk, Ĭ míne' – provides us with an insight precisely into the *unspoken* sub-thought of Ulysses, an insight which a speaking of the line would have us ignore. Ulysses is making a distinction between Telemachus and himself, for the benefit of the listening crowd, with 'he' and 'his' on the one side and 'I' and 'mine' on the other. But more essentially, and for his own benefit, he is making a distinction between two different conceptions of 'work', on the one hand the dutiful, pedestrian, gradual work of his son, and on the other his own adventurous, questing, grasping kind of work. And the condemnation of his son's 'work' is contained in the heavily pleonastic ring of 'He *works* his *work*'; it is a work whose only achievement is more work, it is work for work's sake, and the unexpressed, but apprehended, iambic stress-pattern underlines the unimaginative futility of it all. Ulysses keeps his own work to himself and does not directly name it; the assonant ī ('*I* m*i*ne') suggests perhaps that his work is indissolubly linked with his heroic identity, that it is an expression of his deepest self, and beyond comprehension for that very reason. Our reading of the line would be incomplete without an awareness of the temporarily abandoned iambic. Recitation promotes natural speech most where natural speech is metrical variation; in this sense recitation may distract the reader from a still active, though inaudible, verse-design. Recitation is only in a very diluted sense an analysis of the poem, and the justifications for such-and-such a recitation are ten times closer to what the process of reading is than the 'reading' they beget. The rhythmic unit of the French line, the 'measure', has not provoked the same disquiet as the foot, simply because it corresponds by and large with natural word-groups and is bounded by syntactic junctures. The qualification 'by and large' is necessary however; there are instances where the measure-boundary (*coupe*) seems as fictitious, as artificial, as unhelpful, as the foot-boundary, precisely when it falls *within* a word; it should also be said that the prosodic demands of the French verse-line frequently do create more junctures or pauses in the syntactic sequence than would be normal in ordinary speech (for example, between a noun and its adjective, a verb and its adverb); conversely they may require the voice to glide over and minimise certain normal junctures.

Finally, we might add that attitudes to foot- and measure-divisions may well be influenced by attitudes to the nature of the central interval division of the line, the caesura. For those who argue that caesuras always coincide with major syntactical junctures – as the English analyst with a moveable caesura at his disposal probably would – foot-divisons which do not also fall at junctures will make a nonsense of the rhythmic hierarchy created by juncture itself. For those who argue that the caesural division will usually occur at a natural syntactical juncture, but need not, and that it will be redundant as an expressive resource if it is compelled to – as the French analyst working within a tradition of a *fixed* medial caesura might – then the measure-division will not attract incredulity if it falls in a syntactically uncomfortable position. That this latter position is offered as a French one is ironic, since French versification is very much geared to self-identifying, natural word-groups; it may indicate a desire to shake off, from

time to time, the imperatives of syntax, to let prosodic
structure make its own suggestions.

(b) *Stress and syllable.* Rhythmically the most stable elements
in English verse are dissyllables. The most volatile elements, the elements which provoke a healthy wavering of
rhythm and recitational rumination, are the 'naturally'
unstressed monosyllables, which nonetheless have stress
potential, and abundant polysyllables. A line like Ernest
Dowson's:

> Áll thăt Ĭ kńow ĭn áll mў mínd shăll nó mŏre háve ă
> pláce

> ('The Sea-Change')

is indeterminate enough to throw itself constantly into
doubt. Might we not scan it alternatively as:

> Ăll thăt Í knów ĭn áll mў mínd shăll nó móre hăve ă
> pláce

or in many other ways? How do we determine these
equivocations? By reference to rhythmic context, by the
plausibility of contrastive accentuation – in the above, 'ăll
thăt Í knów' (as opposed to what you don't) or 'áll thăt Ĭ
knów' (as opposed to some fraction of my knowledge) –
often by word-grouping. In other words, just as, in broader
terms, scansion may need to seek the advice of recitation,
so, more narrowly, the foot may need to seek the advice of
the larger units of syntax. Foot-scansion cannot afford to be
far distant from the word-group, though it will not always
find easy answers. If we look at the Larkin lines again, we
may feel troubled about 'And so we rise'. The dominant
iambic tells us to read 'Ănd só wĕ ríse'; to give the clause its
proper contrastive force, we may feel more inclined to read
'And sŏ *wé* ríse' (as opposed to the travellers). If we try to
resolve this dilemma by juncture and word-group, we
cannot get much further: 'And so / / we rise' ('And so' =
consequently, because we have been challenged to do so by
those arriving) or 'And/so we rise' ('And/so' = in due

course and proper season; people arriving tell us that the
time for getting up has also arrived). Word-groups themselves may be so difficult to define that they deny the foot
the help it seeks. This discussion lets us see that there may be superstructural motives for stress. While words bring their own
stress-patterns to a line, the phrase or line will impose, in its
turn, its stress demands, and these will be either of the
contrastive kind, or derive from pitch-change (the rising
and falling of the voice as it shapes the syntactical units of
the sentence), or will be associated with pause (pauses of
sense, pauses of punctuation, pauses of emphasis, pauses to
lengthen a preceding syllable, or the pauses of the line –
caesura and line-ending – which will often coincide with
sense pauses). And of course these stress demands can rarely
be dissociated one from another, in most instances they are
functions of each other and converge on the same syllable.
To distinguish these superstructural stresses from word-
stresses, and to indicate that they relate to phrasing and
intonation, we call them 'accents'. Accents will either re-
inforce stresses already in existence or they will endow
with stress words which normally make up the unstressed
particles in a line, but which have stress potential.

The other source of metrical ambiguity we have mentioned is the abundant polysyllable. Arthur Symons's poem
about Nini Patte-en-l'Air, 'Intermezzo', is fundamentally a
poem of iambic tetrameters (lines of four iambs); but when
he speaks of:

> The insinuations indiscreet
> Of pirouetting draperies

this pattern is submerged momentarily in the ill-defined
byways of syllabic superfluity. Our confidence in reading
these lines derives not from their being a continuation of a
familiar metre, but from their being of the same basic shape
(though the order adjective + plural noun is reversed in the
first of the lines) and from their both having two un- •
equivocal stresses. In other words, we are treating two lines

temporarily as instances of pure-stress metre (the metre in which the number of stresses in the line, regardless of syllables and feet, is the determining factor). And this tendency will be strengthened by our doubts about elision and, consequently, syllabic values. Do we say 'The insinuations' or 'Th'insinuations', 'draperies' or 'drap'ries'? If we read by the metre (iambic tetrameter), then it would be:

Th'insĭnŭátĭons ĭndĭscrέet
Ŏf pĭrŏuéttĭng drápĕrĭes.

Reading by metre and somewhat against the natural impulse is defensible when the metre compels us to give prominence to words we might overlook as carriers of meaning, when metre reveals to us a new point of view, releases unsuspected designs in language; but it can hardly do this in the upper reaches of polysyllables. English may have an innate tendency towards alternating stresses (see Chomsky and Halle, 1968, pp. 77–9), but where readers perceptually foreground only a word's primary stress, where there is some doubt about the proper syllabification, the metric outline drifts towards indeterminacy; Roger Fowler (1971) puts the case: 'Now polysyllabic words are a particular challenge because, to speak impressionistically, they level out the stress-contrasts and smooth the transitions between syllables. The impact of many polysyllabic words on the verse instance is to soften and relax it (and also speed it up)' (p. 193). What we *can* say here is that the lines do not positively disturb the metre, while they do not affirm it either.

Something similar might be said of French polysyllables, which leave the voice without accentual support for long sequences of syllables (monotonement, majestueusement, plénipotentiaire). The voice responds by introducing its own accentual supports, relay-accents on the antepenultimate syllable of the word (see Chapter 2). But the status of such accents remains problematic and it is not easy to know how consistently they should be identified. Thus the substantial French polysyllable lets the rhythmic frame expand to its limit (hemistich) and in so doing instals moments of rhythmic limbo, abstraction, moments of meditative slackness.

Many would argue that it is in lines such as those from Symons's 'Intermezzo' that traditional scansional methods show their real, and indefensible, coarseness. Traditional scansion seems to leave us with unacceptable alternatives: to say that the lines do not relate properly to the dominant metre, but instead are an isolated instance of pure-stress metre; or, on the other hand, to say that the metre may distort current pronunciation in order to maintain its own unequivocal existence. The argument would continue thus: traditional scansion assumes that all stresses are of equal value, and of equally maximal value at that, just as it assumes that all iambs or trochees or whatever are of the same length, and syllables likewise. The analysis of recitations by oscilloscope or spectrograph demonstrate the falsity of these assumptions. As a first step to making scansional method more sensitive, why not distinguish different degrees of stress and accent, why not adopt George Trager and Henry Smith's (1951) four-stress system (´primary, ^ secondary, ` tertiary, ◡ weakest) and read, for instance:

Th(e) insinuâtions indiscréet
Ŏf piroŭétting drápĕries?

The traditional scanner counter-argues in this fashion:
1. If you are aiming at accuracy and distinguishing between different degrees of stress, why stop at four degrees? Won't any number be as arbitrary as another? Where *do* you stop?
2. If you are aiming at accuracy, aren't you under an obligation to take into account other stress-factors as well – loudness, length, emotional colouring – which no *manageable* set of stress/accent signs can cope with?
3. (a) The very perception of rhythm is a regularising, standardising process. Rhythmic units simply would not be experienced as rhythmic if there was not a high degree of identity between them.

(b) Too much reliance on instrumental evidence, on the analysis of recitation, will blur the distinction between 'scientific' reality and 'psychological' reality, between recitation and reading. The oscilloscope registers all the accidents of the human voice, all the contingencies of a voice *performing* at a particular time in a particular context. A recitation is a poem heard by others, created for others, and the relation between cause and effect much too hazardous. The voice plays to its own specialities, looks to interpose and develop its indispensability. When we read a poem inwardly, we try to realise our total perception of it, as operations of mind and senses, as all modes of utterance. This perception involves our psychological need to discover rhythm (i.e. to regularise), our psychological ability constantly to compensate for inequities, accidents and so on. Even if syllables, stresses, feet, are not scientifically speaking equal, they may be perceived as equal and their effectiveness as rhythmic units may *depend* on their being perceived as equal. Besides, our faculties are hardly as sensitive as scientific machines; scansion is coarse because our conscious faculties are coarse, reducing, simplifying, so that we can quantify and assimilate.

4. A traditional scansion is coarse because it seeks to minimise controversy. Scansion looks for an acceptable *basis* for a reading and for an interpretation. It recognises that in attempting to perceive too much, one is likely to perceive nothing *clearly*. Scansion seeks to create agreement between readers while leaving each reader free to find his own performance, and his own personality in performance.

5. It has been the aim of traditional scansion to mark the occurrence of stress, never to define its strength. To accuse it of not doing what it does not seek to do is an impertinence. It is true that it can *beget* the assumption that all stresses are of equal value, but quite apart from the psychological defensibility of making that assumption, it was never its intention to do so.

These are roughly speaking the two positions which have tended to polarise opinion in modern verse-analysis and, in broad outline, they apply to both English and French versification. In the end, they reduce themselves to this question: is poetry intended to be rationalised as form and structure, or realised as human utterance? Does poetry give most of itself when it is eye-read or when it is recited? Some seem to think that there is an easy answer: 'La poésie prend une valeur beaucoup plus grande lorsqu'elle est dite. C'est une réalité linguistique qui est orale avant d'être écrite, bien qu'elle se transmette par l'écriture' (Monique Parent, 1967, ed. Parent, p. 262). But it isn't just concrete poetry, calligrammatic verse or the kind of typographical ingenuity that goes back to Mallarmé's *Un Coup de dés* (1897) which necessitates a qualification of Parent's view; it is also lyric verse which is multiform, anti-sequential and which expressly seeks to deny the animating human voice ('L'œuvre pure implique la disparition élocutoire du poète' – Mallarmé, *Crise de vers*). Dramatic verse, or narrative verse, particularly the ballad, on the other hand, seem to require the voice categorically. And it may be that for 'verse for speaking' we need a different set of critical criteria from that which we bring to bear on *written* verse. In the former, we may examine the corporate appeal of rhetorical figures, the transparency of the imagery, the sheer speakability of the language, considerations which may be irrelevant to the latter.

There is one further dimension to add to this controversy, namely the case for the relativity of stress. This case runs: yes, lines of verse are made up of many varying degrees of stress, but within the limits of the foot or word, the *weaker* stress(es) is to be rationalised as unstressed and the *stronger* as stressed. That is to say, whether a syllable is stressed or not depends on the relative 'stressedness' of the immediately adjacent syllables. Using the Trager–Smith system, we would want to put 'dĭsĕstáblìsh'; applying the relativity of stress principle, we would say that the first syllable is stressed and the second unstressed because a secondary stress is stronger than weakest; and because the primary stress of the third syllable is greater than either the

weakest, which precedes it, or the tertiary, which succeeds
it, it would deprive the final syllable of the small stress-
value it has by attracting a conventional stress to itself, thus
'disĕstáblĭsh'. Equally, in the Larkin extract, we have discovered in the direct speech a choriambic pattern. But why
not 'Cóme ănd chóose wróng'? Because of the contrastive
principle. 'Choose' may seem to deserve a stress like its
imperative mate 'Come', but it is overshadowed by
'wrong', which is a mocking reversal of what we would
expect to follow an invitation – 'Come along, you can't
lose'. In the event, therefore, we treat two words as equally
unstressed – 'and choose' – when everything seems to point
to the need to differentiate between them. In other verse
contexts, they would, of course, be differentiated.

The assumption of the relativity of stress is very much
what, accidentally perhaps, conventional scansion is con-
structed on. But conventional scansion is not prepared to
take the relativity of stress to its logical conclusion, inasmuch as doing so would seem to deny the possibility of the
so-called 'even' feet, the spondee (/ /) and the pyrrhic (ᴗ ᴗ),
which only ever act as substitute feet in other metres. Again
we should say that whatever the reality, the reading mind
has a special need for these feet and will perceive them if it
wants to; it needs the pyrrhic as an alleviating factor, as a lull
in meaning while relationships between phenomena are
clarified by particles, as a springboard for some densely
stressed material that follows; and it needs the spondee to
cast the mind back to classical metres perhaps, or to give a
special deliberateness to an idea, to solemnise the verse, as in
the final line of Wilfred Owen's iambic 'Hospital Barge at
Cérisy':

> Kíngs pássed ĭn thĕ dárk bárge, whĭch Mérlĭn
> dréamed.

Besides, we cannot allow the choriambic or the ionic or
other extended feet without equally allowing the spondee
and the pyrrhic.

As we have already intimated, the same controversies

beset verse-analysis on the other side of the Channel, though the emphasis is a little different, with as much attention paid to the great unevenness of syllable duration in so-called isosyllabic verse, as to differences of degree and quality in accent. Pierre-Ivan Laroche (1967, ed. Parent, pp. 245–60) gives an oscillographic account of three recitations of Pierre Emmanuel's 'Mes Pas'. I transcribe his findings, omitting terminal pause, for the first two lines (i.e. the first stanza); the rows of numbers underneath each line give the duration in centiseconds of each syllable in each of the three readings; the lines are octosyllabic:

	Mes	pas	si	long/	temps	ont	nei/	gé	Totals
1.	20	*40*	24	24	*25*	6	25	*33*	197
2.	22	*44*	21	26	*38*	13	31	*40*	235
3.	16	*33*	24	25	*30*	16	16	*32*	192

	Sur	ce	pa/	ys	d'im/	mens(e)	at/	tente.	
1.	22	23	25	*26*	17	*30*	26	*35*	204
2.	19	20	23	*25*	19	*34*	16	*54*	210
3.	17	15	19	*21*	19	*32*	12	*51*	186

The italicised centisecond readings mark the principal accents in each line, giving patterns of, for the first, 2+3+3, and for the second, of 4+2+2 (for a fuller explanation of this notational system, see below). If we look at these two lines, certain possibly troubling facts are evident. We need hardly say that the recitations vary in some places more dramatically than in others. What is more surprising is that for each of these speakers the two octosyllables are not of the same duration, and very rarely are any two syllables in the same line of the same length. And if we relate duration to accent-intensity, we may be puzzled to find that in some instances the accentuated syllable is twice as long as the syllable preceding it, or more (e.g. 20/*40*; 16/*54*), and at other times, not significantly different (e.g. 24/*25*; 25/*26*). If we simply asked ourselves what else we would really expect, then I dare say our surprise would disappear, but it is easy to see how the implications of these data, taken to their logical conclusion, might lead one to suppose that there is no such thing as regular verse, and that traditional scansional information is totally misleading. There is no need to repeat the arguments which could be put forward to counter this view. To what we have already said about the reader's natural tendency, if not need, to compensate for inequities, we might add another source of possible compensation, namely the look of the poem. If two lines looked to be of the same length, would we count them as equal even if we could perceive them as unequal aurally? One might also ask the question asked by Mansuy in the discussion which followed Laroche's paper: would the results be the same if one could register a silent, inward reading? Is there in fact any reliable relation between reading aloud to others and reading silently to oneself? And it is not only the difference in duration between syllables and accents that recent analysts have highlighted, but also the existence of secondary accents, non-terminal and non-grammatical, accents of lower degree that makes one want, perhaps, to introduce something like a Trager–Smith notation; of these we shall have more to say in Chapter 2.

(ii) *The essential features of the French line*
    (a) *The syllable.* The length of the English line in standard syllable-stress metre is determined more by the number of feet than by the number of syllables. On the whole, the English are not sensitive to the syllable as a verse-component and we are likely to find iambic pentameters with anything between eight and thirteen syllables in them. And as we have seen with the Symons example, the problems associated with elision have never been satisfactorily resolved. When we meet 'heav'n', for instance, do we assume that the apostrophied e is neither counted nor pronounced, or that it is not counted but may be pronounced? Again, in Byron's line:

All kinds of dress, except the ecclesiastical

(*Beppo*)

we can look to the rest of the stanza to see how many syllables this line *should* have, and what kind of metre. But even
when we discover that it should be iambic pentameter – but
in this particular stanza, twelve-syllable pentameter – it still
does not tell us whether we should say 'the eccles/yastical',
'th'ecclesiastical', or 'the ecclesiastical'. And from this problem we learn that while foot-number is regular, the number
of syllables in the foot and in the line may vary as much as is
consistent with the overall maintenance of the rhythm. We
shall find this order of priorities more or less reversed when
we turn to the French line; we shall find, too, a care for
pronunciation which looks over-punctilious to the English
reader, but without which no syllable-based rhythm can
survive.

The French line is syllabic before it is accentual. That is to
say, its unity is mathematical, and the rhythmic units or
measures resulting from the accents which occur in the line
are significant as fractions of the total number of syllables
the line has. Since the longest *regular* line is of twelve syllables (the alexandrine), since the maximum number of
measures in this line is four, and since no measure is usually
more than six syllables (the half-line or *hemistich* of the
alexandrine), the possible fractional combinations are
limited (3+3+4+2, 2+4+3+3, 4+2+2+4, 1+5+6,
6+3+3, etc.), sufficiently to constitute a recognisable and
circumscribed group of 'working' measures, but not sufficiently to create more than *short-term* expectations in the
reader.

Already we have falsified facts for convenience. We have
begun to suggest that accents are created by number;
accents are, of course, created by language. But given the
customary sizes of measure, to know that one is reading
alexandrines or octosyllables is already to locate oneself in a
certain area of expectations, and to exclude certain possibilities. If we were confronted with octosyllables, for

example, certain combinations of measure would evidently be impossible (6+3, 5+4, 4+5) and others would be more likely than in, say, the alexandrine (3+5, 5+3, 4+4). What we must understand is the centrality of the syllable in French. One syllable more or less means a complete change in the rhythmic structure and balance of the line, and it is only by insisting on syllabic correctness that the French can safeguard the freedoms peculiar to each kind of line. As we shall discover, there are thirty-six basic rhythmic variations of the *regular* alexandrine (that is, the alexandrine with medial caesura and predominantly four measures, the *alexandrin tétramètre*); inadvertently to mix an eleven-syllable or thirteen-syllable line with a series of alexandrines is to make a nonsense of, to render meaningless, the freedom which strict observance of line-lengths bestows. This is the truth that the English reader finds difficult to grasp: that freedom in French verse exists within a system and can only be enjoyed if that system is conscientiously adhered to; or, to put it another way, rigour is, in French verse, a *condition* of freedom. It is only in the light of this fact that we can understand a critic like Robert Champigny (1963) who wonders why free verse is necessary in French: 'Au fond, le moule le plus "libre", celui qui permet sans dommage la plus grande variété dans l'arrangement des mesures, c'est peut-être bien la séquence d'alexandrins qui le fournit' (p. 61).

Thus, while the odd syllable more or less will probably not make much difference in English rhythms, French verse depends for its very existence on agreement about pronunciation. And let us here distinguish between pronunciation and recitation, for the one is the concern of scansion and the other is the concern of performance. To ask how many syllables a word has for rhythmic purposes is not the same as asking how a reader would say a word, with all the concomitant factors of length, loudness and tone. In order to agree about pronunciation, one must necessarily draw up rules, because pronunciation is in a state of constant evolution and is subject to any number of regional variations. Inevitably the rules fall behind the facts, become increasingly arbitrary, and must either be adjusted, abandoned, or accepted as a set of conventions peculiar to verse. To cover every eventuality, the legislator must multiply rules, and in so doing, he multiplies areas of controversy. Messiness is inevitable, and we must attempt to minimise it by concentrating on essentials.

1. The e mute, often called the *e caduc* or the *e atone* by those who feel that these latter appellations more accurately reflect the phonetic instability of this e, is a traditional point at issue. These are the main rules of practice:

(a) The mute ending of a line (usually a feminine rhyme – see Chapter 4) is never counted for scansional purposes.

(b) A final *e atone* within the line, when it is not followed by mute -s or -nt endings, is elided, and thus not counted, before a following initial vowel or mute h. Thus:

Reconnais-tu le Templ(e) au péristyl(e) immense
1 2 3   4 5 6   7   8 9 10   11   12
(Nerval, 'Delfica')

Tout par ce coupl(e) heureux fut lors mis en usage.
1   2 3 4   5 6   7 8   9 10 11 12
(La Fontaine, 'Vénus et Adonis')

(c) But a final *e atone* within the line, when followed by an -s or -nt ending, or by an initial consonant or aspirate h, is counted. Thus:

Apprends-moi de quel ton, dans ta bouche hardie,
1   2   3 4   5 6   7   8 9   10 11 12
Parlait la vérité, ta seule passion.
1 2   3   4 5 6   7   8   9 10 11 12
(Musset, 'Une Soirée perdue')

But if the *e atone* is counted, is it pronounced? This, too, is an ongoing controversy. Many free-verse poets argue that it is no longer currently pronounced and should be ignored or treated as a pause. But if one could agree with this, would it

mean having one rule for classical regular verse and one for
modern verse? Can one simply say that the rules governing,
and which for centuries have governed, regular verse are a
nonsense? A German commentator on French verse,
Theodor Elwert (1965), is in no doubt how to answer: 'Si on
veut lire correctement les vers français et leur garder leur
caractère de vers, il faut sans aucun doute prononcer l'*e caduc*
à l'intérieur du vers' (p. 56). It is certainly difficult not to
sound it in cases of liaison –

> Les brèves voluptés/et les hain*es a*mères
>   I   2 3   4.5 6 7 8 9 1011 12
>   (Leconte de Lisle, 'Maya')

– between identical consonants or after two or more preceding consonants, as below:

> L'homm(e) i*vre* d'un(e) om*bre* qui passe
>   I   2 3 4   5   6 7 8
> Por*te t*oujours le châtiment
> I 2 3 4   5 67 8
> D'avoir voulu changer de place.
> I 2   3 4 5 6 7 8
>   (Baudelaire, 'Les Hiboux')

And it can be argued that the sounded *e atone* has given the
French line its peculiar suppleness, its fluid continuity, and
has contributed to the variety of syllabic definition (we shall
perhaps see this more clearly when we come to deal with the
césure enjambante and the *coupe enjambante* in Chapter 2).

    (d) Within the body of words, e's are counted after con-
        sonants (sinistre ment), but after a vowel are neither
        pronounced nor counted. Thus in Musset's 'La
        Nuit de mai', we meet the lines:

> Crie*r*ons-nous à Tarquin: "Il est temps, voici
> I 2   3   4 5 6   7 8   9   10 11
> l'ombre!"?
> 12
> and:

Clouerons-nous au poteau d'une satir(e) altière
  1   2   3   4   5 6   7 8 910 11 12
Le nom sept fois vendu d'un pâle pamphlétaire?
  1 2   3   4   5 6   7   8 9 10   1112
But of course we still say:
Chanterons-nous l'espoir, la tristess(e) ou la jóie?
  1 2 3   4   5 6   7 8 9   10 11 12

Equally 'avouerai-je' constitutes four syllables, just
as 'gaiement' and 'paiement' constitute two, and
'remerciement' four. Poets with consciences troubled on this score could resort to the acceptable
licence of alternative spelling – 'remercîment', 'fîrai',
'paîment', etc.

(e) But a word *ending* with an *e atone* after a vowel or
combination of vowels should only occur at the end
of the line, unless the *e atone* is elided before a following vowel or mute h. So there is an inconsistency
between the way the vowel + *e atone* is treated within a word and the way it is treated at the end of a
word. This cuts out of use within the line all plural
forms of words with vowel + *e atone* terminals,
because the plural s prevents elision (vies, aimées,
rues) and all verbal forms in -ent or –es where these
endings are preceded by a vowel, again because elision cannot take place. The only exceptions to this
rule are the -aient endings of the imperfect and conditional, and the subjunctive forms 'aient' and 'soient'
which can be used within the line and count as one
syllable only (while the second person singular present subjunctive of 'avoir', 'aies', is allowed only at the
end of the line) (see also the note on these exceptions
in Chapter 4, Section (ii)).

This makes things seem peremptorily cut-and-dried and
peremptorily impoverished. It is Malherbe's attempt to
regularise practice and to resolve another inconsistency:
every terminal *e atone*, whether following a vowel or not,
should be treated the same, but to sound the final *e atone*

after a vowel would involve an even greater disfigurement
of pronunciation than occurs with other terminal e's, and
would also produce an awkward hiatus (see Chapter 3). But
we must still be prepared to meet extremely varied treat-
ments of the vowel + *e atone*. In the seventeenth century, for
example, we shall find Molière breaking the 'rule' from
time to time and reverting to practice more reminiscent of
the sixteenth century:

> La partie brutal(e) alors veut prendr(e) empire.
> I 2 34 5 6 7 8 9 10 11 12
> (*Le Dépit amoureux*, Act I, sc. i)

We must remember, however, when speaking of prosodic
aberrations in neoclassical comedy, that one would expect
as much from comedy; comedy is a lower, less fastidious
genre than tragedy and part of the looked-for comic 'atmosphere' is precisely a certain looseness and lack of taste in
verse-art. But this 'lapse' of Molière's is to be found again in
the twentieth century, in the much-quoted lines from Paul
Valéry's 'Fragments du Narcisse':

> Nulle des nymphes, null(e) amie, ne m'attire
> I 2 3 4 5 6 7 89 10 1112

> Comme tu fais sur l'ond(e), inépuisable Moi!
> I 2 3 4 5 6 7 8 9 1011 12

And in the nineteenth century, we find poets applying the
licence enjoyed by 'aient' and 'soient' to other third person
plural verb-forms:

> Sophistes impuissants qui ne croient qu'en eux-
> I 2 3 4 5 6 7 8 9 10 11
> mêmes.
> 12
> (Musset, 'L'Espoir en Dieu')

As we shall see in Chapter 7, free-verse poets refused to be
embarrassed by these stipulations.

2. Combinations of vowels within words present special problems in syllable-counting, because it is not always easy to know whether they should be pronounced as a single syllable (synaeresis) or as a double vowel (diaeresis). The general principle which should resolve most questions of this nature is: where the two contiguous vowels derive etymologically from two Latin vowels, then they count as two (le*o*nem/l*io*n; delic*io*sum/délic*ieu*x); and where they derive from one Latin vowel, they count as one (n*o*ctem/n*ui*t; p*e*dem/p*ie*d). The trouble is that pronunciation changes over the centuries, and varies between different sectors of society, that the principle just outlined is overlooked, either as a conscious poetic licence, or because a word is assimilated, treated as analogous, to words in a similar group which, however, has different etymological origins. If there is one overall trend, it is the trend of common pronunciation, from the etymological awareness and careful precision of diaeresis towards the lazier, unfussier synaeresis. Thus 'd*ia*ble' (d*ia*bolus), which should be a diaeresis, soon became a synaeresis (by the sixteenth century) simply because the devil was the constant preoccupation of the common folk. Similarly the -*ie*n ending (-*ia*num), originally counted as two syllables, found itself becoming a single syllable in certain oft-used words ('chrétien': sixteenth century; 'ancien': seventeenth century), and this trend continued into the nineteenth century, where we find -ien as a synaeresis in 'comédien', 'quotidien' and 'gardien', for example. In the sixteenth century and part of the seventeenth, the *oè* of 'poète', etymologically a diaeresis (p*oe*ta), became, temporarily, a synaeresis (pwèt) under the influence of the way *oi* was pronounced at the time. The guidelines we give on vowel-combinations in the Appendix are thus very general and riddled with exceptions. Poets seem to delight in being idiosyncratic or simply inconsistent – Hugo has the *ia* of 'miasmes' both as a synaeresis and a diaeresis, and the same is true of Gautier's treatment of the *iu* of 'opium' and of Musset's treatment of the *ui* of 'suicide'. In fact, the only sure way of knowing how many syllables

vowel-combinations are is to refer to the overall line-length as the known quantity and count backwards; in regular verse, after all, it is not the number of syllables in the line which is in question, but whether a vowel-combination should be read as a synaeresis or diaeresis, and what the implications of that fact are, if any. It is in free verse, where the line-length *is* in question, where rules are being treated in a rather cavalier fashion, that uncertainties about synaeresis and diaeresis become even more crucial, as they become more insoluble; we can no longer look to the poet for guidance; we must appeal to our own knowledge and sensibilities, which in one sense may not be a bad thing, but in others . . . But more of this later.

3. A note about 'pays', 'paysage', 'paysan' and 'abbaye'. It is easy to forget that -ay- is a diaeresis (pays/pagensem, abbaye/abbatiam) and to treat it as a single syllable. We have already encountered 'pays' in the quotation from Pierre Emmanuel; we might also quote from Hugo's *La Légende des siècles*:

> Paysans! paysans! hélas! vous aviez tort.
> 12 3   45 6   7 8   9 10 11   12

But in the sixteenth and seventeenth centuries, we often find the diaeresis reduced to synaeresis:

> Et la bonne paysann(e) apprenant mon désir.
> 1   2   3   4   5   6   7   8 9   10 11 12
>   (Molière, *L'École des femmes*, Act I, sc. i)

(b) *Accent*. The line is a number of syllables. The number of syllables in a line creates certain fairly definite expectations about the rhythmic measures which will make up the line. But, ultimately, these measures are created by accent.

We call the points of emphasis in the French line 'accents' rather than 'stresses' because the French do, and because it serves to remind us that French rhythms are essentially phrasal, that is to say, that there is a marked coincidence of emphasis and pitch-change which there is not in English verse. Certainly French accents have nothing to do with beat and very rarely are French rhythmic patterns a surface laid over the line, an extra sense-impression, an onomatopoeic rejoinder to the content of the line, as English metres can so easily seem to be.

Let us look at this more closely. French words do not have inbuilt claims on accent (stress) as most English words do. In composing lines of verse, the English poet is, in a sense, arranging, redistributing, *given* stress-patterns. The French word has only a *potential* accent, if it has the necessary grammatical status (noun, adjective, verb, adverb, pronoun), and this accent, if conferred, always falls on the last syllable (oxytonic) in words of more than one syllable, or on the penultimate syllable if the final syllable is *atone* (paroxytonic) – thus: 'regárd', 'monotóne', 'chercháit', 'sémbles'. But when words appear in grammatical groups in a syntactical system, they yield their individual accent-potential to the group, and the group accent falls on the last accentuable syllable of the last word of the group. Rhythm and syntax thus go hand in hand in French verse, and in scanning French lines, we discover the rhythmic measures and the accents associated with them by identifying the principal grammatical groups. Thus:

> (Il est amér) (et dóux), (pendant les núits) (d'hivér),
> (D'écoutér), (près du féu) (qui palpít(e))) (et qui fúme),
> (Les souvenírs) (lointáins) (lentemént) (s'élevér)
> (Au brúit) (des carillóns) (qui chán)-(tent dans la brúme).
>
> (Baudelaire, 'La Cloche fêlée')

Or, to pick up lines already quoted:

> (Apprends-mói) (de quel tón), (dans ta bóu)-(che hardíe)
> (Parláit) (la vérité), (ta séu)-(le passión).
>
> (Musset, 'Une Soirée perdue')

To describe the rhythmic measures thus formed, we simply

mark up the number of syllables in each group, putting a
plus-sign between them. And so the Baudelaire gives:

$$4+2+4+2$$
$$3+3+3+3$$
$$4+2+3+3$$
$$2+4+2+4$$

while the Musset reads:

$$3+3+3+3$$
$$2+4+2+4$$

I have picked these examples purposely, because they
present no real problems, apart from the rhythmic affilia-
tion of the unelided *e atone* – which measure does it belong
in? – and we shall return to this when discussing the *coupe
enjambante* in the next chapter. But we can already make
some useful deductions from these examples:
  1. The shorter an adjective or noun, the more likely it is
that its position in the word-order will dictate whether it is
accentuated or not, because immediately adjacent accents
are hard for the voice to cope with and usually need to be
justified, in pitch terms, by an intensification of the second
accent. We find it easy to say 'ce gant bléu' or 'ce gánt très
chér'; but 'ce gánt bléu' is more difficult because of our
inherent need to mark accent with a change of intonation; in
order to give our voices a run at 'bleu', we would have to
introduce a pause between the noun and its following adjective. Conversely, of course, intervening unaccentuated syllables make it easy to produce accent – thus 'un soléil éternél'
or 'un éternél soléil', but not so easily 'un éternél crime'. So
the French polysyllable naturally attracts an accent whatever its position. And we can further systematise this observation by proposing that a $1+5$ hemistich will be much
commoner than a $5+1$ one; the $1+5$ hemistich is characteristic, for instance, of enjambed verse where a verb is
carried forward from its subject into a following line:

> Nulle vie et nul bruit. Tous les lions repus
>
> $$3+3+4+2$$

Dorment au fond de l'antr(e) éloigné de cent lieues.

$$1+5+3+3$$

(Leconte de Lisle, 'Les Éléphants')

This is not to say that the 5̆+1 hemistich does not exist; what it does mean is that to facilitate reading and justify the immediately following accent, the voice tends to give more emphasis to the second accent than to the first, to slide up in crescendo; and the pause between the 5 and 1 measures will be greater than the pause between 3+3 or 2+4, so that the voice can gather itself to attack another accentuated syllable immediately. Thus in Corneille's *Polyeucte* (Act II, sc. vi):

(Faisons triompher) (Dieu); (qu'il dispo)-(se du reste) 5+1+3+3

or in *Sertorius* (Act I, sc. i):

(Tour à tour) (le carnag(e)) (et les proscriptions)

$$3+3+6$$

(Ont sacrifié) (Rom(e)) (à leurs dissensions).

$$5+1+6$$

In both instances, the single-syllable measure is a climax, of exultant defiance in the one, of indignation in the other, and these names are certainly worthy of their rhythmic isolation. Already, too, one begins to see how one might speak of different degrees of accent in French verse.

2. Given the coincidence of rhythmic unit and grammatical group, given that the line always ends with an accentuated syllable (the rhyme), it is hardly surprising that the French line has a natural tendency to consist of elements which are grammatically whole, and to be endstopped (to end with some form of punctuation). It is this tendency which, as we shall see later, makes *enjambement* much more of an issue in French verse than in English.

3. It is evident that one scans French verse in basically the same way as one would scan French prose, by the phrase or word-group. In what sense, then, are verse-rhythms any different from prose-rhythms? The French have intermit-

tently been embarrassed by this question for a long time and, it could be argued, have made an *over*-strenuous effort to distinguish between verse and prose. They have insisted for perhaps too long on the indispensability of rhyme to verse, they have encouraged, perhaps too much, the use of indelibly poetic rhetorical structures like inversion, and of a language permeated by abstraction. And the persistence of the counted *e atone* in verse, as opposed to its rapid disappearance in spoken French, may owe something to this same concern. The programme of rigorous division between verse and prose has made it harder for them to fertilise each other; as Thierry Maulnier (1939) puts it: 'La poésie française a, dans le langage français, son domaine propre, elle ne se mêle point à la prose, elle ne lui dispute pas ses thèmes, elle ne lui prête pas son secours dan les grandes occasions, elle ne donne aucune aide à la prose, et elle n'en attend rien' (p. 35). And it is for this reason, perhaps, that that peculiarly French hybrid, the prose-poem, came into existence in the nineteenth century, to act as a mediator between prose and verse, to forge that link between the two which seems to be the necessary preamble to the emergence of free verse.

(c) *The caesura.* So far we have considered rhythmic grouping only in the alexandrine. This, too, is by design. The alexandrine is a good line to practise with, not only because of its absolute centrality to French verse, but because, of the longer lines, it is the one which has the most inbuilt aids. By this I mean that we come to a regular alexandrine expecting to find four measures (*alexandrin tétramètre*) – though alexandrines with six-syllable measures will obviously not have as many – and expecting to find a caesura (marked//), and a fixed caesura at that, after the sixth syllable, dividing the line into two halves (hemistichs) and establishing a permanent accent on the sixth syllable. The term 'césure' derives, of course, from Latin metric, but has little in common with its Latin usage. The caesura is to be found in lines of nine syllables or more. The nine-syllable line has a very mobile caesura which may produce divisions as varied as $3//6$, $6//3$, $5//4$, $4//5$:

Je devin(e), à travers un murmure,	$3//3+3$
Le contour subtil des voix anciennes	$3+2//4$
Et dans les lueurs musiciennes,	$5//4$
Amour pâl(e), un(e) aurore future!	$3//3+3$

(Verlaine, 'Ariettes oubliées II')

The decasyllable usually falls out as a $4//6$ pattern, but might be $6//4$, or, more rarely, $5//5$:

Ce toit tranquille, où marchent des colombes,	$4//2+4$
Entre les pins palpite, entre les tombes;	$4+2//4$
Midi le juste y compose de feux	$4//3+3$
La mer, la mer, toujours recommencée!	$2+2//2+4$

(Valéry, 'Le Cimetière marin')

What further can be said about the caesura? First, that it is not safe to call it a pause, though individual readers may often mark it with a slight pause. It would be much nearer the mark to call it 'a conventionalised point of attention'. It is of course true that the caesura frequently does coincide with punctuation, or with an actualised juncture of some kind. But this is not necessarily so (e.g. Baudelaire's 'Du fond de son réduit sablonneux, le grillon' – 'Bohémiens en voyage'). It might be more justified to speak not about pause, but about the relative significance of the caesural accent, which is second only in importance to the end–of–line accent. And here again, we must be careful not to confuse significance with loudness or intensity. In the second of these lines spoken by Oreste:

Mais un heureux destin//le conduit en ces lieux.	
	$4+2+3+3$
Partons. A tant d'attraits,//Amour, ferme ses yeux!	
	$2+4+2+4$

(*Andromaque*, Act II, sc. iii)

we must beware of believing, because of the decisiveness of

the imperative and the unmistakable punctuation, that the
caesura has been shifted, follows the second syllable, or that
it has been enfeebled by competition from the first measure.
The sixth-syllable caesura, unimpressed by either loudness
or pause, directs our attention to a word – 'attraits' (Hermione's) – which not only reveals the paradox in Oreste's
position and behaviour – 'Partons'/'attraits' – the need to
go, and indeed to leave Épire, and the need to stay, but
contains a piquant dramatic irony: 'Partons' proves inef-
ficacious as Oreste lingers on in the following scene to learn
of the efficacy of 'attraits', as Pyrrhus declares his intention
to marry Hermione. And to celebrate a woman because of
her power to attract and to ask that others are not attracted,
is to make oneself one's own dupe. The caesura is a conventionalised point of attention; it is that which prevents
us being side-tracked by the peremptory 'Partons' and
leads us into the real energy within the line. 'Natural'
language needs to be resisted by certain stable conventions if we are to embed ourselves in it at the level which
counts.

If we are to believe Giraudoux, there is in Corneille the
possibility of transaction, of coming to terms with a predicament, in a way that there is not in Racine. In Corneille's
more argumentative theatre, the balance of the alexandrine
is not the horrifying perfection of unresolvable dilemma,
but the weighing up of alternatives which are real. The
Cornelian alexandrine is often an exercise in analysis and
definition which liberates the speaker into total conviction.
There is a way out of the tragic circle for the bravely
discriminating mind; the tragic circle will continue to exist
only for those who do not agree. In the first scene of *Cinna*,
for example, Émilie needs to sort out what seem to be
conflicting demands: she feels bound to revenge her father's
death on Auguste by the agency of Cinna, but she does not
wish to implicate Cinna, whom she loves, in what might
turn out to be a disastrous enterprise. She resolves this
argument for herself very much with the help of the polaris-
ing force of the medial caesura. She can lay out the pros and

cons, the moral issues, with a clarity and reasonableness which can only convince her of the rightness of her final decision:

> Amour, sers mon devoir,//et ne le combats plus:
>
> 2+4+6
>
> Lui céder, c'est ta gloir(e),//et le vaincre, ta honte:
>
> 3+3+3+3
>
> Montre-toi généreux,//souffrant qu'il te surmonte;
>
> 3+3+2+4
>
> Plus tu lui donneras,//plus il te va donner,
>
> 1+5+1+5
>
> Et ne triomphera//que pour te couronner.   6+6

The expanding measures of the final lines capture only too well Émilie's confidence about her conclusions. The future envisaged in the last two lines is increasingly rid of those doubts that secondary accents might encourage, so thoroughly does Émilie feel in control of it.

Let us stay a little longer with Corneille's dramatic verse, using it to combine our three basic features – syllable, accent, caesura. We shall see how their interaction provides constant shifts in perspective and salience, shifts which variously energise or de-energise lexical items and so bring drama to the verbal surface. And this interaction, these shifts, make better sense in dramatic verse than elsewhere, perhaps, for dramatic verse goes on long enough for us to be able to acquaint ourselves with it as a total set of lexical impulses, developing and relating to each other in continuous metamorphosis. In dramatic verse, we not only become familiar with whole families of rhyme-words (see Chapter 4), but we can enjoy the alexandrine as a sliding scale of differing values on which recurrent words or parts of speech find ever-changing status with their ever-changing positions. A word like 'Rome' has few rhymes, so we find it frequently within the line, and often as the sixth syllable, to maintain its proper prominence. But we may find it in a position without any accent at all:

> Rome seul(e) aujourd'hui//peut résister à Rome
> $$3+3+4+2$$
> (*Sertorius*, Act II, sc.i)

and meet it again in the same position, but this time not conceding its accent to a following word:

> Rome n'eût envoyé//ce noble fugitif. $1+5+2+4$
> (*Sertorius*, Act II, sc.i)

Equally, we may find it elsewhere in the line, for instance as the first measure of a second hemistich:

> Et que j'irais, Seigneur, //à Rom(e) avec plaisir.
> $$4+2+2+4$$
> (*Sertorius*, Act III, sc.i)

And so on. Rome is an ineradicable permanence in the play, but bears on the consciousness of different characters in different ways at different times, and its position on a list of priorities changes constantly; sometimes it is conceived of as an active political protagonist, sometimes as an inert obstacle, sometimes as the yardstick of all conduct, sometimes as a pale imitation. Its instability of role is reflected on the sensitive scale that the alexandrine is.

But such shifting emphases are not only important for proper nouns. As a further example, we might look at *Polyeucte* and see how the use of the alexandrine as a sliding-scale can take the repetition out of repetition, can give a sense of the irregularity and diversity of the impulses which beget repetition, in itself so deceptively uniform. At the end of Act II, Néarque and Polyeucte are on the point of going to destroy the images in the temple. Néarque has hung back to begin with, but fired by Polyeucte, he sets in motion a sequence of first person plural imperatives with the words:

> Allons, cher Polyeuct(e),//allons aux yeux des
>   hommes $2+4+2+4$
> Braver l'idolâtri(e),// . . . $2+4$

This puts the accent unequivocally on the imperative. In Polyeucte's answering speech, this pattern is varied:

> Allons-y du vrai Dieu//soutenir l'intérêt;
> 3+3+3+3
> Allons fouler aux pieds//ce foudre ridicule
> 4+2+2+4
> Dont arm(e) un bois pourri//ce peuple trop crédule;
> 2+4+2+4
> Allons en éclairer//l'aveuglement fatal; 2+4+4+2
> Allons briser ces Dieux//de pierre et de métal;
> 4+2+2+4
> Abandonnons nos jours//à cett(e) ardeur céleste;
> 4+2+4+2
> Faisons triompher Dieu://qu'il dispose du reste!
> 5+1+3+3

To begin with, the accent is on direction and destination; in the second and fifth lines, it is on the violence of their activities when they have reached their destination ('fouler', 'briser'); in the fourth line, the accent returns to the here and now, the overriding sense of impatience. And in the final couplet, the accent is first on a more abstract, more widely communal exhortative imperative, and finally on an infinitive which transfers activity from the two faithful to their God working through them. And it is this last shift of perspective that Néarque incorporates into his final rejoinder, which combines the accentuated imperative of departure with the accentuated infinitive of God's self-manifestation:

> Allons fair(e) éclater//sa gloir(e) aux yeux de tous.
> 2+4+2+4

This is no straightforward repetition; it is a repetitive structure into which the changing accentual patterns of the alexandrine have insinuated the manifold impulses that propel the characters – the attraction of violence, the impatience to prove the self and the faith of the self, the lure of a more abstract and mystical self-sacrifice, the desire to celebrate divine power. There are, as we have mentioned, thirty-six possible combinations of measure in the classical alexandrine (from 6+6, through 6+5+1, 6+1+5, 6+4+2, 6+2+4, etc., to 3+3+3+3); the skilled writer will harness this freedom to telling variations.

If we look at Polyeucte's speech from another point of view, if we consider the pattern of its measures, then we can see that these lines are obviously presided over by 2+4 and 4+2 hemistichs; there are five of each, the 2+4 dominating the first half and the 4+2 the second. The opening lines of Polyeucte's reply which immediately precede the ones we have quoted, instal the 4+2 hemistich before Polyeucte comes on to his 'Allons' imperatives:

> A cet heureux transport que le ciel vous envoie,
> $$4+2+3+3$$
> Je reconnais Néarque, et j'en pleure de joie.
> $$4+2+3+3$$
> Ne perdons plus de temps: le sacrifice est prêt.
> $$4+2+4+2$$

The 3+3+3+3 line which introduces the 'Allons' imperatives sets up the intention in an even, measured fashion; the regularity of the trisyllabic group reinforces the rather restrained and initially unimpetuous language – 'soutenir l'intérêt' sounds a particularly sedate euphemism. Polyeucte then warms to his commitment, taking up the 2+4 pattern supplied by Néarque, then reversing the two measures more frequently as he proceeds, as the voice attacks the hemistich with more gusto, with broader sweeps – 'Allons briser ces Dieux' (4+2), 'Abandonnons nos jours' (4+2), 'à cette ardeur céleste' (4+2). It is as if Polyeucte were reaching through his words to actions. So he comes back to the dominant note on which his speech started, though at the outset the 4+2 pattern was part of a reaction to someone else's energy, rather than an affirmation of his own, filled with pleasurable surprise, rather than destructive intent. The first half of the final line:

Faisons triompher Dieu://qu'il dispose du reste!

$$5+1+3+3$$

acts as a culmination, an *épanouissement* of the $4+2$ hemistich as it achieves the even more extended impulsiveness of the five-syllable measure, with its one-syllable pinnacle 'Dieu'. The second hemistich, as it hands active power over to God, withdraws into the $3+3$ pattern, into a complacent equanimity, into the serenity of anticipated total victory.

It is evident that, by looking at the abstract patterns created by the tabulation of measures in a sequence of lines, we can help ourselves to discover larger rhythmic substructures and thus add to our appreciation of a speech's organisation. In the Corneille example, we came to the pattern of measures after examining the relation of accents to imperatives. What would happen if we took a sequence of lines, or a whole poem, and used the pattern of measures as our starting-point, even before we had properly tried to comprehend the meaning? Would it provide a key to the poem's decipherment?

We can begin to answer this question by briefly contemplating the pattern of measures supplied by a particularly difficult and enigmatic poem, Gérard de Nerval's 'El Desdichado':

Je suis le ténébreux, – le veuf, – l'inconsolé,

$$2+4+2+4$$

Le prince d'Aquitaine à la tour abolie:

$$2+4+3+3$$

Ma seule *étoile* est morte, – et mon luth constellé

$$4+2+3+3$$

Porte le *soleil* noir de la *Mélancolie*. $1+5+6$

Dans la nuit du tombeau, toi qui m'as consolé,

$$3+3+1+5$$

Rends-moi le Pausilippe et la mer d'Italie,

$$2+4+3+3$$

La *fleur* qui plaisait tant à mon cœur désolé,

$$2+4+3+3$$

Et la treille où le pampre à la rose s'allie.

$$3+3+3+3$$

Suis-je Amour ou Phébus?... Lusignan ou Biron?

$$3+3+3+3$$

Mon front est rouge encor du baiser de la reine;

$$2+4+3+3$$

J'ai rêvé dans la grotte où nage la sirène...

$$3+3+2+4$$

Et j'ai deux fois vainqueur traversé l'Achéron:

$$4+2+3+3$$

Modulant tour à tour sur la lyre d'Orphée

$$3+3+3+3$$

Les soupirs de la sainte et les cris de la fée.

$$3+3+3+3$$

There are many analyses available of this poem and it is not my intention to embark on another. I merely wish to indicate some of the observations that might be made, and some of the questions that might be asked, on the basis of the tabulated accentual data. A far more sophisticated and systematic account, along the same lines, of another of Nerval's sonnets is given by Pierre Malandain (1971).

The first thing we might wish to comment on is the gradual increase of the $3+3$ hemistichs, which might be supposed to convey a growing sense of equilibrium and reconciliation; the last two lines of the poem do indeed, we discover, seem to tell of the recovery of the power of utterance with the ability to balance different dimensions of the poetic voice.

The second thing that might strike us is the rarity of the $4+2$ hemistich. We have in fact only two, both as initial hemistichs, one in the first stanza and one in the last (a further one might be argued for in the first tercet, but more of that in the next chapter). If we now look to the text, we find that one $4+2$ tells of deprivation – 'Ma seule *étoile* est morte' – the other of victory – 'Et j'ai deux fois vainqueur'. Does the poet wish us to relate these two hemistichs, not only to underline the upturn of fortune at the close of the sonnet, but also to intimate that the poet has crossed the Acheron into the Underworld precisely to recover his dead star?

We might equally look into the two occurrences of the 1+5 combination. 1+5 is naturally rare and we should beware of suggesting that this alone makes it worthy of comment. But the textual closeness of the two instances here and the fact that they occupy different halves of the verse-line justifies some attention. Once again the two combinations have contrasting values. If the first accent of 'Porte le *soleil* noir' falls on a verb, it is a passive verb (I am not speaking of the verb's voice); the disjunctive pronoun 'toi', on the other hand, is the source of profound action; the abrupt accent on 'Porte' is dissipated in the long measure that follows it; the accent on 'toi' is an upgathering and reorientation of the even, reposeful symmetry of 'Dans la nuit du tombeau', a wonderfully sudden resurrection from the grave, urging a 3+3 of a different kind of stability.

Finally, the idiosyncratic rhythmic structure of the fourth line calls for some explanation. What does this lengthening of measures betoken? Turning again to the text, we may suppose that it betokens a failure of energy, or perhaps the morbid indulgence of sorrow, or perhaps the opening up of cosmic distances, or perhaps something of all these things. Only after many readings might we want to decide.

An examination of tabulated accents does not tell us much about the meaning of the poem by itself, gives no more than hints. But it does indicate to us *where* we should look, it does pick out for us what might be crucial points of structural change or parallelism; it helps to loosen the poem, it opens corridors into enigma. Having identified the areas of possible significance, we need to go to the poem as a whole; but we may find it greatly useful to return constantly to the poem's overall rhythmic structure, to check our findings, to provoke ourselves to new departures.

2

The line (II)

So far the scansion of French verse, aside from the intricacies of syllable-counting, may seem to be reassuringly straightforward. But the confidence to scan, which should derive from this fundamental straightforwardness, must ultimately develop into the confidence to disagree about scansion, or to envisage alternative readings. We must remember two obvious facts: first, that certain scansional concepts, like the caesura and the *coupe* (the line of demarcation between rhythmic groups), are fictions, pure conventions, which usually correspond self-evidently to the linguistic data of a particular line, but often do not; and secondly, that lines will very frequently contain more accentuable syllables that they have available accents – equally a line may contain fewer ostensibly accentuable syllables than it has available accents. Controversy, consequently, is unavoidable.

Before we look more closely into the kinds of controversy and difficulty which arise with the various elements of the line – accent, *coupe*, caesura – we should qualify one other supposition. So far we have made a rigorous distinction between the written and pronounced poem on the one hand, and the recited poem on the other. To summarise roughly, we might say that it is the business of scansion – which concerns itself with the written and pronounced poem – to establish the essential prosodic *données* of the poem, and it is for recitation to interpret those *données* as performance; the act of scansion is a vital counterpart and corrective to recitation, and vice-versa; the scansionalist might argue that scansion is the firm foundation upon which the fantasising edifice of recitation can be built, is the necessary condition of the luxury of recitation. But where the prosodic facts are not self-imposing, not patent, then the scansionalist must refer himself to recitation; he must, to help himself out of doubt, imagine the poem in terms of possible readings aloud. This is not to say that the scansionalist need choose, as the reciter must; he can merely offer alternatives to future reciters, or create a fruitful complexity for the 'inner' reader. A recent and valuable exploration of the ground between scansion and recitation is to be found in F. W. Leakey's lecture *Sound and Sense in French Poetry* (1975).

(i) *Accent*
Generally the position of rhythmic accents in the French line is determined by its syntax and semantic intention, and these will usually be indistinguishable from one another. In lines which contain more accentuable syllables than conventional accents, there may, however, be some conflict between syntax and semantic intention, or, alternatively, we may have to assess the relative significance of grammatical groups and give priority to some at the expense of others. In a line already quoted, from Nerval's 'El Desdichado' –

Mon front est rouge encor du baiser de la reine

– we have opted, without more ado, for a 2+4+3+3 pattern. Certainly there can be no question about the second hemistich. But is the 2+4 reading the most satisfactory account of the first? 2+4 registers the basic syntactic shape, i.e. subject + predicate, but is this perhaps too automatic, too 'dead' a division? The stigma of the queen's kiss, the red mark, is something which, it appears, the poet wishes to hang on to; the queen, most commentators would agree, is the *reine de Saba*, an archetype for Nerval of the 'eternal feminine'. But 'encor' suggests that the trace may fade. To highlight the tension between the poet's desire to prolong the mark and his fear that it will soon disappear, to deepen the red, a 4+2 reading would perhaps make better sense.

Such a reading would not make much difference to what
was said, at the end of the previous chapter, about the
interplay of the different patterns of measure, but to offer it
as an alternative would do more justice to the poet's deducible intentions. In a scansional description of the line, we
would thus include both possibilities, separated by a
diagonal stroke – 2+4+3+3/4+2+3+3.

Let us turn to another problematic example, to be found
in the eleventh stanza of Lamartine's 'Le Lac':

> Hé quoi! n'en pourrons-nous fixer au moins la
>   trace?   2+4+2+4
> Quoi! passés pour jamais? quoi! tout entiers perdus?
> Ce temps qui les donna, ce temps qui les efface,
>   2+4+2+4
> Ne nous les rendra plus?   6

The second line of this stanza contains six grammatical
groups, and thus six potential accents: Quoi!/passés/pour
jamais?//quoi!/tout entiers/perdus? 'Jamais' and 'perdus'
claim their accents by prosodic right, but are we to read
1+5+1+5 or 3+3+4+2? If we opt for the former solution,
we are paralleling our treatment of the exclamation in the
first line, taking account of the more obvious syntactical
divisions and increasing the rhetorical force of the stanza as
a whole. If we opt for the latter, we are consciously damp-
ing down the rhetorical vigour, introducing rhythmic variety to counteract the syntactic repetition within the line and
the symmetry of the chiastically arranged past participles
('passés' and 'perdus'), and focussing attention on words
connected with the passage of time and the unconditional
completeness of its passing; this second reading assumes
that the 'quoi' can be taken as read. Thus 1+5+1+5/
3+3+4+2. To the question 'Why not three accents per
hemistich though (i.e. 1+2+3+1+3+2)?', we shall provide
an answer later.

    The Lamartine example intimates that essential questions
of scansion may depend on *fashions* of envisaging poetic
utterance, as much as non-essential, purely expressive fea-

tures of recitation depend on the poetic persuasions of individual readers. This is certainly true to some extent, but not alarmingly so. There are instances where one can distinguish between different schools of scansion, which may or may not have their origins in different historical periods. Henri Morier (1967, ed. Parent) discusses Victor Hugo's line:

> Montant comme la mer sur le roc noir et nu

and distinguishes between a 'rythme classique', namely $2+4+3+3$, and a 'rythme pathétique', namely $2+4+4+2$. Of the first, Morier writes: 'La diction classique mettra l'accent sur la substance' and further adds: 'Ici la brutalité phonétique du terme "roc", les possibilités sonores de l' "o" ouvert sont pleinement mises en évidence' (p. 105); and of the second:

> Mais le poète, qui est un sensitif par définition, s'attache souvent aux vertus sensibles de la substance. Et c'est pourquoi nous l'entendons accentuer les qualificatifs, quitte à glisser sur le substantif . . . l'intensité de 'roc' s'est effacée devant l'éclatement du symbole hugolien de *noir* marquant la fatalité, l'esprit du mal, la démission divine (pp. 105–6).

The distinction between these two kinds of reading is essentially the distinction we have already made between syntax and semantic intention. But we can say that, however we describe it, this line would naturally be controversial, because it contains a naturally problematic unit: a noun followed by two adjectives, all in the same hemistich (i.e. three accentuable syllables and two accents to distribute). A line presenting a similar problem occurs in Baudelaire's 'La Chevelure':

> Vous me rendez l'azur du ciel immense et rond.

To do justice to the possible readings, one would need to describe it as $4+2+2+4/4+2+4+2$. If we choose the former of these possibilities, we are complying with the more evident syntactical imperative and suggesting that the arching vault of the sky ('rond') *encompasses* its vastness, cathedral-like. If we choose the latter, we are overlooking a noun without weight, the better to insist on its qualities; 'immense' needs an accent to realise its meaning in its acoustic proportions, and with an accent, it is already an exhilarating and liberating ascent for the poet.

The doubts we might have about the position of accents in the alexandrine are, if anything, multiplied in the octosyllable. The octosyllable is perhaps the most mercurial and mobile of lines. Without the structural *point de repère* of a caesura, it situates itself uneasily between a two-accents-per-six-syllables norm on the one hand, and a three-accents-per-decasyllable norm on the other. Of course the octosyllable has its own conventions; 3 + 5 and 5 + 3 are the classic divisions of the line, though 4 + 4 is probably as common. But measures of four and five syllables are already pushing towards the limit of tolerable accentlessness, particularly in a line whose brevity tends to encourage a more attentive reading, a reading that positively looks for accent. There may be some simplification in these assertions, but we can justifiably propose that recitational considerations interfere more continuously with the rhythmic structure of this line than with any other, and this characteristic, resulting from the line's instability, reinforces that instability. In the following stanza from Gautier's 'Symphonie en blanc majeur':

> Le marbre blanc, chair froide et pâle,
> Où vivent les divinités;
> L'argent mat, la laiteuse opale
> Qu'irisent de vagues clartés

the first line presents the noun + two adjectives problem again, though with the accent on the fourth syllable and the brevity of the line, the question is no longer whether the accent should fall on the noun or the first adjective, but whether it should fall on either – if it did fall, the proximity of the fourth-syllable accent would naturally push it on to the first adjective. Do we then encapsulate the appositional group in a single measure – 4 + 4 – or do we give a physical immediacy to the metaphor by allowing 'froide' its resistance, its *noli me tangere* effect – 4 + 2 + 2? The second line is not ambiguous – 2 + 6 – but the third line allows us either to treat its two constituents equally – 3 + 5 – in a conventional octosyllabic pattern, or to give relief to the preposed adjective of the second group, to give support to its opacity, to help it on its journey into the figurative, with a 3 + 3 + 2 distribution. The preposed adjective of the final line and the syllabically extended subject unit probably incline us towards 2 + 3 + 3 rather than towards 2 + 6.

I do not wish to suggest that reading octosyllables is an uninterruptedly harrowing experience. There is, on the contrary, a docile patentness in these opening lines of Baudelaire's 'L'Héautontimorouménos':

Je te frapperai sans colère	5 + 3
Et sans haine, comme un boucher,	3 + 5
Comme Moïse le rocher!	4 + 4
Et je ferai de ta paupière,	4 + 4
Pour abreuver mon Saharah,	4 + 4
Jaillir les eaux de la souffrance.	4 + 4

. . .

But the octosyllable is, as we have said, subject to recitational interference in a way that other lines are not, and it is not always easy to distinguish between prosodic accents and purely expressive ones, that is to say, between accents which indicate the poem's rhythmic structures as system, as an inherent feature of its existence, and accents with which the voice endows the line on an occasional basis, and which do not properly belong to a rhythmic description of the line.

But how many accents can an alexandrine have? So far we have assumed a minimum of two and a maximum of four. But if we listen to Berthon (1948), we might believe otherwise: 'It[the alexandrine] may have as many as six, and even (though rarely) eight' (p.xxv). He goes on to provide an example of a six-accent line:

> Vient, vá, tourne, et, flairánt au lóin la solitúde.
>
> (Leconte de Lisle, 'Sacra Fames')

But before tackling this line, let us look at our own *locus classicus* for this problem, again an enumerative line, from Milton's *Paradise Lost*:

> Rocks, Caves, Lakes, Fens, Bogs, Dens, and shades
> of death.

About this line, not surprisingly, commentators disagree. Enid Hamer (1969) uses the line to exemplify rhythmic units of one syllable (p.95). Joseph Malof (1970) uses the line to exemplify *hovering accent* or *distributed stress*, an English equivalent of the dual notational system we have introduced in this section:

> This is a scansion that establishes the required number of stresses without making a commitment as to exactly which syllables will carry them. When it is said that a stress is distributed over two syllables, what is meant is that the stress is made available to either of those syllables, with the understanding that either may take the role of metrical stress, leaving the other to be slack. This adheres to metrical principles without making a final metrical decision. Distributed stress or hovering accent may be marked:

Rocks, Caves, Lakes, Fens, Bogs, Dens and shades of death.

$$\underset{''}{\bigvee}{}' \quad | \quad \underset{''}{\bigvee}{}' \quad | \quad \underset{''}{\bigvee}{}' \quad | \; x \quad - \; | \; x \quad -$$

(p. 56)

The real problem here, as Malof's words make clear, is not 'Is this line to be read with eight or with five stresses?' – it can be read with as many or as few stresses as the reader

likes, and what the reader likes need not concern the scanner
– but rather 'Where should the five stresses which this line
has, since it is an iambic pentameter, fall?' In prosodic terms,
Hamer's conception of the line does not make sense; one-
syllable feet enjoy no independent existence, there is no
such thing as a rhythm made up of one-syllable feet; one-
syllable units are rather specialised supports of other metres
and usually earn their keep as anacrusis (extra unstressed
syllable at the beginning of a line, acting as lead-in, or what
the Germans call *Auftakt*) or as hypercatalexis (an additional
unstressed syllable at the end of a line, feminine ending).
There is nothing, however, to prevent the reader reading
the line *as though* it were made up of predominantly monosyllabic rhythmic units. Against the eight-stress interpretation we should remember that it is easier to minimise highly
accentuable syllables than it is to maximise normally unac-
cented syllables.

So Malof's basic position – let us treat this line as what it
is, an iambic pentameter, before we treat it as anything else –
and his principle of the available accent, are absolutely
sound. Does he try hard enough to find the position of the
stresses? Perhaps not, since the patterns of assonance in the
line at least suggest ways of rhythmically organising it:

> Rocks, Caves, Lakes, Fens, Bogs, Dens, and shades
> I   2   2   34   I   34   2
> of death.
> 3

That 'Fens' and 'Dens' are rhyming rather than assonant
perhaps gives them some prior claim to stress and should
help the underlying iambic to emerge. But we know that
'Lakes' assonates with 'Caves' before we know that 'Dens'
rhymes with 'Fens', so perhaps ʊ/|/ʊ|ʊ/|ʊ/|ʊ/. We have,
conversely, used the fact that 'Bogs' assonates with 'Rocks'
to keep it unstressed, but this seems justified, because
'shades' and 'death' support the stresses that have been
given to the second, third and sixth syllables.

We have, then, three positions available to us: (a) to

distinguish categorically between prosodic scansion and recitation, and to claim that the demands of the latter are at best secondary, at worst irrelevant, to those of the former; (b) to say that prosodic facts and recitational needs are different, but that a consciousness of each should coexist and be allowed to produce fruitful tensions; it is often the varying nature of this tension alone which enables us to make a rhythmic differentiation between lines prosodically identical; and, as we have seen, doubts about the disposition of prosodic accents may be resolved by reference to recitational probabilities; (c) to argue that prosodic definition should, as far as possible, *determine* recitation, that we should be prepared to let conventionalised patterns of accent and pause reorganise speech habit, even disorientate speech habit, in short, teach us to speak; poetic recitation should, in any case, not be 'normal' speech, but ritualised utterance designed to convey more about the poem than about the reciter; 'normal' speech is, besides, only one way of vocalising the poem, and other methods of enunciation – muttering, mumbling, declaiming, whispering – should be given due weight. In our example from Milton, we can argue that to read the line as we perhaps want to, with eight stresses, is to leave enumeration as enumeration, to take it out of the context of experience and put it into the context of information. Whereas, if we let the prosodic demand for five stresses have its way, if we distribute only three stresses among the six opening nouns, we 'rhythm' enumeration, so that it becomes an inhabiting process, with variation of perception, reaction and association; these natural phenomena cease to be items and become apprehended realities.

The four-accent pattern of the alexandrine is sufficiently conventional for us to speak of the classical alexandrine as an *alexandrin tétramètre*. If we make the problem of the Leconte de Lisle line not one of how many, but of where, we shall find ourselves with a line which reads $3+3+2+4$:

Le sinistre Rôdeur des steppes de la mer

$$3+3+2+4$$

Vient, va, tourne, et, flairant au loin la solitude,

> 3+3+2+4

Entre-bâille d'ennui ses mâchoires de fer.

> 3+3+3+3

And, of course, we find that this glancing over the first two verbs of the sequence captures the swiftness of the shark's movement, leading into the abruptness of its pausing, with the accent on 'tourne'. Berthon's reading gives equal value to each of the movements, thus separating them, and extending each one indefinitely in time. But surely we should see these movements as all part of thc same *élan*, an *élan* which, it transpires, is an expression of frustration at enforced inaction; the greater the suddennes of this sequence, the greater the irony of its contrast with the immobility depicted in the stanza's final line. The reciter may choose to give this line six accents, but this does not entitle him to describe it as an example of a six-accent alexandrine, a kind of line which has no conventional prosodic existence, and it does not entitle him to suggest that Leconte de Lisle is breaking the rules, or liberating verse; this line falls quite happily within the purview of the *alexandrin tétramètre*.

Similar triads of verbs occur in Vigny's 'La Maison du berger', in lines about the train –

Sur ce taureau de fer qui fume, souffle et beugle,

> 4+2+4+2

L'homme a monté trop tôt . . .

– and in lines about Rêverie –

Et, des secrets divins se faisant une étude,
Marche, s'arrête et marche avec le col penché.

> 4+2+4+2

In each instance, there is room for disagreement about the readings. In each instance, the reading chosen is assuming that the *e atone* acts as a liaison agent between the first two verbs ('fume, souffle', 'Marche, s'arrête'), drawing them together, compacting them. In the second example, this assumption is obviously backed up by the sense, the 'pause' at the *coupe* coinciding with a halt in the movement described. In the first example, sense also seems to endorse the division chosen; the first two verbs are about exhalation; they have some connection with sound, but are not concerned with utterance, and presumably aggressive utterance, as 'beugle' is.

Hitherto we have been dealing with lines in which the number of accentuable syllables is greater than the conventional number of accents in the line. I would like to look now at lines or hemistichs in which the number of accentuable syllables is minimal, and to examine two kinds of accent which are essentially support-accents (*accents d'appui*) and whose prosodic status is problematical. Here we encounter what might be regarded as the French equivalent of the Trager–Smith gradation of degrees of stress, for the accents we are to deal with are of a secondary nature, weaker than those they support, weaker than the accents which conventionally occur within the hemistich. The gradation of accent-intensity for the French line might thus look like this: primary – accent at line-ending, secondary – accent at caesura, tertiary – accents within the hemistichs, weak – any *accent d'appui*.

A six-syllable measure is just about as much as the voice can manage without the relief of a juncture of some kind. This, combined with the fact that the classical alexandrine entices us towards four accents, will often lead us to create support accents in words which, in other contexts, we would not think of accentuating. In the opening line of Baudelaire's otherwise untitled poem:

Avec ses vêtements ondoyants et nacrés

we find three uncontroversial accents, 6+3+3. But are we perhaps inclined to rest on the first preposition, in order to endow the line with its proper stateliness, to give relief to the rich adjectives by a tentativeness of approach, even simply to give ourselves a relay-station on our way to the sixth syllable? Will we therefore read 2+4+3+3? A useful

way of indicating the weaker accent on 'Avec' is to paren-
thesise the hemistich in which it appears, thus $(2+4)+3+3$.
A similar example is to be found in Hugo's 'La Rose de
l'Infante':

> Avec la gravité d'une petite reine

where we might read $6+4+2$, or, equally, $(2+4)+4+2$.
One might argue that 'avec' has an acoustic fullness which
itself justifies accent, even though there is little syntactic
justification. It is this last consideration which should put us
on our guard against endowing such support accents with
positive prosodic status, though in certain instances, where
the support accent relates meaningfully to a dominant
rhythmic system, a convincing case might be made for
doing so. Further examples of support-accents on prepositions, conjunctions and the like are not far to seek. In
Hugo's 'L'Expiation', the line:

> Et comme il retournait sa tête pour mourir

gives $(2+4)+2+4$ – and possibly $6+2+4$ – and the same
poet's 'Demain dès l'aube' has the line:

> Et quand j'arriverai, je mettrai sur ta tombe

which we would be inclined to read, I think, as $(2+4)+3+3$.
   A line in which the need for this support-accent is
much more extreme occurs in a poem already referred
to, Gautier's 'Symphonie en blanc majeur', in the eleventh
stanza:

> L'ivoire, où ses mains ont des ailes, $2+3+3/2+6$
> Et comme des papillons blancs, $(2+6)$
> Sur la pointe des notes frêles $3+5$
> Suspendent leurs baisers tremblants. $2+4+2$

What is remarkable about this second line is that 'comme'
should attract an accent, however weak, where 'papillons'
does not – $7+1$ would be unthinkable – and that it acts as
support in a measure which, without it, would occupy the
whole octosyllable. This is perhaps the strongest case we

have met for calling an *accent d'appui* a prosodic accent, not
only because the line has need of two accents and 'comme'
has a better claim than 'papillons', but also because the
two-syllable measure thus formed helps to create, or sustain, the line-initial dissyllabic rhythmic constant which
governs the prosodic structure of the stanza as a whole.
   Another form of *accent d'appui* is to be found when a
syllabically extended measure has as its chief constituent a
substantial polysyllable. This accent is called the *accent
contre-tonique* and falls two syllables before the tonic, or
prosodic, accent, that is to say, on the ante-penultimate
syllable of a polysyllable without final *e atone*. If we look
back over quotations already used, and specifically to those
six-syllable measures made up largely of polysyllables, we
shall see the countertonic accent in action, marked for ease
of identification by ` :

> Tour à tour le carnage et les proscriptions
> Ont sacrifié Rome à leurs dissensions
> > (Corneille, *Sertorius*, Act I, sc.i)

> Et ne triomphera que pour te couronner
> > (Corneille, *Cinna*, Act I, sc.i)

> Porte le *soleil* noir de la *Mélancolie*.
> > (Nerval, 'El Desdichado')

This is not, of course, to say that countertonic accents occur
only in hexasyllabic measures, it is just that their function is
more clearly defined in such measures. But any polysyllable
may attract an *accent contre-tonique*, as 'Éternité' does in
Lamartine's line:

> Éternité, néant, passé, sombres abîmes. 4+2+2+4
> > ('Le Lac')

   But are accents such as these to be looked upon as more
than the accidents of a line realised in speech? The safest, and
in most cases warranted, answer is 'no'. But there are
instances in which a commentator may wish to endow the
countertonic accent with a real rhythmic function and make

it part of the essential prosodic structure of the line. Jean
Mazaleyrat (1974) argues this way about Vigny's line:

> Un navire y passait majestueusement.
>
> > ('La Bouteille à la mer')

He writes:

> Pas de problème pour le premier hémistiche: les
> accents toniques ordinaires en établissent normale-
> ment le rythme (3/3). Problème pour le second:
> il est monogroupe, n'ayant, dans l'ordre tonique,
> qu'un accent. Si l'on s'en tient à la seule accentuation
> tonique, la structure du vers est déséquilibrée: le
> système d'ensemble demeure (6//6), mais les struc-
> tures de détail manquent de cohérence, le premier
> hémistiche ayant une organisation perceptible, le
> second non. Or on constate aux expériences de dic-
> tion que cette organisation des syllabes non donnée
> par l'accentuation tonique, l'accentuation contre-
> tonique peut l'assurer. Un accent secondaire de
> *Nebenton* [German for countertonic accent] se porte
> spontanément deux syllabes avant le tonique, coup-
> ant ainsi le mot en deux mesures (4/2) et introduis-
> ant de la sorte dans l'hémistiche originellement
> massif et inorganique le système de rapport de
> groupes qui lui manquait, lui rendant en somme un
> rythme (majestueu/sement). L'accentuation contre-
> tonique, ordinairement accessoire, est intervenue
> avec *fonction de suppléance* pour assurer le rythme
> que l'accentuation tonique à elle seule ne réalisait
> pas complètement (p. 138).

What is worrying about Mazaleyrat's argument is its implication that six-syllable measures should be discouraged,
unless in pairs, forming balanced hemistichs, and that they
certainly should not be tolerated where their main constituent is a polysyllable. This would be an unnecessary
impoverishment of the resources, structural and expressive,
of the alexandrine, and overlooks the special graces of the

hexasyllabic measure. We have already had occasion to speak of its effects in a specific context, the first stanza of Nerval's 'El Desdichado' (morbid self-indulgence, failure of energy, opening up of cosmic distance). In more general terms, we can say that the six-syllable measure is a coming to rest, an excellent device of closure, that its relaxed, 'inorganic' – to use Mazaleyrat's word – structure may positively release a word, and the polysyllable in particular, into its own mobile and undefined inner rhythms, into its own uncharted depths; the hexasyllabic measure is good at embodying the haunting quality of half-grasped phenomena, or, as in the lines from Corneille's *Sertorius*, the sense of being overwhelmed, unable to organise, and thus withstand, the alien forces at work.

This is not to say that Mazaleyrat's argument might not prove totally convincing in some circumstances; but the instance he has chosen does not seem to me to be the right one, for two reasons, one structural and one stylistic. First, the line quoted does indeed bring a movement of the stanza to a close; it is the last line of the initial alternating quatrain of Vigny's *septain* (*a b a b c c b*) (for a full discussion of this stanza, see Chapter 5, Section (iii)). Because of its suitability to closure, the hexasyllabic reading strikes me as more desirable. Secondly, the intention of the word 'majestueusement' is hard to come at; it is a word with potential duplicity in it, for the ship whose splendid motion reflects the splendour of a tropical Pacific turns out, in the following stanza, to be a slaver, which takes to its heels on the arrival of pirates; the Pacific's 'vagues d'azur, d'or et de diamant' ultimately bring out a gold of a filthier hue in the slaver:

Noyez or et bourreaux du couchant au levant!

Given that a turn-round of values takes place between the stanza describing the ship's magnificent arrival and the following stanza which depicts its undignified retreat, what effect will a 3+3+4+2 reading have?

Un navir(e)/y passait//majestueu/sement

Such a reading, if we can even admit the notion of a mid-word *coupe* which is not a *coupe enjambante* (see below, Section (ii)), embeds 'majestueusement' in the process of *matter-of-fact* description evident in the first half of the line. But it does not deserve to be part of such a process. 'Majestueusement' is as much ironic comment as careful, impartial qualification; the poet jibs at his illusory image just as much as he concedes to it. By not insisting on the transformation of an *accent contre-tonique* into the equivalent of an *accent tonique*, or prosodic accent, we leave to the word and to the six-syllable measure, it recalcitrance, its deviousness and its breadth of sweep. Let 'majestueusement' by all means have its countertonic accent, but let us describe the line as 3 + 3 + 6.

The two kinds of *accent d'appui* we have just examined are essentially accents of diction, rather than prosodic accents, although, as we have said, there may be occasions on which they deserve prosodic status. A sound, working rule of thumb is that tonic, terminal accents are the only true prosodic accents. These *accents d'appui* are also best seen as voice-supports, and not as expressive devices. The final type of accent I wish to discuss·is indeed the expressive accent, the *accent oratoire*, sometimes also called the *accent d'intensité*. This, too, is a recitational accent and only in the rarest instances can it be considered to be rhythmically determining. This accent attacks the first consonant of the word concerned and reverberates through the following vowel, so that it is, properly speaking, a syllabic accent. Where a potential *accent oratoire* coincides with a potential *accent contre-tonique*, it distinguishes itself from this latter precisely by involving the preceding consonant with a force that the *accent contre-tonique* does not. The opening stanza of Baudelaire's 'Les Aveugles' provides two good examples of the *accent oratoire*:

Contemple-les, mon âme; ils sont vraiment affreux!
Pareils aux mannequins; vaguement ridicules;
Terribles, singuliers comme les somnambules;
Dardant on ne sait où leurs globes ténébreux.

Prosodically this stanza reads 4+2+4+2/2+4+3+3/
2+4+(1+5)/2+4+2+4. To this bare description, one
needs to add the probable countertonic accents on
'Contèmple-les' and 'sòmnambules'. But one further needs
to add that 'vraiment' and 'vaguement' seem to require
expressive accents on their first syllables ('vraiment'; 'vaguement'). The poet is horror-struck and deeply fascinated
by these blind men, and mercilessly blunt about them; his
feeling of repulsion is part of his compulsion to look upon
them, his overt contempt is both defence and admission of
his own contemptibility. In this world of punishment and
purgation, the reader will probably want to draw out the
emotional confusion of the poet, to oblige him to commit
himself, the more to dramatise his recognition of himself in
the blind men at the end of the poem:

> Vois! je me traîne aussi! mais plus qu'eux hébété
> Je dis: Que cherchent-ils au Ciel, tous ces aveugles?

One may begin to suppose that certain parts of speech,
certain words even, naturally lend themselves to this
expressive accent, the *accent oratoire*. The adverb seems to
provide the poet with an obvious way to insinuate himself
into his text; while the verb and adjective, along with the
noun, carry the burden of description and basic notation,
the adverb can afford to be all colour, all narrative view-
point, all tone. I am not of course suggesting that adverbs
have no informational function; the informational function
of negative adverbs, for instance, is absolutely crucial. Nor
am I suggesting that nouns, adjectives and verbs may not
have a profound subjective colouring. But adverbs can be
areas of great semantic elasticity. And we shall find that in
poetry of a tragic or elegiac kind, a word like 'jamais' almost
inevitably attracts to itself an *accent oratoire*, an insistence on
its first syllable which explores all poignancy and despair,
which is half cry, as in the Lamartinian line already quoted:

> Quoi! passés pour jamais? quoi! tout entiers perdus?

But can we ever call such accents prosodic? Are not these

accents so bound up with recitational contingencies, so much more so than the *accents d'appui*, that to endow them with an objective status, to suggest that they necessarily inhere in a linguistic structure, would be indefensible? This is really the only reasonable view. But let us leave ourselves with a problem, with a line from Baudelaire's 'La Chevelure':

> Tu contiens, mer d'ébène, un éblouissant rêve.

After the 3+3 of the first hemistich, what? If the adjective 'éblouissant' were postposed, how easy it would be – 3+3+2+4. But can we say 3+3+6 and pass over that adjective, which has all the 'expansion des choses infinies'? Surely not. And how rhythmically unjust a 3+3+5+1 reading would be on the undulations of hair and sea. Should we not perhaps let the *accent oratoire* have its way both recitationally and prosodically and envisage 3+3+3+3?

> Tu contiens,/mer d'ébèn(e)// un é<u>blou</u>/issant rêve.

(ii) *Coupe*

Coupe is a term which we have so far employed sparingly, but only to avoid an awkward inundation of terminology. But it is the standard term for the description of the division between one measure and the next, when the terms 'caesura' and 'line-ending' are not more appropriate. The *coupe* falls immediately after the accentuated, or tonic, vowel, and like the caesura has no necessary connection with pause or break in syntax; it is created by the accent and not by any other factor. It is usually marked by a vertical or oblique line. The problems raised by the *coupe* are few, but have some interpretative implications.

Let us use the first stanza of Nerval's 'El Desdichado' as our starting-point:

> Je suis le ténébreux, – le veuf, – l'inconsolé,
> Le prince d'Aquitaine à la tour abolie:
> Ma seule *étoile* est morte, – et mon luth constellé
> Porte le *soleil* noir de la *Mélancolie*.

It is evident from the first line that when the accent falls on the last or only syllable of the word, and when there is no liaison between the accentuated syllable and a following vowel, the *coupe* takes its place comfortably between the words concerned, thus 'Je suis/le ténébreux,// – le veuf,/ – l'inconsolé'. When there is liaison between the accentuated syllable and the following word, as in 'à la tour abolie' and 'Ma seul(e) étoil(e) est morte', we still place the *coupe* between the words, although it might be more accurately placed between the accentuated vowel and the final consonant(s) of the syllable – so 'à la tour/abolie' and 'Ma seule étoile/est morte' rather than 'à la tou/r abolie' and 'Ma seule étoi/le est morte'. The same holds true of the marking of the caesura. But in the first measures of the second and fourth lines, another problem arises: the accentuated syllables are followed by an *e atone*, not elided, but counted. Which measure do these atonic syllables belong to, the measure created by the word of which they are a part, or the following measure of which they constitute the first, unaccentuated syllable? If we adhere to the principle on which French rhythms are based, namely the terminality of accent, there can be no further argument and we must describe these as *coupes enjambantes*, that is to say, as *coupes* which fall in the middle of a word and are straddled by that word; we require the following measure to complete the word, thus 'Le prin/ce d'Aquitaine' (2+4) and 'Por/te le *soleil* noir' (1+5). And the syntax in each case bears this out: 'Le prince d'Aquitaine' has the natural integrity of a title, while the close kinship between a transitive verb and its object, and the tenacious attachment of the eclipsed sun to the poet's lute, are equally underlined by the *coupe enjambante* of 'Porte le soleil noir'.

Some would argue that this is the only possible way to read measures like these and would refer us not only to the principle of the terminality of accent, but also to the special qualities bestowed on the French verse-line by the *coupe enjambante*: a resilient continuity, a sinuous gracefulness, a sensitivity to pitch-change and broad patterns of intonation, so different from the notion of beat which for so long dominated English versification; the enjambed *e atone* is richly both dying fall and incipient impulse. Henri Morier (1961) summarises thus: 'l'*e* atone enjambant . . . *creuse la mélodie, esquisse une courbe élégante et accentuée; ainsi, la coupe enjambante suggère un mouvement continu, souple et arrondi; elle convient à merveille à la grâce féminine, à la nature voluptueuse et alanguie*' (p. 158). Perhaps, above all, the *coupe enjambante* establishes an incontrovertible role for the *e atone*, is a justification of its being given full syllabic value, as an agent of reconciliation and softened outline. And the stylistic potentialities of the *coupe enjambante*, some of which are alluded to by Morier, are manifold. Another line from 'El Desdichado' shows admirably its conciliatory and softening capability:

Et la treille/où le pampre//à la ro/se s'allie.

And in the first stanza of Baudelaire's 'La Cloche fêlée', already quoted:

Les souvenirs/lointains//lentement/s'élever
Au bruit/des carillons//qui chan/tent dans la brume

one hears in the *coupe enjambante* the dying reverberations of the bells, their being deadened and enwrapped in the mist. And is it over-taxing the imagination to suggest that in Polyeucte's line, again previously quoted:

Faisons triompher/Dieu://qu'il dispo/se du reste!

the *coupe enjambante* exudes the confidence, nay arrogance, of one vicariously enjoying a destructive omnipotence?

The *coupe enjambante* is the normal way of dealing with an accentuated syllable with following *e atone*. But in those exceptional circumstances which warrant it, we may have recourse to the *coupe lyrique*, sometimes also called the *coupe féminine*. We quoted Henri Morier's words on the *coupe enjambante*, but his name comes even more apropos in connection with the *coupe lyrique*, for he it is who has done most to bring attention to it (see his *Le Rythme du vers libre symboliste*, 1943–4, and the relevant entries in his *Dictionnaire de poétique et de rhétorique*, 1975). His own definition (1975) of the *coupe lyrique* runs: 'Coupe ainsi nommée par le métricien Tobler, et qui consiste à "couper" le rythme du vers *après* l'*e* atone précédant une consonne initiale de mot à l'intérieur du vers' (p. 608). In Hugo's poem on weeping in *Les Feuilles d'automne* (1831) – 'Oh! pourquoi te cacher? Tu pleurais seule ici' – the lines:

> Pleure. Les pleurs vont bien, même au bonheur; tes chants
> Sont plus doux dans les pleurs, tes yeux purs et touchants
> Sont plus beaux quand tu les essuies

offer an example of a possible *coupe lyrique*. Do we read 'Pleure./Les pleurs vont bien//. . .' (2+4) (*coupe lyrique*), or 'Pleu/re. Les pleurs vont bien//. . .' (1+5) (*coupe enjambante*)? The points made in support of the *coupe lyrique* might look as follows: (a) there is a clear syntactical break after the second syllable; (b) the pause after the *e atone* is needed to suggest the translation of imperative into action; (c) such a pause would also help to distinguish between the specificity of the verb's purpose and the abstractness of the following noun; (d) it is rhythmically desirable to balance the isolated 'Pleure' against the equally isolated 'tes chants'; furthermore, in the second of these dissyllabic measures, the pattern of the first (accentuated syllable + unaccentuated syllable) is reversed. But the *coupe enjambante* also has some claim: weeping is an ongoing undertone throughout the poem, so that this imperative does not have the force of a sudden command, but is a repeated persuasion, an inbuilt part of the poet's discourse; and the repetition of 'pleurer' in various grammatical guises encourages the reader to create a seamless, continuous structure in which the word is a kind of intoning.

The *coupe lyrique* has perhaps a special significance in dramatic verse, both because of the frequent words of address (proper nouns, 'Madame', 'Sire', 'Traître', 'Ingrate', 'Monstre') and imperatives (particularly 'Parle')

which punctuate speech, and because drama itself so often
derives from the discontinuity of diction and the brusque-
ness of utterance. But here it is easy to get things out of
proportion. These lines from Racine's *Bajazet* (Act V,
sc. vi):

> Vous pouvez de mon sort me laisser la maîtresse,
> Madame; mon trépas n'en sera pas moins prompt

may seem to warrant a *coupe lyrique* after 'Madame' because
of its belonging to the syntax of the previous line, which it
brings to a close. But words of address have a peculiar
amenability and can often be absorbed into following syntactical groups without discomfort; and if conventional
scansion – remembering that the *coupe enjambante* is the
conventional scansion – works in such cases, then there is no
reason not to use it. So 'Madame' in this example will
belong as much to its own line as to the previous one with
which it has its real syntactic link:

> Vous pouvez de mon sort me laisser la maîtresse,
> Mada/me; mon trépas//. . .   2+4//. . .

This particular disposition of a word of address, belonging
syntactically to a previous line, prosodically to the one of
which it constitutes the first measure, is frequently to be
found. In the following lines, successive imperatives make
it easy for 'Œnone' to shift allegiance:

> Va trouver de ma part ce jeune ambitieux,
> Œnone; fais briller//la couronne à ses yeux.
> (*Phèdre*, Act III, sc. i)

But even where the two syntactical units concerned are of
totally different natures – a question and an imperative, say
– with different overall intonation curves, the *coupe enjambante* is still able to reconcile them:

> Est-il temps d'en douter,
> Mada/me? Hâtez-vous d'achever votre ouvrage.
> (*Bajazet*, Act I, sc. iii)

Here, because of the hiatus (clash of contiguous vowels –
'Mada/m<u>e</u>? H<u>â</u>tez-vous . . .'), the *e atone* is minimised,
expressed as a protraction of the consonant m. Nonetheless,
question can become imperative by the agency of the
neutral connective which the *e atone* is.

But the *coupe lyrique* does have its part to play in dramatic
verse, when commands, indictments, abuse are wrenched
out of the flow of fine speech and stand naked as signs of the
barbarity and fragmentariness which threaten, and yet
underpin, the ordered surface of civilised exchange. When
Hermione discovers her inner contradictions, loses her grip
on her own personality, after Pyrrhus's assassination, the
coupe lyrique appears:

> Barbare,/qu'as-tu fait! Avec quelle furie
> As-tu tranché le cours d'une si belle vie!
> Avez-vous pu, cruels, l'immoler aujourd'hui,
> Sans que tout votre sang se soulevât pour lui!
> Mais parle:/de son sort qui t'a rendu l'arbitre?
>   (*Andromaque*, Act V, sc.iii)

A *coupe enjambante* in the last line of this extract would
obviously make a syntactic nonsense of the line. The *coupe
lyrique* equally appears when Mithridate's anger gets the
better of him in a confrontation with Pharnace:

> Traître!/pour les Romains tes lâches complaisances
> N'étaient pas à mes yeux d'assez noires offenses.
>   (*Mithridate*, Act III, sc.i)

Once again, let us close the section with a problem, one
posed by a subtle prosodic commentator, Robert Champigny (1963), a problem which, with its introduction of the
alexandrin trimètre – the three-measure alexandrine – heralds
the next section, on the caesura, a problem which arises
from a line in Rimbaud's 'Le Bateau ivre':

> Et les lointains vers les gouffres cataractant!

Champigny remarks:

Plus utile que ce point d'exclamation serait un signe
de ponctuation poétique qui indiquerait comment
traiter l'*e* atone de 'gouffres'. Si l'on opte pour la
coupe enjambante, on obtient un vers irrégulier,
manquant de cohésion, coupé 4/3/5. La coupe lyrique rétablit en principe la bonne forme du vers
(4/4/4). Mais la prononciation qu'on est alors amené
à donner à 'gouffres' est bien malheureuse (p. 50).

My own view is that the *coupe lyrique* deserves the vote. I
don't accept Champigny's implied equation of irregularity
with lack of cohesion, but nor do I understand his objection
to the pronunciation of 'gouffres' with a *coupe lyrique*. In any
case, these do not seem to me to be the crucial arguments.
With the *coupe lyrique*, the idea of falling, of extension in
space, so necessary to the line, is better conveyed; and by
intercalating the *coupe* (with some pause) *between* the last
two elements, we do not disturb the phonetic integrity of
'cataractant', with its distinctive a̲-centredness, and we
allow the tongue to get round its rather tortuous consonants. The voice needs this run at the final word, too, to give
it an explosiveness proper to it. If we read:

Et les lointains/vers les gouffres/cataractant!

the *e atone* acts as a suspension, a kind of precipice down
which 'cataractant' can suddenly and terrifyingly plunge.
But any case for a *coupe lyrique* must be strenuously argued,
otherwise a *coupe enjambante* will be the assumed reading.

(iii) *Caesura*
The terms used to describe the *coupe*, that is
enjambante or *lyrique*, derive from their use in connection
with the caesura. Since we now have some familiarity with
these notions, we can take for granted some of the basic
characteristics of the *césure enjambante* and the *césure lyrique*.
It should be said, however, that because of the fixity of the
caesura in relation to the *coupe*, because of the much greater
insistence throughout the classical period on the coincidence of rhythmic break and syntactic break at the caesura,

the *césure enjambante* is a much, much rarer phenomenon
than the *coupe enjambante*, and, to my knowledge, is exclusively confined to *vers libéré* and *vers libre*. The *césure lyrique*
presents problems of a rather different nature.

But let us look, without more ado, at some examples. In
Fernand Séverin's 'Le Rêve du voyage' we find the line:

> Le silence, les clo//ches, le silence encore!
>
>   3+3+4+2

where, as in 'La Cloche fêlée', the connecting *e atone* gives
the effect of sound fading into silence. Henri de Régnier's
work has frequent recourse to the *césure enjambante*:

> Une fenêtre sur l'odeur du buis amer
> Ouverte, et sur des ro//ses d'où le vent balance
>
>   2+4+4+2
> Le lustre de cristal au parquet de bois clair.
>
>   ('Le Pavillon')

> Voici le tribut pris aux beaux jardins où pousse
> L'arbre de l'Hespéri//de qu'un monstre gardien
>
>   1+5+3+3
> Regardait s'effruiter parmi l'herbe de mousse.
>
>   ('Prélude')

In both these instances, the first hemistich is closely dependent on a following relative clause. In the lines from 'Le
Pavillon', the *césure enjambante* means that the roses are
already animated by the 'balancement' of the wind. In 'Prélude', a poem about Omphale and Heracles, the *e atone* of
'Hespéride' not only echoes in an amplified way the *coupe
enjambante* of 'arbre' and prefigures the *coupe enjambante* of
'monstre', but sets itself against the *-re* endings common to
these words, so that we experience 'Hespéride' as apex and
goal, surrounded by, defended by, the *coupes*, and con-
demned by them to neglect.

If the *césure enjambante* strikes us as something of a transgression, the *césure lyrique* might seem all but inadmissible.
If the caesura is significant because of the strength of accent

it bestows, because of its place in the gradation of accents in the line, then to put the caesura after an unaccentuated syllable is a nonsense. Another line from Régnier's 'Prélude' will clarify the issue:

Toi pour qui le glaive rutil(e) et la nef rame.
1   2   3 4   5 6 7 8   9 10 11 12

The standard avenues of retreat for the analyst who cannot countenance the *césure lyrique* are: to argue that the caesura is absent (this is often the same as saying that the line in question is a *trimètre*, a three-measure alexandrine), or to argue that the caesura is displaced. We have had a glimpse of the 'displaced-caesura' argument in a line where there was no question of a *césure lyrique*, Racine's

Partons. A tant d'attraits, Amour, ferme ses yeux!

We objected to the 2//4+2+4 reading of this line on the grounds that neither pause nor *phonetic* intensity are reliable indicators of caesura; the caesura is a 'conventionalised point of attention', and it may be that semantic intensity and phonetic intensity do not coincide. By staunchly keeping faith with the medial caesura, we help ourselves to see more deeply into the paradoxes which underlie the line. Our working rule should be: do not suppose shifts of caesura unless you have the best of reasons, or unless the line is in no sense conventionally caesurable; because the effectiveness of the caesura in regular verse, both as a rhythmic *point de repère* and as an explorer of covert meaning, depends on its fixity, on our being able to *resort to it*, for help. But in a line like Régnier's, there is obviously some room for proposing a 5//7 division, with *césure enjambante*. But before opting for this reading, we should understand how versatile the medial caesura can be; it may be a point of phonetic intensity, it may be a point of semantic intensity, it may be a point of intensified doubt, it may be purely imaginary, but no less effective for that; it need not coincide with pause or syntactic break, but it may be the *creator* of pause, whether that pause is syntactically convenient or not. It is this last argu-

ment that we should adopt with the *césure lyrique*; we need
to argue that the caesura in such lines gives a specially
abrupt impetus to the second hemistich, and that the lull in
the line serves other stylistic ends – here 'rutile' is the result
of a blow struck by the sword, a blow struck in the course of
the line; the pause at the caesura imitates the raising of the
sword; and if we fall more heavily, more suddenly, on
'rutile' because of the pause, we fall with the falling blade.
But we must remember that the *césure lyrique* has no prior
claims to existence; in each specific instance it must be
rigorously argued for or against.

The other avenue of retreat we have mentioned is the
assertion of the caesura's absence. Such an assertion might
have been made in connection with a line we have already
met, the third in the opening stanza of Verlaine's 'Ariettes
oubliées II':

> Je devine, à travers un murmure,
> Le contour subtil des voix anciennes
> Et dans les lueurs musiciennes,   5//4
> Amour pâle, une aurore future!

While there are clear syntactical divisions in the other three
lines, the third line compels us to divorce, in our minds at
least, a noun from its adjective. Let us therefore suggest that
a caesura should not, does not, occur in this line. But this is a
feeble argument, not only because the classical alexandrine
has long accustomed us to similar divisions at the caesura,
but because Verlaine positively wishes us to both join and
divorce in our minds the noun and the adjective, for, as in any
metaphor, the force of the fusion of 'lueurs' and 'musiciennes' depends on our feeling at the same time their resistance
to fusion. This line, after all, contains the first real
synaesthetic experience of the poem, a combination of the
visual and the aural – 'contour' in the second line is strictly
speaking visual, but has become so abstract that its
metaphorical charge is exhausted. Furthermore the vague-
ness of the light given off by 'lueurs' contrasts with the
syllabic precision of 'musiciennes' (for a comment on this

feature, see the treatment of these lines in Chapter 4, p.110).
If we bring automatic and rigid attitudes to the nature and
function of the caesura, we shall find ourselves arguing
more frequently, and with less cause, for its displacement or
absence, and consequently we shall find ourselves arguing
unjustifiably that such and such a poet has undermined
classic practice, has flouted convention; the chances are that
the poet in question has simply exploited the versatility
which inevitably grows from the ultimate undefinability of
the caesura, or merely extended it.

The argument for the absence of the caesura in an alexandrine is often, if not usually, backed up by the discovery of a
trimetric, rather than tetrametric, structure in the line. Let
us look at another example from Henri de Régnier's verse,
where again a *césure lyrique* is at stake:

> Et les Princesses fabuleuses aux yeux doux
> Fuirent avec leurs fous et leurs bouffons hilares
> $$1+5+4+2$$
> Aux Nefs de parade qui larguaient les amarres
> D'un or fin et tressé comme des cheveux roux.
> $$3+3+(1+5)$$
> ('La Galère')

I have given the rhythmic shape of the lines which appear to
me unproblematical. The first line of the stanza, with the
sixth syllable falling on the first syllable of 'fabuleuses',
seems to demand a trimetric reading, thus $4+4+4$, with
two *coupes enjambantes*. But what of the third line?

Once again, a case might be made for the displacement of
the caesura, $5//7(2+3+4+3)$ with *césure enjambante*, and
after all, the structure of this line (noun group + relative
clause) is similar to the structure of those lines of Régnier we
have used to exemplify the *césure enjambante*. Alternatively,
we might want to suppose that this line, like the first, is an
alexandrin trimètre – thus $5+4+3$ – and to suppose that the
caesura is absent. This seems to me a totally unconvincing
reading. The syntactical binariness of the line is, I think,
self-evident (and underlined by the fixedness of the phrase

'larguer les amarres') just as the essentially tetrametric
rhythm ('...Néfs... paráde ... larguáient... amárres') is
self-evident. The choice once again, therefore, lies between
a displaced caesura and a *césure lyrique*. Here the pause is
easier to instal after the sixth syllable than in the previous
example, because of the syntactic break, but more justification than that is required. Régnier's poem is a nostalgic
reaching back for the freshness and wealth of childlike
vision, a vision of fine ladies, resplendent in tasteful orna-
ment, accompanied by jester, courtier, tumbler. The incar-
nation of Régnier's Watteauesque dream is the 'galère de
parade', out of which are conjured the ladies and their
Freudian retinue, an emanation of half-buried desire:

> Les Princesses ayant foulé les blondes grèves
> S'en vinrent en cortège à travers les jardins,
> Avec des fous, des courtisans, des baladins,
> Et des enfants portant des oiseaux et des glaives.

But the 'galère de parade', the key to vision, transforms
itself into the 'Nefs de parade' which are the vehicles of the
vision's disappearance, carrying off the princesses. Well
might the poet, then, isolate 'Aux Nefs de parade', in longing and regret, in an attempt to stay the dream and undo the
continuity of ineluctable consequence:

> Aux Nefs/de parade//qui larguaient/les amarres.

Similar problems of choice between displaced caesura,
absent caesura (*trimètre*) and *césure lyrique* are posed by
another line from 'Prélude':

> Et le voici maître//du Sceptre et du Trésor

where the argument for *trimètre* (i.e. 5+3+4) is slightly
stronger than in the previous example, and by another line
from 'La Galère', where the case for *trimètre* is stronger still:

> Vint aborder une//galère de parade.   4+4+4(?)

The *alexandrin trimètre* has already elbowed its way into
our reflections, without our stopping to give it special

consideration. This should be remedied. The *trimètre*, sometimes called the *alexandrin ternaire* or the *alexandrin romanti-
que*, because of its connection with Romantic, and particularly Hugolian, practice, comes into existence when the
caesura is either minimal or apparently absent, and is
superseded by a straddling measure with a stronger syntactic integrity; the binary, four-measure structure is submerged beneath a new self-imposing three-measure structure, which at its most regular creates a $4+4+4$ disposition,
but which may vary immensely ($4+5+3$, $5+3+4$, $2+6+4$,
etc.). Examples of the *trimètre* are to be found in the work of
Molière, Racine, La Fontaine, Chénier, but it is the Romantics who are properly credited with its popularisation. The
Romantics, however, distinguish themselves from subsequent poets in ensuring that their *trimètres* are still caesurable; that is to say, the sixth syllable is still prosodically
accentuable, though not in fact accentuated, which is not the
case in Régnier's:

Et les Princesses fabuleuses aux yeux doux

$4+4+4$

nor in Verlaine's celebrated:

Et la tigresse épouvantable d'Hyrcanie. $4+4+4$
('Dans la grotte')

The *alexandrin trimètre* draws much of its significance
from the regularity of contextual lines; it acts like a syncopation. Hugo's verse, for instance, tends to gather a powerful
forward momentum, as his vision seeks to encompass a
world which is constantly growing, changing, diversifying;
the syncopation of the *trimètre* helps to capture something of
the fear, panic even, which intermittently takes hold of the
poet as his visionary energy lures him into hallucination,
or into vertiginous cosmic spaces. We can feel this in the
following lines from 'La Pente de la rêverie':

Quand j'eus, quelques instants, des yeux de ma
pensée, $2+4+2+4$

Contemplé leur famille à mon foyer pressée,

$$3+3+4+2$$

Je vis trembler leurs traits confus, et par degrés

$$4+4+4$$

Pâlir en s'effaçant leurs fronts décolorés,

$$2+4+2+4$$

Et tous, comme un ruisseau qui dans un lac s'écoule,

$$2+4+4+2$$

Se perdre autour de moi dans une immense foule.

$$2+4+4+2$$

Hugo first conjures up in his mind his friends of the *Cénacle*, then those travelling in distant lands, and finally, in this extract, those who have died. And as these last appear, so he loses his grip on their individuality, they become a nameless crowd, a chaos, governing him. The point of transition, when the poet's heart misses a beat and his subject assumes a disturbing autonomy, is the *trimètre* (but note also the temporary mesmerisation of the poet by the rhymes in *é*). And this *trimètre*, with its use of the word 'confus', looks regretfully back to an earlier *tétramètre* in the same section:

Mes amis, non confus, mais tels que je les voi.

As we have mentioned, Hugo's *trimètres* are still caesurable, and it would not be unreasonable to suggest that this *trimètre* is in fact a *tétramètre* $(4+2+2+4)$, with an *enjambement* at the caesura, throwing into relief the word 'confus', which, as we have seen, has a special piquancy. To the implications of this approach we shall return.

Other *trimètres* are less problematic because the sixth syllable is not accentuable in the same way. We have already met such instances in Régnier and Verlaine. We might equally point to a line in Leconte de Lisle's 'Sacra Fames':

La Faim sacrée est un long meurtre légitime

$$4+4+4$$

Des profondeurs de l'ombre aux cieux resplendissants,

$$4+2+2+4$$

Et l'homme et le requin, égorgeur ou victime,
                                        2+4+3+3
Devant ta face, ô Mort, sont tous deux innocents.
                                        4+2+3+3
Leconte de Lisle uses the *trimètre* to highlight his awful
truth, a truth the more powerful for its moral, as well as
rhythmic, awkwardness. The *trimètre* here also serves a
larger structural function; this is the final stanza of the
poem, and the *trimètre*, by momentarily erasing the tetrametric norm, allows it to re-establish itself with renewed
vigour and certainty, as finale; this emergence of the poem
as if from its own ashes is made easier by the syntactic
continuity of the stanza.

But confidence in the identification of the *trimètre* too
easily leads to an overeagerness in its discovery. We need to
caution ourselves. First, prefer the term *alexandrin trimètre* to
alexandrin ternaire, because while *trimètre* contrasts with
tétramètre, *ternaire* contrasts with *binaire*; in other words,
trimètre encourages us to see the divisons between measures
as *coupes* (4/4/4), whereas *ternaire* encourages us to see them
as caesuras (4//4//4). If we opt for *coupe* divisions – and there
is plenty of room for debate here – it is because a *trimètre*
only makes sense as deviation, is dependent for its effect on
our either setting its three measures against a *potential*
binary, tetrametric structure (as in the Hugo example), or at
least imagining the caesura which has been superseded. This
is not to disqualify the notion of a displaced caesura, which
may well find its place in a trimetric structure; the trimetric
reading of Régnier's 'Aux Nefs de parade qui larguaient les
amarres' is more convincing as 5//4+3 than as 5/4/3. And in
defence of this general view, let us remind ourselves once
again of the versatility and tolerance of the medial caesura.

In our treatment of accents, we looked at those situations
in which prepositions and conjunctions may carry a weak
accent, indicated by a bracketing of the hemistich. If such
words can bear an accent, though weak, can they not bear a
caesural accent? 'Comme' and 'avec' were two of the words
that occupied us. Consider the following set of lines:

(a) Ton Souvenir est comme un livre bien aimé
                              6

(Samain, 'Ton Souvenir est comme un livre bien
                                            aimé')

(b) Ah! maintenant c'est comme un vol d'oiseaux
        meurtris   6
        (Richepin, 'Les Trois Matelots de Groix')

(c) Qui l'observent avec des regards familiers
                        6
                (Baudelaire, 'Correspondances')

(d) Agile et noble, avec sa jambe de statue
                        6
                    (Baudelaire, 'A une passante')

(e) Mon dernier souffle, avec l'odeur des foins
        nouveaux.   6
                        (Theuriet, 'Les Foins')

One might be inclined to see all these lines as *trimètres* – (a)
4+4+4, (b) 4+4+4, (c) 3+6+3, (d) 4+4+4, (e) 4+4+4 –
not surprisingly. But certainly not all traces of the *tétramètre*
have been effaced, and it could be plausibly maintained that
the lines, all of which have compound nominal groups in
their second hemistichs, would benefit from a momentary
pause, or a suspension of the voice, at the sixth syllable; such
a pause, or suspension of the voice at the crest of a pitch
curve specially created, would convey a hesitancy in the
poet as he seeks, and happily chances upon, the apposite
image (b), or as he prepares to savour a self-indulgent,
sentimental moment (e), or as he insinuates a slight feeling
of eeriness (c), or as he strives to give an image full weight as
tribute (a), or as he attempts to reconcile potentially conflicting epithets in a resounding equilibrium (d). I am not
suggesting that trimetric readings of these lines should not
be preferred; the structural argument for reading 'Agile et
noble, avec sa jambe de statue' as a *trimètre*, to take but one
example, is overwhelming; it is the first line of the sonnet's
second quatrain, a quatrain whose remaining lines are con-

cerned with the poet's depiction of himself, and his reaction to the passing woman; in fact, this line looks like an afterthought which did not find room for itself in the first quatrain, where it logically belongs, with the rest of the woman's description; it should be said, however, that the first line of the poem is similarly detached, a glimpse of the urban environment. Furthermore, the syntactical anomalousness of 'Agile et noble, avec sa jambe de statue', the absence of any verb, squares well with the rhythmic anomalousness of the *trimètre*. No, what I am suggesting is that, in these instances, the trimetric reading should by no means be a foregone conclusion.

And even where there seem to be no grounds at all for marking the medial caesura, as in Régnier's line:

> Et les Princesses fabuleuses aux yeux doux

and in Verlaine's line:

> Et la tigresse épouvantable d'Hyrcanie

we need to think twice. True, the sixth syllable falls in the middle of long adjectives; but it falls precisely upon those syllables which we might wish to endow with an *accent oratoire* – 'fabuleuses', 'épouvantable'. In other words, the caesura has exchanged its prosodic role for a recitational one; and precisely because of its being so deeply embedded as a prosodic *donnée* in our consciousness of the line, it has the power to *impose* itself in another, purely expressive guise.

As will be evident from examples already encountered, an over-insistent use of the trimetric reading, or at least of an exclusively trimetric reading, tends to impoverish the classic *alexandrin tétramètre*, by making *enjambement* at the caesura almost unenvisageable. Before pursuing this point, we must clearly distinguish between the *césure enjambante* (where a single word 'enjambs,' or straddles, the caesura) and a caesura with *enjambement* (where a closely knit syntactical group enjambs, or straddles, the caesura). *Enjambement*, the non-coincidence of syntactic and prosodic juncture (of any kind, *coupe*, caesura or line-ending), will be dealt with as

an end-of-line phenomenon in the following chapter, and
there, too, the terms associated with *enjambement*, namely
rejet (what is pushed forward by the prosodic break) and
contre-rejet (what is left behind by the prosodic break) will be
more fully defined. But from our discussion of the lines
from Hugo's 'La Pente de la rêverie', and of the caesural
possibilities of prepositions and conjunctions, we have
gained a fair view of what a caesura with *enjambement* might
look like and what its effects. might be. Two further
examples will suffice.

Let us first return to Hugo, to 'Le Sacre de la femme'
from *La Légende des siècles:*

> La création sainte, à son tour créatrice, $5+1+3+3$
> Modelait vaguement des aspects merveilleux,
> $3+3+3+3$
> Faisait sortir l'essaim des êtres fabuleux, $4+2+2+4$
> Tantôt des bois, tantôt des mers, tantôt des nues.
> $4+4+4$

The trimetric reading of the final line underscores the tri-
pleness of the enumeration, too meekly, too undramati-
cally, too unenquiringly it might well be claimed. What
consequences would follow from the restoration of the
medial caesura and a tetrametric reading $(4+2+2+4)$? First,
and most basically, it would envigorate the enumeration by
rhythmically diversifying it. Secondly, this last line would
rhythmically echo the line preceding it, making the process
of creation coherent and concerted. Thirdly, it would
dramatise the emergence of the 'êtres fabuleux' by enacting
at the caesura a *surgissement*. The *enjambement* of the phrase
'tantôt//des mers', by creating a pitch-apex on 'tan<u>tôt</u>', and
a momentary pause, would embody not only the explosiveness of a bursting into life, but also the apprehensive
anticipation of an onlooker. And if this reading seems to do
too much violence to the natural (linguistically governed)
enunciation of the sentence, then we can at least suggest that
an awareness of the caesura with *enjambement* should organise our perception of the line, however we recite it.

My second example comes from Baudelaire's .'Chant
d'automne':

> Courte tâche! La tombe attend; elle est avide!

A trimetric reading, following the indications of the punctuation, would run 3+5+4 (or possibly 4+4+4 – I do not
here wish to enter into the pros and cons of a *coupe lyrique* at
'tâche', but if I opt for the *coupe enjambante*, it is to capture
something of the tomb's impatience). But is this as satisfying as a more conventional tetrametric reading with medial
caesura?

> Courte tâche! La tomb(e)//attend; elle est avide!
>
> 3+3+2+4

We would normally associate 'attend' with a certain passivity, a passivity which the trimetric reading tends to confirm.
But does not 'elle est avide' make it clear that passivity is the
last thing the poet has in mind? Only by practising *enjambement* at a restored caesura can we endow 'attend' with an
assertive force, positively experienced by the reader, which
will not be gainsaid. Thanks to the caesura, what might be a
colourless circumlocution, a dead metaphor, in other contexts, is re-awakened and charged with nervous energy.
One other argument for the full marking of the caesura in
this line might be easily overlooked. If we read back
through the poem, we shall find that Baudelaire has previously related the sounds ɔb (to<u>mb</u>e) and ã (att<u>end</u>), in the
third line of the first stanza:

> J'ent<u>end</u>s déjà to<u>mb</u>er avec des chocs funèbres

and again in the first line of the third stanza:

> J'écoute en frémiss<u>ant</u> chaque bûche qui to<u>mb</u>e.

In both instances, the ã not only precedes the ɔb, but
belongs to the poet, while the ɔb belongs to the funereal
phenomena which surround him. In our original line, the
order is reversed, and the two sounds both belong to the
same hostile forces. The caesura with *enjambement* captures,

it seems to me, both the vestigial, if now ironic, tension between these sounds, and the overcoming of that tension in complicity.

In his discussion of the caesura's position in a line from Ronsard, F. W. Leakey (1975) maintains that: 'the demands of sense are imperious and overriding: they *must* override the eye's desire to impose, where possible, the "rule" of the median caesura, or indeed any other rule; on no account can we allow ourselves to read the poet's verses in such a way that they become *non*sense'. In this connection, he speaks of the 'irrelevance' of the caesura: 'by "irrelevance", I mean simply that the "obligatory" division at the hemistich only becomes significant, in the performance of the poem, when it coincides with a main division (or pause) imposed by the sense or syntax of the line' (pp. 8–9). It will be clear from the foregoing pages that I must either totally disagree with these opinions or regard them as a classic instance of the yawning gap which separates the business of scansion from the concerns of recitation. Of course we cannot 'allow ourselves to read the poet's verses in such a way that they become *non*sense', but we can read them in such a way that they reveal a sense *within* sense, dimensions of meaning which we would miss were we to read only by meaning.

3

Enjambement, hiatus and word-sound

(i) *Enjambement*

As we saw in the previous chapter, the notion of *enjambement* can be applied both to the caesura and to the rhythmic *coupe*. But it is most generally used of line-endings, when the line-ending catches the syntax off balance, when the reader must read on to the next line if he is to complete the interrupted clause or phrase. The other terms necessary to a discussion of *enjambement* are:

(a) *rejet*, which refers to the word, or small group of words, *rejeté* by *enjambement* into the following line, when the larger part of the syntactical entity is in the first line, e.g.:

> Dieux! dans ma lourde plaie une secrète sœur
> <u>Brûle</u>, qui se préfère à l'extrême attentive.
> (Valéry, La Jeune Parque)

(b) *contre-rejet*, which refers to the word, or small group of words, initiating an *enjambement*, when the larger part of the syntactical entity is in the following line, e.g.:

> Le vent de l'autre nuit l'a jeté bas! <u>Le marbre</u>
> Au souffle du matin tournoie, . . .
> (Verlaine, 'L'Amour par terre')

Since word-quantities are at stake in these definitions and since quantities are often hard to differentiate, there is some case for using *rejet* and *contre-rejet* with rather more licence, simply to refer, respectively, to the part of the enjambing unit, however long, which appears in the second line and to the part of the enjambing unit, however long, which appears in the first line.

But there are, unfortunately, disagreements about these terms, which makes necessary their constant re-definition. My own particular view is that *enjambement* is a general phenomenon – the run-on of sense over certain prosoidic divisions – which encompasses many different manifestations, and within which the notions of *rejet* and *contre-rejet*, can help the commentator simply as descriptive tools. But Jean Mazaleyrat (1974), for example, distinguishes between, on the one hand, *rejet* and *contre-rejet*, and, on the other, *enjambement*, seeing in the first a desire to give prominence, and in the second a desire to efface:

> Sur le plan du style, la discordance par rejet ou contre-rejet met en valeur un élément du discours; pas la discordance par enjambement. Sur le plan phonétique, l'éclairage spécial de l'élément mis en relief par rejet ou contre-rejet se marque par renforcement – voire par création délibérée – de l'accent rythmique indiquant l'articulation métrique; tandis que l'enjambement affaiblit cet accent et voile cette articulation. De sorte que le rejet et le contre-rejet assurent le mètre en soulignant les contours; l'enjambement l'ébranle en les effaçant partiellement (p. 127).

But let us return to the broader context of *enjambement*. It will perhaps be difficult for the English reader, so accustomed to *enjambement* in his own verse, to understand why it should have been the subject of so much controversy among French verse-analysts. In English verse, *enjambement* only serves to endorse the potential continuity of English rhythms; if the rhythm is noticeably regular, then the chances are that the last foot of one line will be the same as the first foot of the next. What more natural, then, than that the syntax should constantly cast doubt on the sanctity of the line-ending? No doubt dramatic blank verse, with its inclination to traffic in the fluency of normal speech, has had something to do with the minimisation of the sense of a line-ending, quite apart from the prosodic fact that *enjambement* helps to push blank verse into the larger groupings of the verse-paragraph, a kind of free, blank-verse stanza, and to accentuate what is perhaps the main rhythmic resource of blank verse, namely the caesura, by transferring important syntactical stops to the interior of the line, and by tending to displace the caesura, given the usual brevity of a *rejet* or a *contre-rejet*.

Odd experiments apart, France has had no blank verse tradition; and besides, French rhythms are not, as we have seen, built on the continuity and recurrence of certain measures. A sequence of alexandrines is, in a sense, a series of autonomous lines which relate to each other not by continuity, by commonness of measure, but because they are all dispositions of measures with the same twelve-syllable structural perspective. The last measure of one alexandrine is significant not because it indicates what the first measure of the following line will probably be, but because with the three measures preceding it, it adds up to twelve syllables; measures within a line may be said to determine other measures in the same line, but they in no way influence the measures in the succeeding line. This self-contained quality of the line – a function of the phrasal nature of French rhythms – is obviously jeopardised by *enjambement*. And once *enjambement* has established itself, it is not long before the unaccentuable word or syllable finds itself in a position, the rhyme position, where it must be accentuated:

> Or, voilà des spleens infinis que je suis en
> Voyage vers ta bouche, et pas plus à présent
> Que toujours, . . .
> (Laforgue, 'Complainte du Temps et de sa com-
> mère l'Espace')

Classical legislators would not have envisaged this last eventuality, but concentrated their argument against *enjambement* on the need to maintain the inviolability of the line, the pre-eminence of rhyme and the unison of rhythmic

measure and sense-unit. As so often, the principal legislators we look to are Malherbe and Boileau. Boileau writes
that, thanks to Malherbe:

> Les stances avec grâce apprirent à tomber
> Et le vers sur le vers n'osa plus enjamber.
>
> (*Art poétique*)

But what, after all, counts as *enjambement*? Not much of
that so-called *enjambement* which, in fact, in no way harms
the phrasal coherence of the line, where the division between lines, though not marked by punctuation, is a division between grammatical groups; such divisions are those
between noun and accompanying adjectival phrase, between noun and relative clause, between verb and adverbial
phrase, between noun and coordinating conjunction
followed by a second noun. In other words, the absence
of punctuation is no real indication of *enjambement*. L. E.
Kastner (1903), in his chapter on *enjambement*, quotes two
examples from the work of André Chénier:

> Et près des bois marchait, faible et sur une pierre
> S'asseyait. . . .   ('L'Aveugle')

and

> Il ouvre un œil avide, et longtemps envisage
> L'étranger. . . .   ('Le Mendiant')

To my mind, only the second of these is a genuine *enjambement*. The phrase 'et sur une pierre' certainly leaves one
suspended, awaiting a resolution, but both 'sur une pierre'
and the *rejet* 'S'asseyait' are complete grammatical groups,
and the line-ending only makes stronger a pause that one
would make if one were reading the lines as prose, a pause
not so much created by the line-ending as by the inversion.
In the second quotation, there is a rupture of the close ties
between a transitive verb and its object; the line-ending
persuades us to make a pause where normally we would
not. And this is perhaps the best test for *enjambement*: would
you make a pause in 'normal' reading where the line-ending

asks you to make a pause? Or, translated into intonational
terms: does a pitch juncture occur at a point not required by
the syntactic groupings? Do we meet a pitch break which, *in
prose*, could only be justified by a parenthetical insertion?
It is only natural that the incidence of *enjambement* should
be greater in shorter lines, in the octosyllable, for instance,
where the prosodic structure constantly outruns the syntax
and leaves the reader in a pretty constant state of vivid
anticipation, so that such lines strike one as being inherently
nervous. But even here impressions can so easily be false. In
the following stanzas, which constitute the fourth of
Gautier's 'Fantaisies d'hiver', there are, in my view, no
instances of *enjambement*:

> Sur la mode parisienne
> Le Nord pose ses manteaux lourds,
> Comme sur une Athénienne
> Un Scythe étendrait sa peau d'ours.

> Partout se mélange aux parures
> Dont Palmyre habille l'Hiver,
> Le faste russe des fourrures
> Que parfume le vétyver.

> Et le Plaisir rit dans l'alcôve
> Quand, au milieu des Amours nus,
> Des poils roux d'une bête fauve
> Sort le torse blanc de Vénus.

In all these unpunctuated lines, the line-endings bring no
extraordinary pauses, either because one can imagine a punctuation mark (ll. 1, 7), or because the line is syntactically
complete (l. 9), or because of inversion (ll. 3, 11), or because,
though verb and subject are separated, they are not so much
separated by the line-ending as by an extended parenthesis
(l. 5).
    Before looking at a few of the positive functions of
enjambement, we should caution ourselves against a mistaken supposition contained in remarks like that made by
Garnet Rees (1976) about the fourth stanza of Baudelaire's

'Le Cygne': 'The tone is now narrative and the verse is hastened by *enjambement*' (p. 25). Two things should be said here. First, all comments about the speed of verse should be made with the utmost tentativeness. The speed of verse depends entirely upon the reader. One can argue that certain linguistic/prosodic features do produce variations in the pace of utterance – a sequence of unstressed syllables in English will be 'quicker' than a sequence of stressed ones, just as, in French, the fewer the accents in hemistich or line, the more forward momentum utterance will have; but even in asserting this, we must admit that we may only be speaking of the *impression* of speed, and that the reader still has it within his power to disregard these indications. One can propose that verse should be read at a certain speed, but the verse itself is rarely able to dictate speed (see, however, the comments on Valéry's 'Les Pas', p. 93). Similarly, one should not say categorically that one line is longer than another because it has more syllables in it; syllabically it may indeed be longer, but reading-speed may iron out that difference and even reverse it. A line is not just as long as it looks, but as long as it sounds, and its length may equally depend on the 'weight' of its subject, on its emotional charge, on its grammatical or intellectual complexity.

Secondly, it is by no means automatic that *enjambement* involves a reading-on with the sense; here again we should say that it is up to the reader, but we might add that there is some argument for marking the pause at the line-ending with even greater vigour than we would if the line were end-stopped. We know that neither Hugo nor Banville, both prolific enjambers, were fond of actors reading verse, and actors are, by profession almost, renowned readers-on. But let us look at this issue more closely.

Leaving aside considerations of speed, which depend on too many imponderables, we might wish to argue that *enjambement* is a blow struck for the liberation of verse, and that only by reading straight on with the sense can we give proper prominence to that fact. By reading on, we begin to undermine the ascendancy of rhyme, 'ce bijou d'un sou' as

Verlaine called it in his 'Art poétique', and to create free-verse patterns within regular verse – the lines quoted from Valéry's *La Jeune Parque* constitute *in the reading*, it might be claimed, one line of thirteen syllables and one of ten syllables (supposing the *e atone* of 'Brûle' to be the feminine ending of the line newly formed, and thus uncounted). But, paradoxically, this view ends by denying *enjambement*. Some free-verse theorists argue the corollary, namely: *enjambement* is undesirable because, if verse were less hidebound and regular, it would simply be unnecessary. Much free-verse theory turns out, ironically, to be far from liberated, and what Gustave Kahn (1897) has to say about *enjambement* – 'les libertés romantiques . . . sont fausses dans leur intention, parce qu'ils [the lines quoted] comportent un arrêt pour l'oreille que ne motive aucun arrêt du sens' – sounds very much like classical dogmatism. But we shall have more to say of this later. One would hardly expect a poet to use *enjambement* merely for the purposes of discrediting it, or to reduce poetry to prose. The function of *enjambement* is to let into syntactic sequence extra modal values, to compel syntax to admit the primacy of poetic structure at the same time as syntax celebrates or discovers its own deep intentions.

Enjambement requires us to make a pause where we would read on. And rhyme, needing to be perceived, helps us make that pause. The beauty of the situation is that rhyme momentarily cedes its function as the creator of anticipation and fulfilment to the enjambing words, precisely by insisting on itself, by asking to be heard. My own view is that *enjambement* is a nonsense without pause, that its power as a poetic convention depends on our installing a division between syntactically related words, so that suspension and resolution, curiosity and satisfaction or surprise, trepidation and reassurance, are mutually intensified. That is why, perhaps, some of the most compelling *enjambements* are those which translate suspended tension, savoured tension, into explosive affirmation, in verbs like 'éclater', 's'épanouir', 's'élancer', 's'envoler', in *rejets* which seem to

collect into themselves all the energy of preceding lines and
then to release it again in a single current:

> Mais il vieillit enfin, et, lorsque vient la mort,
> L'âme, vers la lumière éclatante et dorée,
> S'envole, de ce monstre horrible délivrée.
>
> (Hugo, 'Les Malheureux')

(If the absence of punctuation is no guarantee of *enjambement*, its presence equally is no guarantee of *enjambement*'s
absence; the punctuation here is not what creates the pause).

A similar, if rather more short-lived concentration of
energy occurs in the fourth stanza of Leconte de Lisle's
'Midi':

> Parfois, comme un soupir de leur âme brûlante,
> Du sein des épis lourds qui murmurent entre eux,
> Une ondulation majestueuse et lente
> S'éveille, et va mourir à l'horizon poudreux.

Here, the very force of the *rejet*'s self-projection makes
more binding, more disempowering, its subsequent
absorption into a pattern of death. What false hopes
enjambement can awaken in verse like this, given up to a
depiction of the 'néant divin'! And in the two lines from
Valéry's *La Jeune Parque*, the explosiveness of the *rejet* is
much more repressed and insidious; the pause at the line-
ending encourages us to lengthen the û of 'Brûle', bespeaking assiduity as well as strength, drawing us down into
some unidentified centre of force.

The *contre-rejet*, on the other hand, does not release energy
so much as withhold it, so that a word is left in a state of pure
virtuality, of multiple potentiality, fully gathered into itself.
In Chénier's lines:

> Les belles font aimer; elles aiment. Les belles
> Nous charment tous. Heureux qui peut être aimé
> d'elles
>
> ('Jeune fille, ton cœur. .')

not only has the poet intensified 'belles' by repeating it, in a position where its accent is upgraded (at line-ending instead of at *coupe*), but he has isolated it – 'aiment' would attract to itself a *coupe lyrique*, I think – the better that we should endow it with a meditative aura, should fill the word with the accumulated efficacy of all its connotations. And when the moment of meditation is interrupted by the onset of the following line, the spell itself is not broken, the verb gives nothing away by defining nothing.

Enjambement has many functions, beside the expressive. It has an important rhythmic function inasmuch as it will frequently create with the *rejet*, as in the Valéry example and as we have previously mentioned, a 1 + 5 hemistich, not an especially common hemistich, a welcome variation. It has also an intonational function; instead of falling with the end of the line, to give the characteristic 'accent circonflexe' pitch-outline of the endstopped line, the voice rises to meet its suspension and remains high as the suspense is resolved with the first word(s) of the following line. And as we have already said, in rhymed verse, *enjambement* begets a new kind of rhyme-word; the grammatically inconspicuous, a particle perhaps, even just part of a word, is thrust into the limelight of the rhyme position, is endowed by rhyme with an accent which in normal circumstances it would not expect. Particular instances take us back to expressive considerations. We shall deal at more length with the particle rhyme created by extreme kinds of *enjambement* in Section (iii) (c) of the following chapter, but, for the present, we can look at the first stanza of Gautier's 'Les Néréides':

> J'ai dans ma chambre une aquarelle
> Bizarre, et d'un peintre avec qui
> Mètre et rime sont en querelle,
> – Théophile Kniatowski.

In writing about Kniatowski, Gautier is actually compelled by the verse to write about the difficulty of writing about him. 'Qui', accentuated by rhyme and position, expresses, with its accompanying pause, Gautier's vain attempts to think of anything positive to say about the painter. In the

end, the accentuation leads us to expect a parenthesis after
'qui' – this does not materialise – or, more pointedly,
encourages us to imagine a concealed question mark; the
poet insinuates retrospectively that Kniatowski is as
unknown as his name is outlandish.

The *enjambement* of the first two lines is also intriguing,
because it is an *enjambement* only after the event. At the end
of the first line, all conditions of syntactical completeness
have been satisfied. The discovered *rejet*, 'Bizarre', is the
overriding concern masquerading as afterthought; statement of fact cannot sustain itself against the evidence,
becomes, suddenly, all opinion, apologetically, ironically,
waspishly. The pause provides an element of disbelief as
much as of malice.

Enjambement will occupy us again in the context of free
verse. As a conclusion to this section, we might look at an
example of the concerted use of *enjambement* within a stanza,
a concerted use which reveals much about the perceptual
mode of the poet. The following stanza comes from Verlaine's 'Dans les bois' (*Poèmes saturniens*), in which he
describes the rather banal fears aroused in him by the
woods:

> Surtout les soirs d'été: la rougeur du couchant
> Se fond dans le gris bleu des brumes qu'elle teinte
> D'incendie et de sang; et l'angélus qui tinte
> Au lointain semble un cri plaintif se rapprochant.

All these *enjambements* are by way of being qualifications,
which either render vivid sensation indeterminate, blur the
edges of acute perception ('la rougeur du couchant/Se
fond'; 'qui tinte/Au lointain') or do the opposite, restore to
an etiolated or imprecise impression a new immediacy and
power ('elle teinte/D'incendie et de sang') – incidentally, the
loss that is suggested in the progression from 'qui tinte' to
'Au lointain' is reversed *within* the final line of the stanza:
'un cri plaintif *se rapprochant*'. Of course we can explain this
phenomenon by referring to the oft-quoted lines of 'Art
poétique':

Rien de plus cher que la chanson grise
Où l'Indécis au Précis se joint.

But we need to underline the peculiar contribution of
enjambement. By instituting a pause, by opening up a
moment which both savours the past and anticipates the
future, *enjambement* prevents one perception from blending
indiscriminately with others and being superseded by them;
the excitement of intense sensory experience and the lure of
an unthreatening, anonymous lack of differentiation are
held in a stable state of tension across the line-ending. The
marked dominance of either one or the other would
endanger the poem's quality: vivid sense-perceptions, cul-
tivated for themselves, would lead to fragmentation and
randomness; the fusion of perceptions in an all-
encompassing mood would lead to a dulled passivity.

I have argued for observing the pause at the line-ending
in cases of *enjambement*, because, among other things,
enjambement brings a new kind of rhyme into existence. The
contrary view – that we should read directly over the line-
ending with the syntax and thus undermine the tyranny of
the line-ending and the overbearingness of rhyme – should
not be ignored. I would have more sympathy with this
view, and believe more in Verlaine's castigation of rhyme as
'ce bijou d'un sou', if I had reason to think that those
late-nineteenth-century enjambers who were concerned
with the liberation of verse did not thoroughly enjoy the
intellectual and imaginative exercise of rhyming.

(ii) *Hiatus*
   Hiatus is simply the clash of two contiguous vowels,
either within the word ('aéroport') or between words ('et il
a arrangé ce morceau'). We have already encountered two
kinds of hiatus: the *e atone* in conjunction with other vowels
(livrée, vie, pluie) and diaeresis. Pierre Guiraud (1970) calls
hiatus 'contraire au génie phonétique du français' (p. 92) and
points to the reduction of double vowels to single ones
(reïne, aage) and to the development of elision and liaison as

evidence of this; another commentator, A. Gosset, be it said, mentions the French delight in hypsilonised (preceded by u) and iotised (preceded by i) vowels (quoted by Berthon, 1948, p. xli). But whatever the fundamental proclivities of the French language, hiatus is an enduring feature of it, a feature which poets appear to exploit precisely because of its connection with the exotic and the bizarre.

If the third of the following lines from Musset's 'La Nuit de Mai' –

Et le bleu Titarèse et le golfe d'argent
Qui montre dans ses eaux, où le cygne se mire,
La blanche Oloossone à la blanche Camyre

– has, along with Racine's 'La fille de Minos et de Pasiphaé' from *Phèdre*, been one of the *loci classici* of pure poetry, it is because the line typifies a poetry which means nothing and yet is somehow heavy with meaning. And this heaviness of secret design does not derive solely from the repetition of the figurative, pre-posed 'blanche', but from the tantalising opacity of names which *can* only be full of history, and more specifically still, from the procession of full, rounded vowels in 'Oloossone', beautiful in their aloof single-mindedness, in their refusal to make concessions to a vulgar demand for variety or to French habits of pronunciation; the medial double o compels the voice to echo the o, to linger over it, to probe it, to make it the corridor to a new space. Does it matter, then, that Oloossone, an *inland* town of Thessaly, cannot, geographically, do what the lines say it does? And the Racinian line has a hiatus in 'Pasiphaé', which points up and intensifies the vowel modulation (a-i-a-é) and, in so doing, helps to summon the image of an elusive, volatile, morally contradictory woman, the daughter of Helios *and* the sister of Circe, the wife of Minos, Hadean judge-to-be, *and* adulterous lover of the bull. Phèdre tries to hang on to the vestiges of her father's moral probity; but 'Minos' is only part of a four-syllable measure *within* a hemistich, and the accent on his name is only caesural; 'Pasphaé', on the other hand, has a whole hemistich to herself, has an enveloping density, and has the authority of a line-terminal accent with supporting coutertonic accent ('Pasipháe').

But the foreignness of hiatus is not confined, of course, to foreign names alone; the common noun containing hiatus and having a foreign etymology, or reference, works in much the same way, even though it means more limitedly.

Heredia's 'Soir de bataille' makes something of the name of Antony's unsuccessful opponent, the Parthian king 'Phraortes' (Phraates IV); but Roman military terminology also has its uses:

Le choc avait été très rude. Les tribuns
Et les centurions, ralliant les cohortes,
Humaient encor dans l'air où vibraient leurs voix
    fortes
La chaleur du carnage et ses âcres parfums.

It is too easy, when dealing with so-called Parnassian poets like Heredia, to account for rather pedantic technical borrowings like 'tribuns', 'centurions', 'cohortes' – as one might account for Leconte de Lisle's cultivation of Greek spellings of mythological figures – as instances of an unimaginative historicism, a pursuit of authenticity for its own sake; for such a poet, the 'unnaturalness' of hiatus is merely a pledge of the genuine character of the local colour. It would, however, be fairer to assimilate these borrowings to the usage of the contemporary Symbolists, as an effort via the archaic, the technical, the *recherché*, to revitalise linguistic perception and to lure the mind away from the overt and accepted to the infinity of the imperfectly comprehended and the wholly challenging.

But this is to stray from our stanza. Such lofty ambitions aside, 'cohortes', with its internal hiatus, does at the very least evoke something of the labour of battle. It is the culmination of a set of words – 'tribuns', 'centurions', 'cohortes' – which remind us of the Roman military hierarchy and in so doing, bring home to us more forcibly its disarray. It is the culmination of two lines difficult to read and rhythmically disorientating: there are lesser hiatuses in 'centurions' and 'ralliant'; the stanza does not settle down to an unequivocal four-measure pattern until the third line – do we read the first line as 2+4+2+4, with an enjambing caesura, so that the voice falls more heavily on the *rejet* 'très rude'? Or do we read it as 2+6+4, to try and give more emphasis and isolation to 'choc', and to endow the medial measure with more matter-of-fact compactness? And there is a potential *coupe lyrique* at 'rude', to convey the dying reverberations of the 'choc' and the pause that is needed as the troops catch their breath. (The second line, of course, reads 6+3+3). And finally, it could be argued that 'cohortes', demanding as it does a separation of like vowels – kɔɔʀt(ə) – is a word which itself needs to be rallied.

The very attention we have paid to internal hiatuses reveals something of a contradiction. Internal hiatus, unmitigated by the pause between words, at line-endings, between rhythmic groups, unobscured by the force of grammatical agreement (this will be explained), presents the confrontation of vowels at its most abrupt and uncompromising, at its most stark and therefore maybe at its most expressive. But internal hiatus has not attracted the legislative attention that hiatus between words, which is subject to all the qualifications listed above, has; indeed, in the language of many prosodic handbooks, the term 'hiatus' is rarely used of the internal kind at all.

Ronsard is credited with the first objections to hiatus between words, though he never practised absolutely faithfully what he preached. Malherbe took up the demand for the avoidance of inter-word hiatus, but Boileau's lines on the matter, in his *Art poétique*, are probably the best known formulation of this principle:

> Gardez qu'une voyelle, à courir trop hâtée,
> Ne soit d'une voyelle en son chemin heurtée.

These lines are justly famed, because they show the wry humour of one so often thought of as a stick-in-the-mud, and because they reveal, by the agency of that humour, the

contradictions within the rule they enunciate. It is clever of
Boileau to position the word 'voyelle' at the caesura in both
lines, by discreet recourse to inversion, so that the 'voyelles'
are in a sense juxtaposed, do come face to face with each
other in a kind of hiatus. It is even more ingenious of him to
exemplify the transgression itself without actually breaking
any rules: 'trop hâtée' and 'chemin heurtée' *sound* like hiatuses, and to all intents and purposes are hiatuses, but the
presence in each case of an aspirate h, which originally did
have consonantal value, prevents the hiatus, or at least
makes it allowable. This would not be so if the h were mute.

A similar kind of anomaly has already been encountered.
Mute e cannot occur immediately after another vowel at the
end of a word within the line, unless it is elided before a
following vowel; but this elision inescapably means that the
vowel which precedes the mute e and that which follows it
are brought into direct contact, as in this line from François
Coppée's 'Petits Bourgeois':

> Oui, cette vi(e) intime est digne du poète.

Guiraud (1970, p. 92) expresses the view that the interposed
mute e lengthens the preceding vowel and thus creates a
transition which deadens the collision with the succeeding
vowel. This may indeed be so, and certainly the inequality
of the vowels makes their contiguity less hard on the ear;
but in an area where there are so many anomalies, it is
hardly worth trying to rationalise every one of them. It is
one of the hazards of prosodic legislation that in attempting
to plug one hole, one inadvertently opens another.

Anomalies similar to those created by the changes in
pronunciation of the aspirate h are to be found with the
nasal vowels (-an, -en, -in, -on, -un) and other endings (e.g.
-ier, -et, -ard). Originally, the consonants in both these
groups would have been pronounced in liaison and the
question of hiatus would not have arisen. Boileau, for
instance, writes:

> Mais pourtant on a vu le vin et le hasard
>
> > (*Art poétique*)

expecting the n to be sounded in 'vi-n-et'. And indeed the consonants after nasal vowels were liaison agents well into the eighteenth century. But since then, like the other endings mentioned, the nasal vowels have lost the support of their final consonants in all circumstances; and hiatus, but permissible hiatus because of this history, is the result. Confusions are likely to arise about which hiatuses are permitted exceptions and which are liberties taken – this is particularly so of fixed phrases with inbuilt hiatus (e.g. peu à peu, ça et là, sang et eau); Berthon (1948) treats these as liberty, Kastner (1903) as exception. And the problem raised by interjections (ah, eh, oh) followed by vowels – actually permissible hiatus – may provoke some amused disbelief. It is the legislator's burden that he must envisage all eventualities. But the whole system is undermined by one inescapable fact: rules made from the evidence of the ear have imperceptibly found themselves applying to the evidence of the eye.

More is to be gained, perhaps, by considering not different kinds of hiatus, but different degrees of hiatus, that is to say, by considering the ways in which the syntactic or prosodic structure can render hiatus either more or less obtrusive. Many effects can be attributed to hiatus; Henri Morier (1975, pp. 488–90) gives examples in which, according to him, hiatus conveys ideas of rupture, suffering, cruelty, dissonance, connection, prolongation, duration, idleness, voluptuousness, variety, colour, light. But most of these appear to derive as much from the overt meanings of the words themselves as from the hiatus – as Morier is not ashamed to half-admit himself – and they seem to be based on the assumption that the force of hiatus, aside from purely phonetic considerations, is always the same, that hiatus is always equal to itself.

But grammar may diminish hiatus; we have spoken of hiatus being 'obscured by the force of grammatical agreement'; the first line of Apollinaire's 'Zone' will make clear what we mean:

A la fin tu es las de ce monde ancien.

The hiatus 'tu es' does not really warrant the name; its inevitability, its propriety, are overwhelming. (One might erect a principle here: the more avoidable inter-word hiatus is, the more it deserves the name.) In this instance, the hiatus is a guarantee of grammatical fittingness; the hiatus acts as an agent of reciprocal confirmation.

But it is not just grammar which may take the edge off hiatus; pause and accentuation also have their part to play. One of Morier's examples, presumably of the idea of connection or 'liaison', is Racine's line:

C'est Vénus tout entière à sa proi(e) attachée.

3+3+3+3

That this is permissible hiatus should not concern us at present. What should concern us is the fact that this hiatus occurs over a *coupe*, that one of the vowels is thus accentuated and the other is not, that a slight pause may coincide, in some readings, with the *coupe*, a pause made more probable by the regularity of the trisyllabic measure, which the voice may wish to underline with clear demarcations. The *coupe*, the absence of easy transition between 'proie' and 'attachée' give to 'attachée' a firmness of outline which bespeaks the tenacity of attachment, rather than attachment itself, and the kinship between the vowels (pʀwa(ɑ)ataʃe), when put together with the accentual inequality and the pause between them, evokes rather Phèdre's own contradictoriness, the conflict between her feelings of guilt and her desire to indulge desire.

In a similar way, one might, on reading the first line of Baudelaire's 'A une passante' –

La ru(e) assourdissante autour de moi huɪlait

2+4+4+2

– be inclined to interpret the (permissible) hiatuses as evocations of the painful and discordant din of the Parisian street. And, of course, this is very much to the point. But once again, the positions of the *coupes* (and pauses) might lead one to modify this view slightly. The accentual inequality of the vowels, the absence of easy transition between them, not only engenders a sense of discord, but conveys the poet's isolation from it; he is indeed surrounded by a numbing din – as 'autour de moi' finds itself caught between words of noise – but he is also, in a strange way, insulated against it by the very vividness of his internal and psychic existence. One of the remarkable things about this poem is the speed with which the poet turns from his environment to the mysterious passing woman and the ease with which the protagonists seem able to ignore the clamour of the street in their self-absorption:

> La rue assourdissante autour de moi hurlait.
> Longue, mince, en grand deuil, douleur majes-
> tueuse,
> Une femme passa, . . .

L. E. Kastner (1903, p. 120) observes that pause annuls hiatus, but does not make any distinction between different kinds of pause. Two things should be said. First and most obviously, Kastner's observation may be true of vowels separated by the line-ending – though *enjambement* may serve to divide opinion:

> J'entre et je sors, accoutumée
> Aux blondes vapeurs des chibouchs
>   (Gautier, 'Ce que disent les hirondelles')

– and it may be true in stichomythic dramatic verse, where contiguous vowels are separated by a change of speaker:

> *Agnès*   Et qu'avec lui j'aurai de satisfaction.
> *Arnolphe*   Avec qui?
> *Agnès*   Avec . . . , là.
>   (Molière, *L'École des femmes*, Act II, sc.v)

But it will not do for potential pauses at the *coupe* and cannot be relied upon to be true of hiatuses at the caesura. In these latter cases, pause does not annul hiatus, it modifies its function as it makes it more tenuous.

Secondly, the converse of Kastner's axiom needs to be imagined, namely that hiatus, inter-word hiatus that is, itself creates pause. P.-O. Walzer (1966, p. 266) suggests that Valéry's attempt in 'Les Pas' to slow down the moment of moments, the 'Douceur d'être et de n'être pas', the moment which is the brink of contact with the visitor, whether she be Muse, poem, idea or mistress, is helped by the rhythmic disposition of the first line of the last stanza:

> Ne hâte pas cet acte tendre,
> Douceur d'être et de n'être pas,
> Car j'ai vécu de vous attendre,
> Et mon cœur n'était que vos pas.

Walzer writes that this first line 'peut être dit comme un vers ïambique (2+2+2+2), d'où un allongement extraordinaire qui est en parfaite conformité avec l'impératif d'attente qui s'y trouve contenu'. If the line is indeed slowed by the insistent rhythm, then the insistence of that rhythm is due in large measure to the physical difficulty of reading the line. No doubt the accumulation of t's has much to do with this. No doubt, too, the (permissible) hiatus 'Ne hâte' also plays its part, giving a tentativeness to enunciation which is itself an enjoyment of the coming consummation.

In conclusion, then, it is best to stick with common sense. If hiatus is equated with cacophony, it is natural to wish to avoid it, unless cacophony is the source of the effects desired. Elision, liaison (consider the creations 'mon amie', 'cet homme', 'ira-t-il') and the tendency to reduce double vowels to single sounds, do point to an aversion to hiatus in the language, but poetry so often heightens its expressiveness precisely by resisting the dictates of linguistic habit and the ear's desire to be comfortable. In the process of interpretation, the rules about hiatus are best left to one side, unless it is apparent that a central part of the poet's intention is to infringe them and that the poem's meaning is dependent on our perception of that fact. The work of phoneticians, from the late nineteenth century onwards, has shown that where factors of accent and pause are not operative, there is no difference between internal (tolerated) and external (prohibited) hiatus and has further reinforced the view that 'permissible' forms of hiatus (aspirate h, nasal vowels, certain other endings) are built on illusory, purely visual features which in no sense affect the reality of the hiatus. Since hiatus is by definition an acoustic phenomenon, the only principle of identification to which we should refer ourselves is sound – 'Do you hear hiatus?' If the answer is affirmative, if there is no reason to suppose that pronunciation complicates the question, then one should feel free to comment on the hiatus as a *bona fide* hiatus.

(iii) *Word-sound*

This heading could be an invitation to enumerate, endlessly, felicitous and intriguing examples of the music of words. I wish to treat the subject quite briefly and in a cautionary manner.

Observations about assonance and alliteration are extremely difficult to control. To the student embarking on the hazardous business of verse analysis, no evidence seems more available, no test of interpretative sensitivity more challenging, than a sequence of identical vocalic or consonantal sounds. But usually we either accept the challenge on our own terms, drawing upon the arbitrariness of our emotional response to the poem, or we rationalise prominent sound-patterns by making them an inevitable concomitant of the poem's semantic base. No sounds have an inbuilt potential for meaning. And even the poem's overt meaning is not sufficient to justify the isolation of certain sounds; there must be prosodic justifications as well, sounds supported by accent or other features of verse-structure, or highlighted by repetition; above all, no sounds should be deemed to have a special function until it has been ascertained that other, perhaps contrasting, sounds do not have an equal, if not prior, claim to attention.

And, besides, it would be surprising if assonance and

alliteration did not occur quite by accident; language is by no means inevitably various. It would be even more surprising if writers did not resort to assonance and alliteration almost on principle, simply to make their poems more readable, slip into the mind or ear with greater fluency and persuasiveness. In these lines from Goldsmith's *The Deserted Village*:

> For him no wretches, born to work and weep,
> Explore the mind or tempt the dangerous deep

the alliterations bind the pairs of words ('work' and 'weep', 'dangerous' and 'deep') in an indestructible embrace and make the rhymes polyverbal compounds. But in attending to these pairs, let us not overlook the assonant sequence 'For', 'born', 'Explore', 'or', which unobtrusively counterbalances the emphatic line-endings and creates convenient *points de repère* for the voice. One might also suggest that such assonances have a 'phatic' function, that is to say, they establish the kind of communication that poetry is, the suppositions on which it is built.

Theories of expressive sound have attracted increasing scepticism; stylistic phonology has given ground to phonetics, concern with *Lautsymbolik* to concern with the purely formal function of phonemes: 'Plus les appareils dont disposent les phonéticiens se perfectionnent, plus leurs analyses séparent les constituants du langage, et plus leurs conclusions s'éloignent des interprétations psychologiques ou stylistiques.' The book from which these words are taken – Michel Gauthier's *Système euphonique et rythmique du vers français* (1974, p. 13) – and Graham Chesters's *Some Functions of Sound-Repetition in 'Les Fleurs du Mal'* (1975) are interesting examples of this general trend.

It is, of course, true that poets themselves have proposed that phonemes, and not just repeated ones, are significant, the begetters of image and mood. Rimbaud sowed the seeds with his 'audition colorée' ('Voyelles'), René Ghil's 'instrumentation verbale' (*Traité du verbe*) developed connections between phonemes and orchestral instruments, and Mallarmé, too, showed an interest in this area (*Les Mots anglais*). But these departures should be put in their late-nineteenth-century context and seen as part of an attempt to create a language which might synthesise all sensory faculties and thus become an ultimate reality, a pattern of *total* experience, a transfiguration of an ill-organised and Babel-like world. In Rimbaud's words: 'Cette langue sera de l'âme pour l'âme, résumant tout, parfums, sons, couleurs, de la pensée accrochant la pensée et tirant' (letter to Paul Demeny, 15 May 1871).

In general terms, then, the only kinds of alliteration and assonance whose effects can be spoken of with some confidence are those which are patently imitative, those which beget significant kinships, as the alliterative pairs in the Goldsmith example, and those in which the related sounds create a definite pattern, a substructure to set against the more apparent or conventional structures of the poem.

An example of imitative alliteration of the simplest, onomatopoeic kind is to be found in Oreste's vision of the Furies, complete with hissing snakes, in Racine's *Andromaque*:

> Eh bien! filles d'enfer, vos mains sont-elles prêtes?
> Pour qui sont ces serpents qui sifflent sur vos têtes?
>
> (Act V, sc. v)

But even these lines are not so straightforward. What makes this alliterative sequence so powerful is the fact that it appears in dramatic verse. We expect lyric verse to realise, in the concrete world of acoustics, its own solitary fictions. But the dramatic poet, when he is not concerned with the 'poems' of messengers and soliloquisers, gives voice to the reality of on-stage confrontations. Oreste's alliterative sequence in the second line has both a dramatic and a lyric function; it is *intended* by Oreste as a vocal gesture of scorn and bitterness for on-stage figures, the Furies, whom he alone sees; it appeals to the audience, on the other hand, as the embodiment of a totally fictional image, hissing snakes. Alliteration here highlights our difficulty, when faced with a mad man, in distinguishing between the dramatic and the lyric, address and soliloquy.

It is not always easy to say whether a set of acoustic kinships has become an organised substructure or not. The two examples I wish to examine next exist in this no man's land between meaningfully related, but unstructured sounds, and related sounds which have achieved a real structural coherence.

In the second stanza of Baudelaire's 'La Chevelure':

> La langoureuse Asie et la brûlante Afrique,
> Tout un monde lointain, absent, presque défunt,
> Vit dans tes profondeurs, forêt aromatique!
> Comme d'autres esprits voguent sur la musique,
> Le mien, ô mon amour! nage sur ton parfum

the rhymes set a short, sharp ik against the deadened nasal œ. These two sounds, it could be argued, project two conflicting worlds: on the one hand, a world of alert, vivid mental activity, and on the other, a sultry, lethargic, primitive world. This latter world fully occupies the second line of the stanza, which is almost totally given over to nasal vowels – œ (un), ɔ̃ (monde), ɛ/ɛ̃ (lointain), ɑ̃ (absent), œ̃ (défunt) – and the nasal recurs intermittently throughout the rest of the stanza (dans, profondeurs, mien, etc.). But no sooner is this world exclusively established in the second line, no sooner does it reach a fitting climax in 'défunt', than it is denied, in both sound and sense, by 'Vit', which retaliates with the incisive i of the rhyme. And however much the poet has tried to install his exotic, indolent world in the first line, not only by his choice of adjectives (not also the nasal ɑ̃ in both of them), but in his pre-posing of them, the very continents he calls forth betray him by having the i at their very heart, as the accentuated syllable – Asie, Afrique. And this i is perhaps best explained by another word in which it appears, 'esprits'; the i is the Westerner's vigilant intellect and penetrative imagination. And the poet is not looking for a resolution of this conflict in the ultimate supremacy of one world over the other; he is looking, rather, for their paradoxical coexistence. He can find no peace in his exotic world because of his unquiet, inquisitive, memory-filled Parisian mind; but exotic peace without the Parisian mind would be death.

Another poem of exotic wanderlust, equally beset by contradiction and difficulty, is Mallarmé's 'Brise marine', from which I quote the final lines:

> Et, peut-être, les mâts, invitant les orages
> Sont-ils de ceux qu'un vent penche sur les naufrages
> Perdus, sans mâts, sans mâts, ni fertiles îlots. . .
> Mais, ô mon cœur, entends le chant des matelots!

As we read through these lines, we are likely to be struck by the close assonant groups 'vent penche', 'ni fertiles îlots', 'entends le chant'. What seems evident is that we should once again set the nasal ɑ̃ against the i; but they have by no means the same connotations as in the Baudelaire stanza. In its first appearance here, the ɑ̃ is connected with a malicious wind driving ships to shipwreck; the i, on the other hand, is connected with the rich vegetation of tranquil tropic isles. But with the final line and the further development of the assonant ɑ̃ ('entends le chant'), we are invited to relate the song of the sailors with the destructive wind; this sailors' song, it seems, irresistible as it is, is a sirens' song, the suicide of aspiration or evasion; the search for spiritual fullness turns out to be a courting of deprivation (here 'sans' adds its nasal vowel to the assonant group).

In 'La Chevelure', linkage by assonance reinforces and diversifies a structure already available in the rhyme-scheme, while in 'Brise marine', it creates a covert substructure. Structural assonance like this latter may operate within an even more circumscribed space, the single line.

A single-line instance is provided by Lamartine's 'L'Isolement':

> Je promène au hasard mes regards sur la plaine
> $$3+3+3+3$$

where the chiastic pattern è-ar-ar-è (ai) runs counter to the

easy *advance* of the trisyllabic measures; within a movement
of infinite extension across a landscape, is a pattern of return. Are we meant to see the chiasmus as a sign of the
pointlessness of the eye roaming over a meaninglessly mul-
tifarious landscape only to return empty-handed to its point
of departure? Are we meant to see in the chiasmus a *hope* of
return built into a uniform experience of distance and separation? One might even argue, more fancifully, that the
chiasmus describes the shape of the summit – as in the
near-assonant chiasmus 'Au sommet de ces monts' of the
same poem – on which the poet is seated, a summit which
thrusts him purposefully towards a realm which has little to
do with the flat and changeable plain below him.

One area of acoustic study as yet little investigated (but
see Gauthier, 1974, pp. 99–100, and Chesters, 1975, pp.
34–5) is the relationship between homophonous phonemes
and the accentual make-up of the line. Does the fact that two
or more accentuated vowels (excluding the rhyme-vowels),
within a line or group of lines, are phonetically identical
intensify their accentuation? Can a primary accent (at caesura or line-ending) draw a secondary accent up to its
own level by virtue of homophony? Can the primariness
of an accent be threatened, indeed undermined, by the
homophony of elements in secondary accents (vowels or
pretonic consonants)? How does accent affect our perception of, and reaction to, alliteration and assonance? Graham
Chesters, for instance, argues that medial clusters of similar
sounds in a line, straddling the caesura, tend to push the
tétramètre in the direction of the *trimètre*; an example of his is:

> Je fermerai partout portières et volets
> (Baudelaire, 'Paysage')

where the 4+2+2+4 pattern is pushed towards 4+4+4 by
the p. .rt coupling of 'partout' and 'portières'. This analysis
might be developed. The syntactic disposition of the line is
too strong to allow the trimetric usurpation, but the intima-
tion is sufficient to make the line a pointed allusion to those
other lines in the poem which are properly trimetric:

Et les grands ciels qui font rêver d'éternité 4+4+4

and

Il est doux à travers les brumes, de voir naître.

3+5+4

These two lines, separated only by a stanza division, express, apparently, a reaction to the urban environment which has little in common with that to be found in:

Je fermerai partout portières et volets.

As Baudelaire's pan-urban-cum-cosmic consciousness reaches a peak at the end of the first stanza, so the line broadens out into three measures, loses the analytic arbitration of the medial caesura, and seems to penetrate into another realm of perception, another rhythm of existence:

Et les grands ciels qui font rêver d'éternité.

A *trimètre*, of slightly less regular contour, is equally the impulse of the second stanza, whose first five lines maintain the drift of the first stanza:

Il est doux, à travers les brumes, de voir naître
L'étoile dans l'azur, la lampe à la fenêtre,
Les fleuves de charbon monter au firmament
Et la lune verser son pâle enchantement.
Je verrai les printemps, les étés, les automnes;
Et quand viendra l'hiver aux neiges monotones,
Je fermerai partout portières et volets
Pour bâtir dans la nuit mes féeriques palais.

The writer of eclogues, as is proper, comes round to the pattern of changing seasons; with the arrival of winter, the urban eclogue must give way to the rural variety, the physical evidence of the senses must give way to the fictions of the imagination, the open window must close to ensure a fruitful privacy. The submerged, subliminal, trimetric structure in the seventh line implies, perhaps, that the change is only nominal, that the poet seals himself within the better to expand within, that the pastoral idyll is no less essentially an urban product than the fairyland of workshops, lamps, pipes. And if we return to other examples, we may make equally useful connections between phonetic and accentual structure. In Racine's:

> Eh bien! filles d'enfer, vos mains sont-elles prêtes?
> $2+4+2+4$
> Pour qui sont ces serpents qui sifflent sur vos têtes?
> $2+4+2+4$

the sequence of s's in the second line – after the adumbration of 'sont-elles prêtes' – turns out be a careful organisation. The absence of accent on 'sont ces ser-' drives the initial consonants together and produces a continuous, if subdued, undercurrent of sound; the strong caesural accent on 'ser/pénts' asks us to regard the hissing as a *function* of the reptile, as a potentiality of the agent, rather than as an explicit action, and indeed this may encourage us to read the whole muted sequence 'sont ces ser-' as unexpressed threat rather than as actualised aggression. But in the second hemistich, s is part of an accentuated syllable which belongs, precisely, to the verb of action. This, then, is the culmination of menace and hallucination; after the brief respite of the caesural pause and repeated 'qui', the hiss is fully actualised, as part, almost, of the snakes' strike, so that action is at once sound and movement. And the action as quickly settles back into dormancy, on the dying, unaccentuated 'sur' which follows the defusing *e atone*.

And in the stanza from Baudelaire's 'La Chevelure', it is noticeable that the i of Western vigilance always falls at points of prosodic vigilance, at the caesura or line-ending, so that its accent reinforces its connection with discipline, with the structures of consciousness and intellect. 'Vit dans tes profondeurs' is the exception, but even here there are compensating factors. The *enjambement* and $1+5$ pattern give unusual relief to the secondary accent which 'Vit' strictly speaking has. And this rare $1+5$ hemistich is shown, retrospectively, to be influential, to have authority, for it is taken up twice more; in the hemistichs 'voguent sur la musique' and 'nage sur ton parfum'; in these latter instances, however, the force of the first accent is softened by its leading into a *coupe enjambante*, and by its being post-caesural rather than line-initial. In contrast to the prosodic prominence of the i sound, the nasals of sensual indolence occupy the whole accentual scale from primary accentuation to non-accentuation.

The art of phonetic and phonological interpretation is advancing at great speed, as any glance at periodicals such as *Littérature* and *Poétique* will show. Here are a couple of examples, which take us deep into the intricacy of structural phonemics, a mode of inquiry whose sources are probably to be found in Saussure's researches (1906–9) into the anagrams concealed in Greek and Latin poetry (see Starobinski, 1971):

La densité de l'écriture mallarméenne est extrême puisqu'on voit ces considérations touchant le problème de l'ouverture enfermées dans les deux premiers mots du sonnet: LE VIERGE amène lever, levier, le vers, le verre (du glacier), l'hiver qu'on retrouve anagrammatisé dans *ivre* et *givre* et qui conduirait au Livre. Comment faire lever le vers, voler la plume? Par un 'coup d'aile', à coups, de L-E-V: LEV ierge, LEV ivace et LEB aile . . .
(Daniel Bougnoux on Mallarmé's 'Le vierge, le vivace et le bel aujourd'hui', 1974, p. 85).

Tout le jeu est sur l'*e* 'muet': absent/présent comme l'*e* de Médé(e) – précisément; ce qui m'amène au titre: 'colchique' est la plante de Colchide, pays de Médée l'*empoisonneuse*: dont le nom *tu*, sousjacent, est évoqué *in absentia* par les trois é initiaux qui y font assonance: 'le pré est vénéneux. . .' (Médé(e))
(Michel Deguy on Apollinaire's 'Les Colchiques', 1974, p. 453).

This makes interpretation look like the strenuous decipherment of hieroglyphs, the struggle towards an infra-text which constantly threatens to supersede the ostensible text, even though it is unjustified without it. While such examinations of phonetic fragments may provide exciting *aperçus* about the mysterious concertedness of language, about the subliminal patterns which make every inch of the poem resonant and self-multiplying, we should beware of letting the inexhaustibility of detail deprive the poem of a total design, obscure the whole utterance which the poem is, and of crediting the arbitrary with more plausibility than it deserves, simply because technical expertise is responsible for its selection.

4

Rhyme

(i) *Degrees of rhyme*

'In the first place, rhyme is, of course, an accident rather than an essential of verse' (J. L. Lowes, 1939, p. 159). Although English critical interest in rhyme has been intensifying (e.g. Lanz, 1931; Wimsatt, 1944; Perloff, 1970; Pendlebury, 1971), Lowes's remark reminds us of the traditionally apologetic attitude to rhyme common among English poets and critics. On this side of the Channel, rhyme has never seemed to be an indispensable ingredient of verse, particularly of stichic verse, and in explanation of this view, the English have been in the habit of pointing to the poverty of their rhymes; they find themselves always thrown back on the monosyllable to get their stressed rhyme-syllable, because stress in English polysyllables is rarely terminal; they have not been aided by a wealth of accentuable inflexions, as the French have. A typical expression of this predicament is to be found in the work of Thomas Gray:

> Another thing which perhaps contributed in a degree to the making our ancient poets so voluminous, was the great facility of rhyming, which is now grown so difficult; words of two or three syllables, being then newly taken from foreign languages, did still retain their original accent, and that accent (as they were mostly derived from the French) fell, according to the genius of that tongue, upon the last syllable; which, if it had still continued among us, had been a great advantage to our poetry. Among the Scotch this still continues in many words; for

they say, envȳ, practīse, pensīve, positīve, etc.: but
we, in process of time, have accustomed ourselves
to throw back all our accents upon the antepenultima, in words of three or more syllables, and of our
dissyllables comparatively but a few are left, as
despāir, disdāin, repēnt, pretēnd, etc., where the
stress is not laid on the antepenultima. By this mean
we are almost reduced to find our rhymes among
the monosyllables, in which our tongue too much
abounds, a defect which will for ever hinder it from
adapting itself well to music, and must be consequently no small impediment to the sweetness and
harmony of versification ('Some Remarks on the
Poems of John Lydgate').

But English verse criticism does contain concepts parallel
to those used by the French. The English speak of feminine
endings, that is, rhymes (or lines) which end with an
unstressed syllable (e.g. patter/batter, pity/city) and can
refer to the richness of a rhyme, that is, where *several* elements in a pair of rhyme-words are identical. But these
descriptions have nothing to do with verse-principles as
they have in French; they do not fit into a total scheme of
things from which they ultimately derive their significance.
And English feminine endings, though unstressed, *are*
sounded (unlike French mute e's) and for that reason, and
because every rhyme must involve a stressed syllable,
feminine rhymes in English are necessarily rich where they
are not so in French. We shall discover shortly what rich
rhyme means for the French. Rich rhymes of monosyllabic
words, whether French or English, ineluctably gravitate
towards homonymy and the pun.

Feminine rhymes used in any number in English verse
soon deteriorate into doggerel, both because of the very
laboriousness of their richness and because of the uniformity of their falling cadence. But doggerel finds new life in
ironic motivation. Rich rhymes of this kind are likely to
congregate in verse in which the poet masters the gro-

tesque, in satire, epigram and mock-epic. Doggerel becomes
the measure of the subject's ill-adaptedness, or of the poet's
sublime carelessness:

> But I am but a nameless sort of person,
> (A broken Dandy lately on my travels)
> And take for rhyme, to hook my rambling verse on,
> The first that Walker's Lexicon unravels,
> And when I can't find that, I put a worse on,
> Not caring as I ought for critics' cavils;
> I've half a mind to tumble down to prose,
> But verse is more in fashion – so here goes.
>
> (Byron, *Beppo*, stanza LII)

The French have terms for most degrees of rhyme; the
real difficulty is that this terminology is not entirely stable.
An older system would have us call *suffisante* any rhyme in
which the final accentuated vowels and any consonantal or
mute material following have the same phonetic value (e.g.
bonté/parlé, gouffre/souffre). Such rhymes might also be
called *pauvres*, if one wished to be derogatory rather than
tolerant, in one's description. And if the consonant preceding the accentuated vowel – called the *consonne d'appui* – also
rhymes, the rhyme as a whole is called *riche* (e.g. violence
/balance, main/demain). But this classification, current in
many of the nineteenth- and early twentieth-century handbooks, and essentially neo-classical in inspiration, has dis-
satisfied many, largely because it seems too blunt, and
because it gives undue significance to pre-vocalic consonants at the expense of post-vocalic ones. Is it fair, the objec-
tors ask, to call a rhyme as weak as bonté/cité *riche* and to
call a rhyme as full as tordre/mordre merely *suffisante*? And
so another system has been adopted by more recent verse-
analysts, which attempts to be nicer and more just in its
distinctions:

> *rime pauvre*: where only the tonic (accentuated) vowels
> are identical (i.e. where there are no following letters
> apart from mute ones). This kind of rhyme is in reality no
> more than assonance (eau/blaireau, doux/toux).

rime suffisante: where two elements (the tonic vowel + consonant, either preceding or succeeding) are identical (père/frère, génie/monotonie).

rime riche: where three or more elements in a single syllabic group, the syllabic group of the tonic vowel, are identical – this in fact covers a very wide range of possible combinations (arche/marche, patrie/flétrie, rêve/trêve).

Both of these systems of classification would refer to rhymes involving more than one *syllable* as *rimes léonines* or, possibly, as *rimes doubles* (abonder/inonder, divers/univers, rime ailleurs/rimailleurs), though these terms, too, need to be used with some circumspection. *Rime léonine* of the kind just defined may be confused with the *rime léonine* or *vers léonin* of the Middle Ages, where the two hemistichs of a line rhyme with each other. And *rime double* has a habit of being muddled with *rime redoublée* which refers to a rhyme-sound employed more than twice in a single scheme.

Handbooks and histories contain definitions and examples of other species of rhyme – *rimes batelées, brisées, couronnées, emperières, entrelacées, annexées, rétrogrades, senées, fratrisées, enchaînées, équivoquées* – most of which describe relationships between end-rhyme and elements within the line. These are the rhymes of the fifteenth-century poetic virtuosi, the *Grands Rhétoriqueurs*, and have begotten little in the way of a progeny. Of these byzantinisms, only *rimes équivoquées* – rhymes where the rhyme-sound covers more than single words (see back to the quotation from *Beppo*) – are really worth keeping in mind. We often find this kind of rhyme in those poets concerned to push *enjambement* to its limits. In his parody of Villon, 'Ballade des célébrités du temps jadis', Banville 'laments' the passing of, among others:

> . . . ce Rhéal qui mit Dante en
> Français de maître d'écriture.
> Mais où sont les neiges d'antan!

The ill-fittingness of the rhyme apes the ill-fittingness of the

translator's work. Banville discloses Rhéal's hopeless
clumsiness in a masterly display of his own prosodic
acrobatics. But in Mallarmé's 'Prose pour Des Esseintes',
we find *rimes équivoquées* with a graver intention: the pair
'désir, Idées/des iridées', for example, suggests the ability of
the flowers to absorb and reconcile the physical and the
metaphysical, to express their quiddity ('Idées') at the same
time as the poet's longing for them to do so ('désir'). The
virtuality of objects, which is a form of human desire, finds
itself 'enflowered'. In the twentieth century, *rimes équivoquées* crop up in the work of Louis Aragon and Tristan
Dereme.

Since this study is not intended as a guide to correct
writing, but as an aid to correct description, it will not
concern itself with all the intricacies of allowed pairings,
apart from indicating the rules that obtain in the difficult
area of mute consonants. The following groups of mute
consonants can rhyme together: (i) s, x, z (ii) d and t (iii) c
and g (iv) ds, ts, cs, gs – these last can also rhyme with s, x or
z (thus: échos/inégaux, nid/unit, blanc/rang, etc.) The principle that lies behind these rules is simply this: only those
final mute consonants which would sound the same as agents
of liaison between vowels may rhyme together – thus grand-
t-homme/chant-t-éternel,   sang-k-abondant/blanc-k-ébat.
These rules are by no means strictly adhered to; we shall
find plenty of poets who feel free to rhyme 'sang' and 'rang'
with words ending in -ent or -ant, or to rhyme any vowel
or diphthong without following consonant with an homophonous vowel followed by any mute consonant apart from
s, x or z. And these rules may seem to imply that singulars
cannot rhyme with plurals; this is basically true, but we
must not overlook examples such as morts/mors, morts/
corps, morts/remords, and so on.

   (ii) *Rhyme gender*
      Rhymes in French verse are called feminine when
the tonic vowel is followed by a mute syllable. Those
without a terminal mute syllable are correspondingly called

masculine. In classical prosody, no masculine word should rhyme with a feminine, even though their sounds may be identical in the rhyme (mère/amer, embaumée/aimé), nor should a pair of rhyme-words of one gender be immediately followed by a pair of the same gender; masculine pairs and feminine pairs should alternate (*loi de l'alternance des rimes*). This principle of alternation goes back to the sixteenth century, to Ronsard, but no poet now would feel bound by it, and indeed it has created no sense of rigid obligation since Banville and Baudelaire. Can this principle of alternation really be defended? Many would say no, as long as it is treated as an automatic imperative. As a safeguard of variety, it has lost much of its force with the muting of the e. Of course we continue to be aware of masculinity and femininity without *hearing* the difference, but even if this is so, the potential expressive or tonal distinction between masculinity and femininity is lost when alternation is a mechanical process, when the placing of masculine and feminine rhymes is not a strategic act.

One way of resolving this problem is developed by Maurice Grammont (1965). He argues that since the distinction between masculine and feminine words is phonetically meaningless, another, phonetically meaningful, distinction should be made: from henceforth, all rhymes ending with an accentuated vowel should be called masculine, and those ending with a consonant after the accentuated vowel – a sounded consonant, that is – should be called feminine, the final mute e's being completely disregarded. Grammont left it a little late to establish his alternative and prevent poets ignoring the rule of alternation on their own initiative; besides, his hypothetical classification makes a nonsense of the words 'masculine' and 'feminine', depriving them of any hint of gender. And Grammont himself does recognise that conventional masculine and feminine rhymes have modal or tonal values, and in this respect he places himself in an already long tradition – we may cite an eighteenth-century figure, Marmontel, who defends alternation not in the name of phonetic variety, but in the name of modal variety: 'Les vers masculins sans mélange auraient une marche brusque et heurtée; les vers féminins sans mélange auraient de la douceur, mais de la mollesse.' But at the very least, Grammont provides us with another way of looking at line-endings, another source of structural counterpoint. All the rhymes in Verlaine's ninth 'Ariette oubliée' (*Romances sans paroles*) are feminine, but in terms of the vocalic/consonantal distinction, they produce the scheme VVCC//CCVV, and encode the mirror-effect the poem is about.

Marmontel has some sense of the expressive potentialities of masculinity and femininity, but like most neoclassical poets and critics, he is looking only for that variety which, by its very regularity, begets a mean, a just proportion of all human faculties. It is only later poets who are interested in isolating moods and exploring their extensions into obsession and neurosis. Baudelaire uses exclusively masculine rhymes in 'Ciel brouillé' and 'A une mendiante rousse', for instance. Verlaine is known for his predilection for feminine series – we have just mentioned the ninth of his 'Ariettes oubliées', and we might equally refer to the second, whose first stanza runs:

> Je devine, à travers un murmure,
> Le contour subtil des voix anciennes
> Et dans les lueurs musiciennes,
> Amour pâle, une aurore future!

The effect peculiar to the feminine ending depends largely on the ambiguous status of the final mute syllable. It does not count in the syllabic structure of the line, it is true, but it is like an invitation to the voice to prolong the final sounded syllable, to soothe it into silence gradually, indeterminately. The mute e is an enigma, and for that very reason a symbol of suggestivity. Certainly, too, in this stanza, our awareness of the abrupt nasals of the masculine forms of 'anciennes' and 'musiciennes' enables us to enjoy all the more the vibrancy of the final n's which have, in fact, been brought

into existence as consonants by the following e's. We need
to hear the distant undertone of these voices as we need *no*
aural experience in 'Chanson d'automne':

> Je me souviens
> Des jours anciens
> Et je pleure.

The resonating closure of 'anciennes' gives the word a
crispness of outline which 'anciens' seems to lack and, at the
same time, the final mute e allows the undertone of the
voices to become the overtones of meaning. This crispness
increases, is even more studied and lingering, in the
rhyme-partner 'musiciennes', where the -iennes ending is
dissyllabic (diaeresis), rather than monosyllabic (synaeresis)
as it is in 'anciennes'. This, by the way, is perfectly acceptable rhyming practice.

What this example from Verlaine begins to demonstrate
is how the correspondence of rhyme-gender with grammatical gender can give a new dimension to the rhyme. And
this can happen just as well with alternating rhymes, of
course, when masculine and feminine forms of the same
adjectival (or substantival) ending are set against each other.
The most celebrated and poignant example of this can be
found in Du Bellay's sonnet 'Heureux qui comme Ulysse',
in the last four lines:

> Plus que le marbre dur me plaît l'ardoise fine,
>
> Plus mon Loire gaulois que le Tibre latin,
> Plus mon petit Liré que le Mont Palatin,
> Et plus que l'air marin la douceur angevine.

The systematic antitheses in these lines are distilled in the
rhymes. The brusque, uncompromising nasal vowels
which terminate the two words with a Roman reference –
'latin' and 'Palatin' – convey that sense of inhospitality and
cultural brittleness that Du Bellay finds in Rome. Against
this we have the protracted and relenting endings of 'fine'
and 'angevine', which bespeak the delicacy, the enfolding-
ness, of the Anjou region. This opposition of adjectives

reaches a climax as the -in rhyme invades the last line, in 'air marin', but is completely engulfed by the five lush syllables of 'douceur angevine'. In the end, therefore, the proof of Du Bellay's rightness in lamenting his exile and indulging his nostalgia lies in the acoustic differences between the masculine and feminine forms of the same adjectival ending.

But ironically, rhymes which involve the combination of like parts of speech, as the adjectives in the Du Bellay extract, are generally accounted bad rhyming, particularly by nineteenth-century commentators, and more particularly still by that doyen of rhymers, Théodore de Banville. He advises: 'vous ferez rimer ensemble, autant qu'il se pourra, des mots très-semblables entre eux comme son, et très-différents entre eux comme sens. Tâchez d'accoupler le moins possible un substantif avec un substantif, un verbe avec un verbe, un adjectif avec un adjectif' (*Petit Traité de poésie française*, 1872, p. 75). And so the poet finds himself in the somewhat ridiculous position in which making the most of one *rule* of rhyming necessitates falling foul of another equally important principle of rhyming, and vice-versa. As with so many prosodic revolutions, the change in the habits of French rhyming which took place with the emergence of *vers libéré* and *vers libre* resulted in part from a need to re-clarify the intentions and capabilities of verse at a time when verse had become saturated with a multitude of often conflicting authoritative dicta. The solution of some of these poets was fairly radical; Jules Laforgue wrote to Gustave Kahn in July, 1886: 'J'oublie de rimer, j'oublie le nombre de syllabes, j'oublie la distribution des strophes, mes lignes commencent à la marge comme de la prose.' If we look at Laforgue's *Derniers Vers*, we will see that what he really means by 'J'oublie de rimer' is 'I rhyme forgetfully'; his rhymes are *ad hoc* rhymes, spur-of-the-moment rhymes, disregarding the rule of alternation, pairing singulars with plurals, masculines with feminines. In the attempt to trace the uneven life of the psyche, the different tempi of temperament, the constantly shifting tone, alternation would con-

stitute a barbaric disfigurement. But of these things we shall
have more to say later.

To close this section, two footnotes should be added: (a)
the subjunctive forms 'soient' and 'aient', and the imperfect
and conditional ending -aient, count as masculine rhymes –
see also their special syllabic status within the line, Chapter
I, p. 21 – even though 'paient', 'croient', essaient', etc., are
feminine; (b) another variation of the alternation of rhymes
to be found in Parnassian and Symbolist poetry is the
alternation of rhyme-gender by stanza – see, for instance,
Verlaine's 'L'Amour par terre' or his 'Sonnet boiteux'.

(iii) *Rhyme relationships*

> ... dans notre langue, les vers ne vont que par deux
> ou à plusieurs, en raison de leur accord final, soit la
> loi mystérieuse de la Rime, qui se révèle avec la
> fonction de gardienne et d'empêcher qu'entre tous,
> un usurpe ou ne demeure péremptoirement (Mal-
> larmé, 'Solennité', *Divagations*).

Mallarmé's view of rhyme as watchdog is a view peculiarly
suited to French verse, where the close coincidence of
rhythm and syntax, the phrasal rhythm, gives the line a
natural tendency to seek an autonomy for itself. But in the
end, rhyme justifies the line as well, by demonstrating its
indispensability in a certain scheme of things.

It is in its ability to make lines and words seem indispensable that rhyme shows its rhetorical usefulness. For rhyme
presents arguments as accomplished facts; it contains its
own kind of causality, since immediately we call a word a
rhyme-word, we presuppose the existence of a partner, this
word therefore that word. In the following stanza from
Hugo's 'Pour les pauvres':

> Car Dieu mit ces degrés aux fortunes humaines.
> Les uns vont tout courbés sous le fardeau des peines;
> Au banquet du bonheur bien peu sont conviés.
> Tous n'y sont point assis également à l'aise.
> Une loi, qui d'en bas semble injuste et mauvaise,
> Dit aux uns: JOUISSEZ! aux autres: ENVIEZ!

the poet may seem to do no more than observe God's design: many are miserable and few prosper. But the rhymes 'humaines/peines' and 'aise/ mauvaise' argue and convince, more subliminally than otherwise, that stoicism is the only way to deal with one's humanity, that the human condition, *at all levels*, is a condition of suffering, and that comfort is morally reprehensible, that evil is likely to be found in the lap of luxury. In attempting to rationalise the phenomenon of terminal homophony, the reader constructs a causal relationship. As Samuel Daniel so succinctly puts it: 'Whilst seeking to please our ear, we enthrall our judgement' (*A Defence of Rhyme*, 1602 (?)).

It is easy to forget that the French Romantic poet is often as public-minded and homiletical as this. In more intimate and self-engrossed mood, he is not as eager to convince his reader as himself. Rhyme becomes the vehicle of personal aspiration, the privileged site of wish-fulfilment, poignant for being no more than a trick of language. In the third stanza of Lamartine's 'L'Isolement':

> Au sommet de ces monts, couronnés de bois sombres,
> Le crépuscule encor jette un dernier rayon;
> Et le char vaporeux de la reine des ombres
> Monte et blanchit déjà les bords de l'horizon

the essential Lamartinian drama is presented. Lamartine is the poet of prevarication, ever asking for one moment more, ever being denied it. His poetry takes place on the thinnest of lines between 'encor(e)' and 'déjà', between the still just there and the already gone. As things wilt and fade, bringing home to Lamartine his personal losses, he hangs on to them for all he is worth; it must be their last moment if they are to be properly treasured, but it must be a moment long enough to be fully savoured. Lamartine dreads being taken by surprise. He knows the facts – 'couchant/attend'; has before him evidence of the impossibility of disengaging the end from the beginning – 'se lève/s'achève'; the passing from the persisting – 's'évapore/encore'; and out of a kind

of combination of the positive halves of these last two pairs
of rhymes, he creates his own dream – 'aurore/encore', the
at least verbal fulfilment of a prayer – 'aurore/implore'. The
dawn that Lamartine would protract or have return is not
the dawn of 'Le Lac' which dissipates night and the blissful
encounter, but the mystic dawn of 'L'Isolement', 'Le Soir'
and 'Le Souvenir', the dawn which is a charge of spiritual
energy, a projection of the soul heavenwards, towards a
reunion with his past and Elvire. It is the vision of a persistent or recurrent dawn which helps stave off the encroach-
ment of despair:

> Le soleil de nos jours pâlit dès son aurore;
> Sur nos fronts languissants à peine il jette encore
> Quelques rayons. . .
>
> ('L'Immortalité')

Even as erosion takes place, Lamartine cheats it, makes
rhymes which render the dream as good as invulnerable.
And ironically, even as the dream is achieved, the rhyme, in
one sense the instrument of its achievement, becomes also
the taunt with which the poet reproaches himself for his
continuing dissatisfaction:

> Comme deux rayons de l'aurore,
> Comme deux soupirs confondus,
> Nos deux âmes ne forment plus
> Qu'une âme, et je soupire encore!
>
> ('Le Souvenir')

Rhyme can be an almost unconscious attempt to effect
desired conjunctions, and in this respect it has connections
with a free-wheeling, self-improvising, association-of-
ideas mechanism. But rhyme can also be a hyperbolically
conscious act, where language has a mirror held up to it, a
mirror which casts back an adjusted image. Some rhymes
seem inescapable; others have their inescapability thrust
upon them. One form of the highly conscious rhyme, a
rhyme in which the rhyme-partners *undergo* their part-
nership as a trial by fire, is the *rare* rhyme. Here the

acoustically consonant compels us to take a new look at the semantically, and often grammatically and linguistically, dissonant. The rare rhyme is the *recherché* rhyme, exquisite or bizarre; it serves serious purposes with a characteristically witty nonchalance. Rare rhyme is the rhyme which takes pleasure in outraging conventions, even as it maintains them. I would like to exemplify briefly hereunder three kinds of rare rhyme: the rare rhyme involving the technical (often foreign) word, the proper noun, and the particle.

(a) *The technical word*

> Penser qu'on vivra jamais dans cet astre,
> Parfois me flanque un coup dans l'épigastre.
>
> (Laforgue, 'Clair de lune')

Rhyme here unmasks the hypocrisy involved in technical jargon. The more precise defintion becomes, the less direct and familiar it is; precision shades off into preciosity, and analysis is taken to the point where it begins to embroider on the necessary, becomes euphemistic. And it is the very rareness of the rhyme that suggests the contradiction: the self-mockingly pretentious, if specific, 'épigastre' (which is here no more than a cod-learned way of saying 'stomach') face to face with the unassuming 'astre', tells us that exactitude has nothing to do with truth, and that the truth is more often told by the word that makes no show of telling it. Here, of course, the technical word 'épigastre' is the word that is striving to maintain the dignity of the theme of the first line against the disrespectful familiarity of the remainder of the second line, so that the second line is a wonderful mixture of true burlesque and mock-epic. And if the poetical word and the technical word are equidistant from the target of the plain truth, the technical word finds it harder to suppress its own pedantry and lack of taste. But whose fault is it, Laforgue would ask, that such words are admitted? Poetry's own, of course; rhyme invites irreverence, has a blind spot in its very rhymingness; it blindly accepts all its acoustic relations, be they fools or sophisticates. Anyway, somehow the frail subject 'astre' is overwhelmed and digested by the poet's more meticulous concern with his own anatomy. Here the ornate technical word has the power to expose a whole tradition of morbid and bathetic Romantic egocentricity.

(b) *The proper noun.* The mystery of the proper noun has busied philosophers, linguists and literary critics. Does a name mean, does it refer, is it a shorthand for a description and therefore made otiose by description? How much does its referential power depend on prior knowledge – and in the area of reference, we must make a distinction between the comparatively limited circulation of surnames, the unmistakable specificity of nicknames, the more intimate, but more indefinite nature of christian names? If a proper noun can mean, how much does its ability to mean depend on its etymological transparency (professional names, towns, etc.), how much on the currency of circumstantial data (biography, connections with events, etc.)? If a proper noun describes, can its descriptive function work unless the name's referent has been so simplified, so mythicised, that paradoxically the name's ability to encompass a total historical personality descriptively has been removed – 'That fellow is a regular Judas'?

It is around the name that takes place the conflict between the desire to fix an image and the desire to render the relativity of experience – 'Tom' refers to many, but with an urge for singleness of knowledge; 'Rommel' refers to one, but has different associations for many. When a name-rhyme is repeated, but with a different rhyme-partner, in a non-developmental structure (i.e. in lyric verse, rather than in epic or dramatic verse), then relativity is implied in our simultaneous perception of different aspects or associations of the name – names beget rich worlds of connection and connotation to which they are the only key and which they alone can encompass and synthesise. In Baudelaire's 'Moesta et Errabunda', for instance, we find 'Agathe' rhym-

ing first with 'éclate' and then with 'frégate'. A similar effect
is achieved when a name-rhyme appears only once, but in
the company of more than one rhyme-partner; among
many examples in Samain's 'L'Ile fortunée', one might pick
out the group 'terre/solitaire/Cythère'.

But it is in the interests of many kinds of verse, especially
satirical kinds, to reduce the name (as in the 'Judas' case
above) to a single, unequivocal existence. Because they may
mean so much and need mean nothing in particular, proper
nouns have a peculiar helplessness. The proper noun *invites*
definition, and that definition which has the closest phonetic kinship with it, the rhyme-word, has very strong claims
to priority. Little need be said of Verlaine's rhymes
'Moréas/hélas' and 'Graivil/vil', but they do demonstrate
how the slanderer can imply that his abuse is not his own,
but is prescribed by the very make-up of language itself;
rhyme assumes the responsibility and at the same time lends
its authority to the assertion.

But the poet's purpose in limiting the range of the name
need not be so vindictive; it can help express a tragic
self-mockery, as the rhyme 'Saharah/nagera' does in
Baudelaire's 'L'Héautontimorouménos':

> Je te frapperai sans colère
> Et sans haine, comme un boucher,
> Comme Moïse le rocher!
> Et je ferai de ta paupière,
>
> Pour abreuver mon Saharah,
> Jaillir les eaux de la souffrance.
> Mon désir gonflé d'espérance
> Sur tes pleurs sales nagera.

Baudelaire's irritation is with a world that will not live up to
his imaginative or emotional ambitions, which merely
reflects his own powerlessness. His sadism is an expression
of his exasperation, his contempt, his desire to recover his
will and bully existence into an infinity. Suffering itself
is of course, a valuable corridor to self-knowledge, self-
expansion, and to real compassion; in inflicting suffering,

the poet looks to suffer. But the chances of success are small. The infinity that Baudelaire may so easily stumble on is the infinity of the desert, rather than the infinity of the sea. And besides, Baudelaire's desire is always intercepted before it can realise itself, intercepted by his own ironic self-awareness and consequent self-derision. 'Saharah/ nagera' is literally and figuratively a mirage, the oasis awaiting Baudelaire is ever 'une oasis d'horreur' ('Le Voyage'); 'Saharah' as inevitably calls forth 'nagera', a cruel delusion, as 'nagera' calls forth 'Saharah', that which explains and destroys the delusion; for the drifting sands of the desert have an uncanny similarity with the waves of the sea. All efforts to escape the human condition are self-defeating, since they only serve to plant one more firmly in that condition with the added consciousness of the presumptuous stupidity of one's aspirations.

(c) *The particle*. Like the proper noun, the particle (articles, conjunctions, prepositions, pronouns) means nothing; but whereas the proper noun does not mean because, if anything, it means too much, the particle does not mean because that is not its job; its job is to clarify, classify and relate other meanings. But in the rhyme position, the particle's function in the syntactical progression is superseded by the purely poetic part it plays as the culmination of the line and as a rhyme, for the accent of the rhyme endows it with a pre-eminence it never enjoys as a simple grammatical drudge.

As we have already seen, under *rimes équivoquées*, Banville is a master of the particle rhyme, often resorting to it for satirical purposes, at other times, as below, investing it with a delightful whimsicality which still manages to reveal a *profundity* in language:

Plus vite que les autans,	2+5
Saqui, l'immortelle, au temps	2+3+2
De sa royauté naissante,	5+2
Tourbillonnait d'un pied sûr,	4+3
A mille pieds en l'air, sur	4+2+1
Une corde frémissante.	3+4
	('A Méry')

In this initial tribute to the celebrated tight-rope dancer
Saqui (1786–1866), on whom Napoleon I bestowed the title
of 'première acrobate en France', Banville pairs, in the
fourth and fifth lines, an adjective with a positional preposition, and it is quite evident that the position is totally
dependent on the adjective: Saqui's remaining *on* her rope
depends on her surefootedness; there is a sense in which
'sûr' transforms itself into 'sur' (just as, in parallel fashion,
the 'mille pieds' depend on 'un pied', just as the stability of a
single foot transforms itself into the height of a thousand).
And how fitting the seven-syllable imparisyllabic line is,
how 'frémissante' it makes the 'corde'; and this rhythmic
imbalance is reinforced by the *enjambement*, not only at 'sur',
but also at 'au temps'. But repeatedly, at the last minute,
Saqui manages to recover her equilibrium, to recover the
straying syntax or find a rhyme. Rhythmically, the penultimate line is particularly wobbly, and the preposition
which tilts perilously over the line-ending is also the preposition which ensures stability. Here it is easy to see why
the particle deserves the emphasis of a rhyme, and its claim
is strengthened by the fact that it is homonymous with its
rhyme-partner. But in other instances, the enjambing
rhyming particle is rather more difficult to account for.

In the last lines of Mallarmé's sonnet 'Au seul souci de
voyager', for example –

> Par son chant reflété jusqu'au
> Sourire du pâle Vasco

– in which we find two typical rare-rhyme partners, the
particle and the proper noun, it is the business of 'jusqu'au'
both to approach meaning and to have no meaning.
'Jusqu'au' means, in as far as it conveys the limitlessness of
Vasco's urge for voyaging; he wishes only to 'voyager
outre', whether it be beyond India or anywhere else; in
other words, 'jusqu'au' does describe what Vasco da Gama's
voyages are about, a constant sailing beyond knowledge,
one 'jusqu'au' following another. 'Jusqu'au' does *not*
mean, in as far as it is merely the link-word between the

poem's aspirations and its goal, which is Vasco, between the poem's wandering and its discovery of the subject which makes sense of it. 'Jusqu'au' sets up, longs for, the rhyme-partner that will give it a direction; by installing the sound that must be answered, by evoking the limitlessness that belongs to 'Vasco' as sailor and as proper noun, 'jusqu'au' itself represents a kind of imperfect para-Vasco.

The particle rhyme works so well here because it institutes a lull in meaning, suspends the intricate network of mood and idea that precedes, the more dramatic and conclusive to make the emergence of that part of speech which is the ultimate in meaningfulness and can contain the whole poem, the name; 'jusqu'au' represents a pause for a final analysis of the data so far collected before its reformulation in a new and inclusive form.

(iv) *Rhyme and genre: rhyme in French classical tragedy*
Rhyme in French classical tragedy is a constant source of tragic recognition. Each time a character speaks, he is, in a sense, brought face to face with an alien will, in the rhyme. Rhyme, too, may be an instrument of dramatic irony; the rhyme may, with its rhyme-partner, speak a language different from the language of the speaker, may speak the language of as yet undiscovered fact; through rhyme, the audience will be able to measure the degree of the character's self-deception. Rhymes in these plays are recurrent moments of irrevocability; the rhyme-words fit together much too snugly for characters to be capable of going back on them; the utter succinctness and grace of it all is utter impotence. The alexandrine couplet is as much an infernal machine as anything the gods can dream up.

Rhyme has a special force in dramatic and narrative works because it can be used so concertedly, can create other protagonists, rhyme-families, in which rhyme-words appear with now one, now another partner, keep quiet for several scenes, reappear with a newly acquired significance. From Corneille's *Horace* we might pick out the obvious families: Romaine/vaine/peine/haine/chaîne; Romain/main/

humain/demain/inhumain/Albain/soudain; Rome/homme/
nomme. Here we can watch the interplay not only between
concepts within individual families, but between families –
the feminine group here is full of passion and of frustration
deriving from ineffectuality, while the masculine group
exudes a kind of impassive power acting through a disembodied agency ('main'), an abstractness, flawed by an
unnerving equivocation about human values (why 'humaine'
and 'inhumaine' do not appear in the feminine group might
excite speculation); the Rome group adds the exclusivity
of its male perspective ('homme') and its notion of supra-
personal obligation ('nomme'). So rhymes act as gravi-
tational centres for dramatic syndromes.

In her two-volume *Le Thème symbolique dans le théâtre de
Racine* (1962–5), Marcelle Blum picks out groups of character rhymes in Racine's plays, e.g.:

> Phèdre se symbolise phonétiquement par le groupe
> *ire*, souvenir de l'étymologie de *colère*, car tout en
> étant coupable, elle est victime de l'ire des dieux
> qui l'ont créée passionnée. Mais parce qu'elle est
> *coupable*, ce terme constitute son thème. Thésée
> s'annonce ou se rappelle par l'*é* féminin en *ée*, tandis
> qu'Hippolyte, le héros misogyne, a pour symbole la
> masculine toute proche en *é* [i.e. includes *er, és, ez*,
> etc.]. Hippolyte a pour thème défiance. Aricie se
> symbolise par *ennemie*, Ismène par le groupe *esse*
> (vol. 1, p. 62).

But this seems a trifle arbitrary, and Blum interprets sounds
rather too elastically: thus 'esprits/mépris' is 'voyelle de
Phèdre' and 'crimes/illégitimes' is 'variation consonale sur
la rime de Phèdre'. As far as the individual plays go, Blum
should only put her faith, I think, in what she calls the 'rimes
nominales' (name-rhymes); the other rhymes belong as
much to the Racinian family as a whole, as to any particular
character.

In the section on the proper noun as rare rhyme, we
mentioned the repetition of name-rhymes in non-develop-

mental structures, and the way in which the name is relativised and its synchronic possibilities multiplied. In developmental structures – drama and the epic, for example – the repetition of name-rhymes has rather different consequences. To begin with, the multiplicity of 'rimes nominales' in drama might indeed seem to present the relativity of character, its elusiveness; but it transpires, cruelly, that these rhymes constitute the dramatic parameters of character or, alternatively, consecutive states; we experience variety no longer as multifacetedness of personality, as a guarantee of autonomy, but as the intricate patience of destiny. Let us look again at Racine's *Phèdre*. When we first hear of Thésée in *Phèdre* –

> *Théramène*: Et si . . .
> Ce héros n'attend point qu'une amante
> abusée . . .
> *Hippolyte*: Cher Théramène, arrête, et respecte
> Thésée (ll. 21–2)

– we might be unable to foresee just how many ironies are contained in the pair 'amante abusée/Thésée', a pairing in which the feminine forms are but a false trail. But we may already suspect the other rhymes which will mark Thésée out as *the* victim, of deceit, of infidelity, of general hostility, even by the end of the first scene:

I, 1 : abusée/Thésée; méprisée/Thésée; opposée/ Thésée
2 : abusée/Thésée
II, 1 : abusée/Thésée; opposée/Thésée; Thésée/aisée
5 : embrasée/Thésée
III, 3 : Thésée/embrasée
4 : opposée/Thésée
V, 7 : excusée/Thésée.

By the end of the third act, Thésée's purely dramatic identity has been fully circumscribed; it only remains to bear its fruit in action during the last two acts. Beyond the recurrent

references to Thésée the victim, we have learned in what
sense he might deserve what he gets: the word 'aisée' is used
by Aricie in a disparaging comparison of Phèdre with herself:

> Phèdre en vain s'honorait des soupirs de Thésée:
> Pour moi, je suis plus fière et fuis la gloire aisée
> D'arracher un hommage à mille autres offert.

(ll. 445-7)

But though 'aisée' refers to Phèdre's moral make-up, that
make-up is seconded by Thésée's own; 'aisée' applies equally
to him, covering a whole gamut of sins, from moral laxity
to over-confidence. We have learned, too, how he will
react to the situation that greets him on his return: the two
uses of 'embrasée' to describe Phèdre's love – first, and
ironically, her love for Thésée, then her love for Hippolyte –
indicate that the heat of Thésée's rage is a direct extension
of, and equal to, the heat of Phèdre's frustrated passion. It is
almost as though Thésée's unconscious jealousy of Hippolyte's increasing prowess and stern virtuousness were
working directly through Phèdre's own jealousy; exacer-
bated, in rather the same way, by Hippolyte's disobedient
courting of Aricie. Thésée is thus haunted by this com-
pact rhyme-family, and each time his name is linked with
one of them, the other's reverberate in it. The final rhyme –
'excusée/Thésée' – which occurs in the very last scene of the
play, after a fourth act empty of such rhymes, is, not surprisingly, the most poignant:

> *Thésée*: Cruelle! pensez-vous être assez excusée. . .
> *Phèdre*: Les moments me sont chers; écoutez-moi,
> Thésée.   (ll. 1621-2)

While Thésée thinks in terms of Phèdre's justification, the
verse thinks in terms of his own justification and forgive-
ness. Has the rhyme-knot that wrought such havoc in the
fourth and fifth acts at last been untied? Has Thésée paid
what he owed to such rhymes? The rhymes that concern
the imponderables, cause and consequence, 'aisée' and

'excusée', occur only once, are surreptitious suggestions for which there is no real dramatic evidence, as there is for the other rhymes. And these rhymes, all together, have pointed to the fundamental kinship of character and motive which exists between Phèdre and Thésée; in a sense, they deserve each other, and Thésée's relinquishment of authority to Neptune is only a continuation of Phèdre's relinquishment of authority to Œnone. Both recover that authority, at a great price. Charles Péguy has some illuminating things to say about rhyme in Corneille and Racine in his *Victor-Marie, Comte Hugo* (1910), and of the name-rhyme he writes: 'Cela donne au vers une facture délibérée, complète, un achèvement plein carré, une absence d'hésitation, une volonté d'emplir.'

Those rhymed English plays which derive so much from French classical practice and which might have profited from the habit of 'rimes nominales', namely Restoration tragedies, show few signs of having done so. Neither Dryden's *Conquest of Granada* of 1670, nor his *Aureng-Zebe* of 1676, nor Otway's *Titus and Berenice* of 1677, follow Racine's example. The principal reason for this would seem to be the difficulty of finding rhymes for intricate Oriental names and Roman names with a feminine ending in -us. It is significant that where, in *Aureng-Zebe*, the names of Aureng-Zebe and Morat appear together in the 'rhyme' position, there also occurs an exceptional passage of blank verse (Act III, sc. 1), and Morat occupies the terminal position in another blank line, a trimeter, in Act V, sc. 1. One can possibly feel *some* attempt to gain the French advantage, in the obvious, if rare, manipulation of a name's sound in order to eke out a rhyme: 'Morat' elsewhere rhymes with 'State' and 'Fate', but also 'that', while Otway's Berenice rhymes both with 'Decrees' and 'this'.

These paragraphs on classical tragedy have been at pains to demonstrate the careful and, by implication, conscious organisation of groups of rhymes, rhymes which are in fact deeply embedded, if not hidden, in texts of at leat two hours' duration. Is this not to stretch credibility to breaking-point and to endow the reader/spectator with a perceptiveness beyond human possibility? Not really. To say that a writer arranges his work in such and such a way is no more than a conventional way of saying that a work *is* so arranged and that for want of evidence to the contrary, we must assume that a writer wrote what he wanted to. Furthermore, to show that a work is arranged is necessarily to suppose that the reader/spectator responds to its arrangedness, whether consciously or unconsciously; and if the critic does care to draw attention to barely perceptible phenomena, he is, by that very act, making them fully perceptible, part of consciousness; the critic, after all, does not write for those who will not read him.

(v) *Conclusion*

We shall have more to say of rhyme in the chapter on free verse, Chapter 7. But three general points can be made in conclusion to this chapter:

1. It is pointless to argue about the naturalness or unnaturalness of rhyme. Much of the debate about rhyme in the eighteenth and nineteenth centuries, and indeed in the seventeenth, certainly centred on this issue. Do we use rhyme in normal speech (the argument against rhyme in dramatic verse)? Rhyme is an artifice, the pretext of difficulty which excuses lame verse (an argument against rhyme used by free-verse poets, Eliot and Pound in particular). But psychology has taught us to see in rhyme a mechanism whereby a mind gets its bearings or finds its way out of tight corners, a totally normal mental resource. The free-verse poet resolves this apparent contradiction by saying that rhyme in regular schemes alone is artifical, because it destroys precisely that impulsiveness, that improvised quality, which should be rhyme's distinguishing feature.

2. There is no such thing as an inherently good or an inherently bad rhyme. There are only rhymes made good or bad by the lines which support them. After all, the tiredest combination might well be the greatest challenge – to put a

strangely profound distance between words too obviously related (e.g. roi/loi, sombre/ombre, larme/alarme).

3. Many would suggest that rhyme creates *unnecessary* difficulties. It is mistaken to come away with the idea that no difficulty attaches to blank verse – at the very least rhyme has to be avoided – and very little to half-rhyme. About the intricacies of half-rhyme we shall have more to say later, but it is not going too far to claim that these intricacies outdo anything the full-rhymer could think up. And Robert Abernathy (1967) has given us a timely reminder that blank verse may be a positive act of *anti-rhyming*, that there may be as much system in the resistance to rhyme as there is in yielding to it.

5

Stanzas

Our first task must be one of terminological differentiation: the English 'stanza' should not be confused with the French *stance*, a fairly specialised term, which dates from the sixteenth century, but is found little after the Romantic period; *stance* is used to denote stanzas, often heterosyllabic, which treat of serious matters (religious, moral, elegiac) – e.g. the *stances* of Corneille's *Le Cid*, of Malherbe, of Voltaire, of Musset, of Gautier; where the English use 'stanza', the French normally use *strophe*; 'strophe', for the English, is limited to descriptions of the stanzas of the Pindaric ode.

But what, after all, is a stanza? Minimally, to cover all kinds of verse, both fixed and free, and to envisage such a thing as a one-line stanza, one would have to say: 'A line, or group of lines, typographically separated from the rest of the poem, or, if itself constituting the whole poem, not sufficiently long or regular to pass as stichic verse' (this last qualification unavoidably begs a question). But minimal definitions, while they may be the fairest, are rarely the most useful or worth applying. Let us stick, for the moment, to a regular-verse context and ask ourselves a negative question: why is a sequence of eight alexandrines with the rhyme-scheme *a b a b a b a b* an unsatisfactory stanza? Because, with its potentially unlimited alternation, the scheme creates no inner tensions, has no designs upon itself. Nor is it a fruitful compound of different rhyme-schemes, as so often happens in the longer stanzas. Nor do the rhymes limit themselves to a *minimal* schematic fulfilment, which is what makes the alternating *quatrain* a stanza. Nor is there any variation in line-length which would warrant the title 'stanza' (it goes without saying that distinctive patterns of line-length, like patterns of measure or rhyme, can be the structural bases of stanzas). In short, a stanza is a group of lines – or, indeed, a single line – whose special identity makes it repeatable, but not continuable. So, though it is difficult, if not impossible, to define 'stanza' in any thorough way, it is possible to pick out some of the principles which would need to be taken into account if such a definition were attempted. As in other chapters, I do not here plan to give a wide-ranging catalogue of different varieties, but to examine some of the ways in which observations about stanza can contribute to interpretation.

(i) *The basic schemes*

> Les strophes de cinq vers de la *Chevelure* ne produisent pas sur notre poitrine une pareille impression de légèreté vive et d'envol. Leur ampleur est plus lourde. C'est le même art, mais au service d'une émotion plus intime, plus lente: comme une lente gourmandise respiratoire qui hume les parfums, une joie pensive dont l'expression large et sonore est pourtant toute proche du soupir (Jean Prévost, 1964, pp. 242–3).

Do prosodic devices, be they verse-lines or rhyme-schemes or *enjambement*, really have inherent, independent, expressive capabilities, which the poet calls upon to enhance the ideas he has in mind? Prévost's words might lead us to think so, as indeed might the logical facts of the matter: if we can argue that forms pre-date, have an existence anterior to, the poems in which they appear – and even where a form is used for the first time, we can say that it was a *deducible possibility* prior to the poem – then we can argue not only that forms exist in their own right, in a metaphysical world of Platonic Ideas, and that therefore the poet is working as much to communicate the form as himself, but also that the poet does at least choose his means of expression, and he would hardly choose them if he did not feel that they would help him. But even if we feel happy to argue like this, do we still feel happy about asserting that the five-line stanza of Baudelaire's 'La Chevelure' (*a b a a b*) evokes 'une lente gourmandise respiratoire' or 'une joie pensive', or, as Prévost later proposes, 'l'atmosphère à la fois tropicale et marine de son rêve'? Can this bald pattern of *a*'s and *b*'s be that subtly suggestive? The plain answer is 'No', and Prévost, perhaps feeling he has gone too far, retracts a little: 'Ces effets sans doute sont puissamment aidés par le sens et les images, mais ils les suscitent, ils les rendent plus faciles et plus puissants' (p. 245).

Prévost is not wrong to attribute certain expressive potentialities to a rhyme-scheme; it is just that he has gone about it in the wrong way, as many others do; he has derived the expressive potentialities from a specific example and has not been able to prevent qualities of that example actually becoming the expressive potentialities of the scheme. If we are to do proper justice to a rhyme-scheme's ability to mean, we must analyse the data in a pre-poem state, because in that way only will the findings have more than single-poem validity; but we must, of course, resist the temptation to equate abstractness with absoluteness – in analysing a rhyme-scheme as a set of letters, we should not conclude that the interpretations have an incontrovertible and universal applicability. And we must also accept the fact that, in describing schemes in the abstract, we must necessarily resort to metaphors, and that metaphors are always prejudicial.

The first thing that can be said about rhyme-schemes is that they *are* schemes, organisations of meaning, and it is not a bad idea to apply tactical terminology to them. A rhyme-scheme is a strategic deployment of forces designed to stamp a mode of relating, an intention, which may amount to a 'personality' or an 'atmosphere', on a group of lines. The enclosed *a b b a* scheme (*rimes embrassées*), for instance, can be described as a stanza in which the *b* couplet is outflanked, even out-manoeuvred, by the *a* couplet. This would lead one to suppose two things: first, that the second *a* line might revel in its finality, might have something self-congratulatory about it; secondly, that the *b* couplet might seem somewhat parenthetic, like an insertion, an observation superseded by the fourth line. It is equally evident that the *a b b a* pattern forms a chiasmus, that *b a* is a mirror-image of *a b*, so that it also suggests an inturnedness, a self-absorption, which creates a reposeful symmetry, and an 'inner' activity. For the Symbolist poets, this narcissistic quality was particularly available in the enclosed quatrains of the Petrarchan sonnet (see below, Chapter 6, for a description of the Petrarchan sonnet); the Symbolist sonnet, like the mirror, is a surface which remains decorative surface while reflecting a perspectival depth, which lures one into its impenetrability, which allows consciousness to consummate itself in its own image, an ideal virginity; and the steady reflected light of the quatrains, which are both self-reflecting and mutually reflecting, is animated, rendered infinitely problematic, by the refractions and distortions of the probing, exploratory asymmetries of the tercets. The Belgian Symbolist, Émile Verhaeren, remarks of the Mallarméan sonnet: 'Pourquoi ne dirait-on pas qu'un sonnet de Mallarmé est un palais tout en verrières glorieuses qui reçoivent leur lumière non du dehors, mais du dedans?' ('La Poésie', *L'Art moderne*, 4 June 1891), and Mallarmé himself writes of his own 'Ses purs ongles très haut dédiant leur onyx': 'J'ai pris ce sujet d'un sonnet nu se réfléchissant de toutes les façons' (letter to Henry Cazalis, July 1868).

But in considering another of Mallarmé's sonnets, 'M'introduire dans ton histoire', it is not the self-reflecting quality of the enclosed quatrain I wish to demonstrate, but the feature referred to earlier, the outflanking of the *b* couplet by the *a* couplet, the latent aggression of the *a* couplet:

> M'introduire dans ton histoire
> C'est en héros effarouché
> S'il a du talon nu touché
> Quelque gazon de territoire

A des glaciers attentatoire
Je ne sais le naïf péché
Que tu n'auras pas empêché
De rire très haut sa victoire

Dis si je ne suis pas joyeux
Tonnerre et rubis aux moyeux
De voir en l'air que ce feu troue

Avec des royaumes épars
Comme mourir pourpre la roue
Du seul vespéral de mes chars.

The meaning of this poem is not easy to come at; either we
look upon it as a love poem in which the erotic, if tentative,
advances of the poet, wrapped in a veil of self-effacing
euphemism ('M'introduire', 'histoire', 'talon nu', 'gazon',
'attentatoire', 'rire'), are repulsed, and the poet finds alternative, defiant relief in his own fiction (sunset and triumphal
chariot), or, alternatively, the 'glaciers' denote not the
cold inaccessibility of a mistress, but the pure, forbidding
heights of art itself, heights which the poet is happy to
abandon – morally reprehensible though it may be – for odd
excursions into an artistic splendour of his own concoction.
But what we can safely say is that the reticence, not to say
timidity, of the quatrains becomes the violent ecstasy of the
sestet. This change has a purely linguistic manifestation: the
octave opens with the infinitive 'M'introduire', the most
neutral and inactive part of the verb, while the sestet opens
with the imperative 'Dis', that part of the verb which is
most assertive, most peremptory. Throughout the octave,
the poet makes no headway, he appears as a failure, even as a
coward. But the rhyme-scheme contradicts this evidence
and prefigures the martial triumph of the sestet. The *a b b a*
pattern may represent, as we have said, a movement of
envelopment, in which the *b* couplet becomes an insertion,
bracketed, and it is significant that the *a* lines here have the
more sonorous rhymes – the generous aureola of '-toire'
against the prim and brusque '-ché' – and that the *b* lines

contain the clearest expression of the poet's vulnerability and impotence. It is significant, too, that the *a* lines have the authoritative, not to say pedantic, words, and that the *b* lines contain the active verbs and are therefore the motors of syntactic, though not of prosodic, meaning. Ultimately, we must feel that the *a* lines, by enclosing the *b* lines, underline the provisional nature of the *b* lines and nullify their influence. The last *a* line of the octave leaves us, appropriately, with an infinitive on the very point of bursting into energetic finiteness:

> De rire très haut sa victoire.

If the *a b b a* scheme, in one of its guises, presents us with a picture, self-regarding, inviting us to a contemplative stance, the other common quatrain scheme, *a b a b* (*rimes croisées*), presents a more cinematographic experience, a sequence of 'shots', as the eye and/or ear wander over their subject. We have already had occasion to refer to the panoramic opening description in Lamartine's 'L'Isolement'; I quote the second stanza:

> Ici gronde le fleuve aux vagues écumantes;
> Il serpente, et s'enfonce en un lointain obscur;
> Là, le lac immobile étend ses eaux dormantes
> Où l'étoile du soir se lève dans l'azur.

Here the alternating scheme works like a narrative dynamo, embodying the coming and going of the eye. It is not all forward progression, of course, it is essentially forward progression with hesitation, with room for circumstance and qualification; sometimes it is more oscillation than progression.

In reading the opening stanzas of 'L'Isolement', one might well be struck by their similarity with the opening stanzas of Gray's 'Elegy Written in a Country Churchyard', which also present a wide prospect as evening closes in:

> The curfew tolls the knell of parting day,
> The lowing herd winds slowly o'er the lea,

The ploughman homeward plods his weary way,
And leaves the world to darkness and to me.

Because of its use in this poem, Gray's stanza, a quatrain of
iambic pentameters with alternating rhymes, has assumed
the title of 'elegiac stanza'. It would not be difficult to find
subsequent elegies written in stanzas other than this (e.g.
Shelley's 'Adonais', Arnold's 'Thyrsis'), but we can see in
what sense the title is fitting. The *a b a b* scheme is a scheme
of parry and thrust, or put more quietly, of give and take; in
other words, it is a constantly relenting scheme, even-
paced, without the conflict which often characterises the
enclosed scheme. And elegy is precisely a mode which
removes the sting from death, by its reflective equilibrium,
which uncovers consolation and reconciliation at the heart
of lament. Elegy is a growth to understanding through the
contemplation of loss, and the whole secret of elegiac
reconciliation is that the lamenter should not be stinted of
sights and sounds, of memories, of a continuing enjoyment
of those images which are the very cause of his acute sense
of loss. The elegy generalises particular loss into a broader
sense of the patterns of existence; the poem which sustains
the particularity of loss is more likely to be a form of ode.
Unlike Gray, Lamartine is usually bemoaning personal loss,
but he can look for comfort in the indestructibility of love,
of which his anguish is continuing proof, and can take
refuge in the valley-womb of Nature:

> Mais la nature est là qui t'invite et qui t'aime;
> Plonge-toi dans son sein qu'elle t'ouvre toujours:
> Quand tout change pour toi, la nature est la même,
> Et le même soleil se lève sur tes jours.
>
> ('Le Vallon')

The third line of this stanza reveals another secret of the
alternating scheme. It is a scheme of change with a small
dose of recurrence built into it, sufficient recurrence to give
courage. This relenting scheme creates perhaps a certain
amenability, passivity, in the poet, making him vulnerable

to his own impressions and to change; but, at the same time, as *a b* moves away from us, so we know that it must come back to rhyme, as memory or as alternative. The *a b a b* scheme is a scheme of losing *and* remembering, of changing in order to recur.

The final basic scheme is the couplet (*rimes plates*), or, in its stanzaic form, the distich. Here the rhyme occurs without interruption, conveying, among other things, self-satisfaction, dismissiveness, feeling under pressure, depending on the tone animating the poem. In its intellectual dimension, it will usually express the agility of a mind delightedly feeding off itself, a mind almost outpacing itself in the discovery of an apt rhyme, so that the rhyme strikes the reader as occurring right in the front of the consciousness, as an instrument of irony:

> Déguster, en menant les rites réciproques,
> Les trucs Inconscients dans leur œuf, à la coque.
>
>   (Laforgue, 'Complainte du Sage de Paris')

The poet is always keen to show that his wisdom is written in the will of language itself, that truth, in the guise of rhyme, must have its way. Not unnaturally therefore, this 'dance of the intellect among words' (Ezra Pound's definition of 'logopœia') will often shade into a more elementary form of sagacity, the proverb, where the degree of linguistic patterning ('A stitch in time saves nine', 'Least said, soonest mended') is proportional to the age-oldness of the wisdom it contains:

> Nature est sans pitié
> Pour son petit dernier.
>
>   (Laforgue, 'Complainte du pauvre corps humain')

Here already is a graver note. Where the feelings are concerned, the distich represents the sustained nature of the emotional pressure; the poet or protagonist is so subject to feeling that he can do no more than complete the rhyme, mark time, in a temporary paralysis; he does not change the rhyme-sound because he has not sufficient control of himself, or of his destiny, to do so:

– 'Quel silence, dans la forêt d'automne,
Quand le soleil en son sang s'abandonne!'
(Laforgue, 'Complainte de l'orgue de Barbarie')

All these examples are taken from Laforgue's *Les Complaintes* (1885), and demonstrate how one poet, in one collection, can explore and exploit the capabilities of a rhyme-scheme, with the effect that, as we read through the collection, we find each capability reverberant with other capabilities, building up an ever more complex texture of tone and intention; the distich quickly becomes the sum of the different pressures on meaning it can exert. By constantly re-defining the distich, the poet refuses to define himself. But the expressive scope of the distich is still limited enough for us to feel that it, and more especially the poet, add up to a discernible personality: the poet has an intellectual ingenuity which shades into sentimental commitment, an analytical mind which often surrenders its powers to an aphoristic fatalism, a will to dominate others which is a will to dominate himself, his own emotional paralysis.

How, then, does this kind of analysis differ from that offered by Prévost? It suggests a close relation between the expressive power of form and the syntactic meaning of the poem as Prévost's does. But it does this only after affirming that form irresistibly implies that syntactic meaning by the special ways it organises and articulates language, by the generative pulse it gives to the patterning of utterance. An arrangement of rhymes influences the way that language functions.

In the following pages, I wish to come back to the question of how far a poet may be defined by his use of stanza. But I would like first to consider the relationship between a genre – the ode – and the stanza. And finally I would like to examine the way in which a movement or period can give special privilege to a particular stanza.

(ii) *Stanza and genre*

That the iambic pentameter quatrain with alternating rhyme is peculiarly elegiac is an English view; it can be applied with some justification to French elegies, assuming that we substitute alexandrine for iambic pentameter. But no generical imperative attaches to this stanza; there are elegies which do not utilise the stanza, just as the stanza appears in many contexts beside the elegiac. The French ode stanzas, on the other hand, are unmistakably ode stanzas, though this is not to say that all odes (discounting free-verse odes) are written in them. Before examining these stanzas, we should describe the ode more generally.

We can make a rough distinction between a major and a minor ode, a distinction which corresponds to the two main ode varieties, the Pindaric and the Horatian. The major or Pindaric is a poem with large-scale ambitions, situated between lyric fire and epic grandeur, between personality and the disembodied, inspired voice, a poem usually of celebration (Pindar's odes are celebrations of games or religious festivals), solemn, sublime, mythologising and mythicising. It is the supremely public poem, glorifying man, his achievements, his essential dignity. The minor or Horatian ode is a more thoroughly occasional poem, often epicurean in inspiration (cross-fertilised by the Anacreontic ode), an intimate discourse on the pleasures of wine, or women, or friendship, but characterised by a moderation which frequently dips into the laconic or ironic. The Horatian ode has the reflective sobriety of the Pindaric, though its philosophical aspirations may not be so great.

The classic English Pindaric uses the strophic divisions of Pindar, a strophe and an antistrophe, complex heterosyllabic or heterometric stanzaic structures, in the same mould, followed by an epode of a different structure. But after the eighteenth century, such a pattern is rare. The Horatian ode took many forms. But the ode always had a reputation for irregularity and complexity and became a natural agent of the liberation of verse – the 'free-verse ode' has never really been a contradiction in terms (see, for example, the works

of Coventry Patmore and Francis Thompson). The degree
of irregularity which the French were prepared to tolerate
might have been less, but the ode stanzas were frequently
heterosyllabic and, in the nineteenth century, became increasingly heterostanzaic (see Hugo's odes in *Odes et bal-
lades* (1828 – written 1822–6)). The rhyme-scheme of the
major ode stanza is *a b a b c c d e e d*; the rhyme-scheme of
the minor ode is simply the last six lines of the major, i.e.
a a b c c b.

The rhyme-scheme of the major ode is a compound, in
one sense, of all the basic schemes we have looked at, and of
all their capabilities. After the forward-moving, developmental phase of the opening quatrain, it seems to gather
itself together, to reach a pinnacle or fulcrum, with the
couplet, which suspends movement and redirects the
expository energy of the first four lines into the inturned,
enclosed quatrain, the quatrain of resounding finality. What
can two such stanzas, one taken from Ponce-Denis
Écouchard-Lebrun's (often referred to as Lebrun-Pindare)
'Ode à Monsieur de Buffon sur ses détracteurs', and the
other from Hugo's ode 'A Ramon, duc de Benav.(ente)',
tell us further about the resources of this disposition? Both
poems are written in the so-called *dizain isométrique classique*:

> Mais si tu crains la tyrannie
> D'un monstre jaloux et pervers,
> Quitte le sceptre du génie,
> Cesse d'éclairer l'univers.
> Descends des hauteurs de ton âme,
> Abaisse tes ailes de flamme.
> Brise tes sublimes pinceaux,
> Prends tes envieux pour modèles,
> Et de leurs vernis infidèles
> Obscurcis tes brillants tableaux.
>
> (Lebrun)

> 'Esclaves d'une loi fatale,
> Sachons taire les maux soufferts.
> Pourquoi veux-tu donc que j'étale

La meurtrissure de mes fers?
Aux yeux que la misère effraie
Qu'importe ma secrète plaie?
Passez, je dois vivre isolé;
Vos voix ne sont qu'un bruit sonore;
Passez tous! j'aime mieux encore
Souffrir, que d'être consolé!'

                                                    (Hugo)

The beauty of Lebrun's stanza lies in the way in which the
changing rhyme-scheme gives changing emphasis and
direction to the repeated imperative. The stanza is a taunt.
The first four lines explore the logic of the position, should
Buffon concede to his detractors, if this, then that, an
argumentative progression. The couplet intensifies the jibe,
reformulates it twice, amplifies the paradox of disdain and
tribute that the stanza is. The last four lines develop a
metaphor of the naturalist's work, the naturalist being
depicted as a painter; the enclosed scheme provides a natural
opportunity to introduce a lull in the sequence of imperatives in the inner couplet by the expedient of inversion, and
allows the poet to concentrate his comments on the
unworthiness of the detractors also in the inner, parenthes-
ised couplet, the better to focus his attention exclusively on
the gifts of his subject in the outer, outflanking couplet. The
imperatives of the final quatrain have a coherence of reference, and thus a conclusiveness, which the preceding
imperatives do not have.

In the Hugo stanza, the rhyme-scheme corresponds to
changes in syntax and perspective. The first four lines are
mixed first-person plural imperative and rhetorical question addressed, presumably, to the poet. The couplet continues the rhetorical question approach, but now the
speaker is looking beyond the poet, his question begins to
embrace a larger community of listeners. The final quatrain
develops the form of communal address, but is now
imperative again. The confraternity suggested in the imperative of the second line of the stanza has given way to an
imperative which isolates the speaker from his fellows.

One of the attractions of compound schemes like this is that their various parts can relate to each other in different ways. Punctuation will usually provide a reliable indication as to how we should group the lines, where we should put what Henri Morier calls the 'césure strophique'. We have so far treated the ode stanza according to the divisions *a b a b/ c c/d e e d*, and in the examples quoted, the punctuation endorses this disposition. But an equally plausible disposition, and one which, in my experience, is noticeably commoner, is *a b a b/c c d/e e d*. The following stanza from Lefranc de Pompignan's ode on the death of a fellow eighteenth-century ode-poet, Jean-Baptiste Rousseau, will serve as an example:

> Oui, la mort seule nous délivre
> Des ennemis de nos vertus:
> Et notre gloire ne peut vivre
> Que lorsque nous ne vivons plus.
> Le chantre d'Ulysse et d'Achille,
> Sans protecteur et sans asile,
> Fut ignoré jusqu'au tombeau.
> Il expire: le charme cesse,
> Et tous les peuples de la Grèce
> Entre eux disputent son berceau.

This begins to give the ode stanza the look of a contracted sonnet. The opening quatrain still plays its developmental role, carrying the argument forward. The sestet which follows exemplifies that argument with its reference to Homer. The *c c d/e e d* pattern evens out the force of the couplets, the *c* lines no longer acting as a suspension and instrument of intensification, but as a springboard for the *d* line; the *e* couplet is no longer a potential parenthesis, but endorses the *c* couplet, adding to it a note of expectancy, even impatience, as the second *d* rhyme is looked for, reached for, in a final impulse. In the stanza we have before us, the pattern of parallel couplets is skilfully complicated. The *c* couplet sets up the subject and then qualifies it with a discouraging, syntactically 'dead' line. The *e* couplet starts on a note of discouragement, acts as an after-effect of the first *d* line, and then picks up, in the second line, with a superlative nominal group. The contrary directions of the couplets are picked up in the *d* rhyme: we descend to 'tombeau' and then experience a renaissance as we reach for 'berceau'. And the underlying parallelism of the tercets, the equality of their value, is revealed in the fact that, for the poet, 'tombeau' and 'berceau' are synonyms, that physical grave is artistic birth.

We have had cause to mention Thomas Gray in relation to the elegy, and his work is by no means irrelevant to a discussion of the French ode. Gray's familiarity with French verse seems to have been fairly extensive, and to judge from his correspondence, it was the poet Jean-Baptiste-Louis Gresset who, of his contemporaries, particularly caught his attention. Roy Fothergill (1929) has explored what Gray has in common with Gresset and what he may owe to him. Among other things, Gray uses the French major ode stanza in 'Ode on the Spring' and 'Ode on a Distant Prospect of Eton College'; and his choice of the traditional English tail-rhyme stanza *a a b c c b* (where *a* and *c* are tetrameters, *b* a trimeter) for 'Ode on the Death of a Favourite Cat' may well owe much to his knowledge of the French minor ode stanza:

> Eight times emerging from the flood
> She mewed to every watery god,
> Some speedy aid to send.
> No dolphin came, no Nereid stirred:
> Nor cruel Tom nor Susan heard.
> A favourite has no friend! (Sixth stanza)

Here are the humble occasion, the irony, the reflective turn, the decorative ease we associate with the Horatian ode. That the *a a b c c b* scheme here acts itself out as tercets is not to be wondered at, given the syllabic structure of the stanza, with its shorter third and sixth lines. Obviously syllabic variation is to be added to punctuation as an indicator of the stanzaic substructure. And the shortening of the line at the end of the group has a deflating effect; the *b* lines are not launched by the couplets, but counter the couplets' mock-epical eloquence by interposing an important reminder of home truths. The *a a b/c c b* division is the more common division in the minor French ode, which often takes on the grander tones of the major and is able to capitalise on the broad periods of the three-line unit:

> Un précipice affreux devant eux se présente,
> Mais toujours leur raison, soumise et complaisante,
> Au-devant de leurs yeux met un voile imposteur.
> Sous leurs pas cependant s'ouvrent les noirs abîmes,
> Où la cruelle mort, les prenant pour victimes,
> Frappe ces vils troupeaux dont elle est le pasteur.
> (J.-B. Rousseau, 'Sur l'aveuglement des hommes du siècle')

The first *b* line momentarily evades the insistence of the opening couplet, leavens rhetoric with a sagacious level-headedness, steps aside from the certainty of personal conviction to a certainty of wearied knowledge, tonally different, distanced, half-pitying. But the second *b* has nothing of all this. Now eagerly looked for as a rhyming partner, it becomes the very apex of rhetorical pressure, endowed with the full force of an inescapable destiny. While the first *b* retains something of an understanding of human frailty, the second *b* has all the pitiless rigour of divine justice. So it is still tonally different from the preceding couplet, but its tonal difference is no longer a resistance to emotional pressure, but a transformation of it into a higher, impersonal wrath.

Jean-Baptiste Rousseau also uses a shorter *b* line:

> Mais une dure loi, des dieux mêmes suivie,
> Ordonne que le cours de la plus belle vie
>   Soit mêlé de travaux;
> Un partage inégal ne leur fut jamais libre,
> Et leur main tient toujours dans un juste équilibre
>   Tous nos biens et nos maux.
> ('A Monsieur le comte du Luc')

But it has, of course, nothing in common with Gray's crisp interruptions. For these short lines are receptacles aspired to, into which substantival facts can settle, solid and four-square, or in which the energy of a verb can be stabilised, given defined purpose, even as it is released.

One might suppose that the division of the minor ode stanza into a couplet followed by an enclosed quatrain would create too halting and concentrated an opening, and thus impair the stanza's momentum. But this division is to be found:

> La nuit, quand les démons dansent sous le ciel
> sombre,
> Tu suis le chœur magique en tournoyant dans
> l'ombre.
> L'hymne infernal t'invite au conseil malfaisant.
> Fuis! car un doux parfum sort de ces fleurs nouvel-
> les;
> Fuis, il faut à tes mornes ailes
> L'air du tombeau natal et la vapeur du sang.
>
> Qui t'amène vers moi? Viens-tu de ces collines
> Où la lune s'enfuit sur de blanches ruines?
> Son front est, comme toi, sombre dans sa pâleur.
> Tes yeux dans leur route incertaine
> Ont donc suivi les feux de ma lampe lointaine?
> Attiré par la gloire, ainsi vient le malheur!
>
> (Hugo, 'La Chauve-souris', fourth and fifth stanzas)

I have quoted two stanzas because they give some hint of what 'heterostanzaic' might mean. Hugo's shifting octosyllable endows this ode with a structural volatility which is part of the form's zestfulness and part of the subject's disturbing and elusive nature. But this is a timid irregularity compared with some of his other odes; 'Au vallon de Cherizy', for example, has four four-line stanzas, two five-line stanzas, five six-line stanzas, and one eight-line stanza; 'Premier soupir' has two four-line stanzas, one five-line stanza, one seven-line stanza, one nine-line stanza; and so on. At all events, the two stanzas before us have strong syntactic breaks after their second line. The halting quality of which we spoke obviously suits the gothic subject; each stanza opens with a powerlessness, a paralysing apprehensiveness, in the face of the bat's sinister and mysterious habits. But Hugo has minimised the break between couplet and quatrain by rendering the third line structurally equivocal. Syntactically self-sufficient, it has a foot in both camps; without interfering with the stasis of the couplet, it delays the onset of the quatrain and masks its outline. An ode in the 'genre frénétique', as this is, takes us a long way from Horace, but tells us something about the adaptability and scope of the ode stanza.

(iii) *Stanza and poet*

It would be stretching a point to call Laforgue the poet of the distich. If we limited ourselves to the poetry of *Les Complaintes*, this might be more justified, but it would probably tell us more about the collection than about the poet. But nevertheless, a student looking for the secret of Laforgue's poetic personality could do much worse than start with the expressive scope of the distich and work carefully inwards towards the poet.

A more obviously identifying stanza is Alfred de Vigny's *septain* (*a b a b c c b*); of the eleven poems of *Les Destinées* (1864 – written 1838–63), five are written in this stanza and a sixth – 'Le Mont des Oliviers' – has it as a finale. Those who do not find Vigny to their taste would argue perhaps that he derives his lessons too heavy-handedly from his dramatic narratives, that his grip on the direction of his poems is too tight, that the narratives, finely wrought in themselves, are let down, if not superseded, by the condescending moral homilies they beget. How far does a study of his seven-line stanza help to endorse or contradict this view? The second and third stanzas of 'La Bouteille à la mer' will provide a starting-point:

> Quand un grave marin voit que le vent l'emporte
> Et que les mâts brisés pendent tous sur le pont,

Que dans son grand duel la mer est la plus forte
Et que par des calculs l'esprit en vain répond;
Que le courant l'écrase et le roule en sa course,
Qu'il est sans gouvernail et partant sans ressource,
Il se croise les bras dans un calme profond.

Il voit les masses d'eau, les toise et les mesure,
Les méprise en sachant qu'il en est écrasé,
Soumet son âme au poids de la matière impure
Et se sent mort ainsi que son vaisseau rasé.
– A de certains moments, l'âme est sans résistance;
Mais le penseur s'isole et n'attend d'assistance
Que de la forte foi dont il est embrasé.

These two stanzas reveal much that is essential to Vigny's
thinking: that by knowing them, we master the forces
which destroy us, that we disarm destiny by our refusal to
surrender our self-sufficiency, that thought, the invulnerable still centre at the heart of being, outlives, by its high
solitude, the time-bound tempests of existence. 'Grip',
therefore, is not a pressure exerted by an over-careful and
over-patent poet, so much as the key to dignity through
self-sufficiency, to strength through deprivation – one
needs to look more closely at Vigny's use of reflexive verbs
and 'sans' – to which the poems seek to give dramatic
realisation.

The opening alternating quatrain, which Vigny habitu-
ally separates from the last three lines, often conveys, as
here, the vicissitudes of life, tossing man hither and thither,
apparently making him the plaything of chance. In the first
of these stanzas, the only half-isolated couplet intensifies the
findings of the quatrain, accelerates them with its parallel
coordinating clauses – a syntactical feature which also
serves to differentiate these two lines from the preceding
ones. The couplet thus acts as a culmination of narrative, an
exercise in threat, the better to project, *and be withstood by*,
the last line, which is more of a liberation than a succumb-
ing; in fact, the calm of the sailor increases in proportion to
the dangers which beset him. Here, then, the couplet works

in collusion with the quatrain, while preserving something of its autonomy. But it could be convincingly argued that it also works in collusion with the final line, providing just the challenge that the last line needs as it refuses to be brow-beaten, and refuses, too, to dissociate itself from the stanza which, by virtue of contrast, gives it all its significance – its rhyme recovers the link with the quatrain.

In the second of these stanzas, the couplet introduces a more marked break, a turning away from narrative to abstract generalisation, interpreting the narrative by identifying the sailor with the thinker. So the couplet acts both as a brake and as a moment snatched from flux in which to encapsulate a truth, a moment which extends into the last line. From the first-stanza disposition of *a b a b/c c/b*, we move to a quatrain + tercet structure. But, once again, the rhyme-scheme does not allow the philosophical observation to break loose from the narrative, the last rhyme taking us back to the violence of 'écrasé' and 'rasé'.

Already we have uncovered two kinds of Vignyian *septain*. In the first, the couplet is an incitement to courage and disdain, and in the second, the couplet *is* that courage, that hardening of the spirit and flexing of the intellectual muscles. We can hardly explore all the variations possible with this particular stanza, but we can make some tentative generalisations. It is a stanza which has some similarities with the major ode stanza, and like the major ode stanza, it situates itself between the lyric and the heroic, the dramatic and the disquisitional, the quatrain occupying itself with the former, the couplet and final line with the latter. But this is too blunt an account; Vigny varies the mixture of the elements, sometimes excluding one of them altogether.

But however he does it, Vigny is anxious to bring disquisition back into narrative by the loop of the final rhyme. He is glad to use a stanza which allows him to affirm isolation by the separateness of its parts: whether it be the isolation of one individual from another, or from the mass; or the isolation of the couple; whether it be the isolation of thought from involvement, or of self-control from assailment; and at the same time to envisage fraternity and dependence, the fraternity of kindred isolations or the dependence of dignity on an ordered fatalism. It may surprise us to find Vigny idealising Nature and Nature's aloofness, in the latter part of the following stanza from 'La Maison du berger':

Pars courageusement, laisse toutes les villes;
Ne ternis plus tes pieds aux poudres du chemin,
Du haut de nos pensers vois les cités serviles
Comme les rocs fatals de l'esclavage humain.
Les grands bois et les champs sont de vastes asiles,
Libres comme la mer autour des sombres îles.
Marche à travers les champs une fleur à la main.

It may surprise us, because he goes on to express a fear of Nature and to attack it for its inhumanity and incomprehension. Vigny is certainly not above contradiction – how can he damn the servility of cities when he wishes servility from women? how can Delilah and Éva happily coexist in his consciousness? how are we to understand his ambiguous relationship with God? – but Nature attracts his awe as much as his wrath. It has precisely that austerity and taciturnity which he admires in, and enjoins upon, his travelling companion Éva. Nature, on the one hand, and poet/Éva, on the other, become *fellow* separatenesses. And the stanza quoted indeed isolates Nature from the city, in the couplet, yet at the same time, while inviting Éva into this natural environment, isolates her from it in her turn, in the last line of the stanza. This last line, uncharacteristically sentimental perhaps, contains, like the final line of the second stanza of 'La Bouteille à la mer', the ultimate imperative, the proper last-ditch conduct. But we should not overlook the fact that its rhyme carries Éva back into the heart of a toiling humanity which the poet has exhorted her to leave. In view of this, it will not surprise us to find, after this initial castigation of the city and celebration of Nature, a reversal; Vigny turns on Nature, on its complacent impassivity, on its confident durability, to pursue a defiant affirmation of

mortality and to glorify that corporateness of human suffering which isolates mankind as a whole and which the city
surely represents:

> Vivez, froide Nature, et revivez sans cesse
> Sous nos pieds, sur nos fronts, puisque c'est votre
>   loi;
> Vivez, et dédaignez, si vous êtes déesse,
> L'Homme, humble passager, qui dut vous être un
>   roi;
> Plus que tout votre règne et que ses splendeurs
>   vaines,
> J'aime la majesté des souffrances humaines,
> Vous ne recevrez pas un cri d'amour de moi.

Once again the assertion of strength and revolt is housed in
the couplet. But it is strange to find disdain jeered at – by
one who, elsewhere, makes a virtue of disdain – and transience accepted.

'La Maison du berger' is perhaps the most complex of
Vigny's poems, not only because of the apparent shifts of
attitude, but also because of its perambulatory overall structure. Vigny is by no means the easy, accessible poet that
some would have us think. His stanza is a site of struggle, of
isolation in fraternity and in enmity, of withdrawal and
re-assimilation, of challenge met, of knowledge won, but
often cast in doubt.

Apollinaire is another poet who returns with conspicu-
ous regularity to a favoured scheme, *a b a b a*. In his 1913
collection, *Alcools*, this stanza appears in the following
poems: 'La Chanson du Mal-Aimé', 'Marizibill', 'Marie',
'Lul de Falentin', 'Rosemonde', 'Le Brasier' and 'Cors de
chasse'. It is a stanza in which an alternating scheme is
thrown forward another step, into an incipient infinity, into
an undefined continuity. It is a stanza in which the third *a*
line both belongs and does not belong: it brings the stanza
back to its initial rhyme, completes the circle, but if we
think of rhymes as being essentially *pairs* of words, then this
final *a* has no rhyme-partner, or no *specific* rhyme-partner; it

is, in a sense, a word in a rhyming structure without a rhyme, what the Germans would call a *Waise*, an orphan. It is a stanza which has a relaxed, easy-going nature, but which ends on a note of structural interrogation, the final line both rounding off the stanza and awkwardly suspending it.

But how can we say this about Apollinaire's stanza and not about Vigny's, where the *b* rhyme also puts in a third appearance at the end of the stanza? The reason lies in the structural continuity of the Apollinaire stanza, in the strong sense we have that the final *a* is an overlap, a line added to an already complete scheme. Vigny's stanza, on the other hand, is a compound, and consequently we are more prepared to look for a principle of integration; the final *b* line acts as this integrating agent, binding together quatrain and couplet. We may also find it easy to assimilate the final *b* into a notional enclosed scheme, making the second *b* common to both halves of the stanza and thus an alternative integrating agent – (*a b a (b) c c b*).

But let us return to Apollinaire, and to 'Marizibill':

Dans la Haute-Rue à Cologne
Elle allait et venait le soir
Offerte à tous en tout mignonne
Puis buvait lasse des trottoirs
Très tard dans les brasseries borgnes

Elle se mettait sur la paille
Pour un maquereau roux et rose
C'était un juif il sentait l'ail
Et l'avait venant de Formose
Tirée d'un bordel de Changaï

Je connais gens de toutes sortes
Ils n'égalent pas leurs destins
Indécis comme feuilles mortes
Leurs yeux sont des feux mal éteints
Leurs yeux bougent comme leurs portes

This portrait of a prostitute and her pimp has a nonchalance about it which suits the rhyme-scheme (and the half-rhymes of the first stanza). But the note of structural unease, created by the supernumerary final line and by the way in which this line throws the stanza forward into an unspecified continuity, not only leaves Marie-Sybille always out of step, always teetering on the edge of an unfathomable future or an unfathomable past, but seems to draw the whole poem inescapably towards the widening and essentially interrogative reflection of the final stanza, a reflection which, fittingly, takes up the condition of the existentially maladjusted, the spiritually restless, ever reaching for something beyond. The easy give and take of the alternating rhymes is left hanging with this fifth line, as confidence seems to ebb away from the poet, and he is left holding the painfully random. After the sustaining momentum of alternation, Marie-Sybille and the poet come face to face with an existence whose continuity cannot be made sense of, an existence to which they are abandoned.

Finally and briefly, I would like to mention the stanza created by Paul-Jean Toulet in *Les Contrerimes* (1921):

> L'hiver bat la vitre et le toit.
> Il fait bon dans la chambre,
> A part cette sale odeur d'ambre
> Et de plaisir. Mais toi,

> Les roses naissent sur ta face
> Quand tu ris près du feu. . .
> Ce soir tu me diras adieu,
> Ombre, que l'ombre efface.

There is not space in this chapter to deal with all the ins and outs of the heterosyllabic stanza, and the ways in which syllabic variation may counterpoint the rhyme-scheme. But, at least, Toulet's stanza gives us a taste. Against the enclosed rhyme-scheme is set the alternating octosyllables and hexasyllables. The enclosed scheme loses some of its conclusiveness, ends with a hint of surprise; with the lengthening of its second line, the *b* couplet discovers an amplitude in itself, a self-respect, which disarms the final outflanking *a* line; the *b* couplet is no longer the occasion of the *a* line's triumphant return; its fullness gives the final *a* line a quality of undertone, of murmured, puzzled brevity.

And, conversely, the alternating lines surrender their relaxed to-and-fro movement, as they are suddenly caught up short in the medial couplet, as if arrested by a striking or disquieting thought or image; the alternating scheme has to rethink itself in mid-movement, initiate a new impulse with a new first rhyme, so that the stanza seems to present us with two fragments of alternation: *a*8 *b*6/*b*8 *a*6.

(iv) *Stanza and movement or period*

If the preceding attempts to forge meaningful links between rhyme-schemes, interpreted in the abstract, and the poetic make-up of individual poets seems over-ambitious and to rely too heavily on undemonstrable intu-itions, properly put in their place in the section on word-sound (Chapter 3, Section (iii)), then the attempt to make the leap between stanza and movement will no doubt pro-voke even profounder scepticism. Can I defend myself? I must reiterate that intuition and impressionism are un-doubtedly abused in the area of word-sound, but perhaps under-exercised in the area of stanzaic patterning. What drives many away from the study of versification is the apparent intractability, and thus unhelpfulness, of prosodic data. Students are pulled up for comments like 'This poem is written in alexandrines and *rimes embrassées*'; they are told that bare description is insufficient, and yet no interpreta-tive method is available to them. So prosodic data become erudite information of little use in the analysis of single poems, of interest only as knowledge to the connoisseur whose familiarity with French verse is so thorough that any knowledge has significance as point of comparison or his-tory. This should not be so. We can only humanise technical data by attempting the leap, and since there is at present no recognised interpretative procedure, then *careful* metaphor is our only recourse. We are likely to be fairer the less

categorical and single-minded we are; but if our ultimate
aim is to suggest that there *is* some necessary connection
between a particular pattern of stanza and particular directions of meaning, we multiply those directions at the expense
of the necessariness of the connection.

We have already begun to suggest ways in which the
enclosed quatrains of the sonnet may have served the Symbolists' preoccupation with the mirror, both as an image in
its own right and as a metaphor for the structure of the
sonnet as a whole. I would like to stay with the Symbolists
and explore their fondness for another stanza, the monorhymed triplet (*a a a/b b b/c c c/. . .* etc.).

This stanza evokes kinds of *hantise*, rendered more
emphatic by our thwarted expectation of a change of rhyme
after the couplet. It is as if the poet, for the moment at any
rate, is bound by the spell of the rhyme-sound and its
regular, incantatory return. The poet needs the stanza-
ending to release him from the prison of the rhyme; but
once released, he is immediately re-imprisoned, perhaps
only too willingly. And so the poem proceeds in a series of
ecstasies or agonies, of hyperbolised experiences. In poems
of dreamy ecstasy, the hyperbolising effect works in the
direction of spiritualisation; it is as though each stanza were
governed by the privileged tonality of its rhyme-sound, and
as though the third line were a quintessentialisation of the
couplet preceding it, a process of disembodiment opening
up a new dimension of perception:

> Je veux, enveloppé de tes yeux caressants,
> Je veux cueillir, parmi les roseaux frémissants,
> La grise fleur des crépuscules pâlissants
> > (Samain, 'Promenade à l'étang')
>
> O jacinthes des jours meilleurs,
> Parfums-reflets vivants encore ailleurs,
> Aériennes chairs de fleurs.
> > (Nau, 'Jacinthes')

And when we speak of agony in relation to *fin de siècle*
poets, we mean the bonds of apathy, of *ennui*, of spiri-

tual impotence and alienation. The monorhymed triplet shows its other face, as an unprogressive, intransitive, self-consuming monotone. For examples of this species of triplet, we can look across the Channel to English Nineties poets, to Ernest Dowson's 'La Jeunesse n'a qu'un temps', a poem of world-weariness with a more traditional occasion, the passing of youth, or to Arthur Symons's 'Isolation':

> When your lips leave my lips, again
> I feel the old doubt and the old pain
> Tighten about me like a chain.

If we describe the couplet as an arrested state, then the triplet is this state pushed into neurosis or into nihilistic insistence:

> Les âmes dont j'aurais besoin
> Et les étoiles sont trop loin.
> Je vais mourir saoul, dans un coin.
>
> (Cros, 'Conclusion')

The monorhymed triplet is a kind of static parallel of *terza rima*. Where *terza rima* is all rolling momentum, the monorhymed triplet is continually caught up in the whirlpools of its stanzas. *Terza rima* needs a single final line for closure (*a b a/b c b/c d c/. . . . .y z y/z*), to tie off the outstanding thread of its final tercet. Samain uses a single final line in his 'Promenade à l'étang', from which we have already quoted, but it is not to bring a self-perpetuating poetic mechanism to a halt, it is to restore the equilibriating binary structure of the couplet:

> Comme pour saluer les étoiles premières,
> Nos voix de confidence, au calme des clairières,
> Montent, pures dans l'ombre, ainsi que des prières.
>
> Et je baise ta chair angélique aux paupières.

Samain uses his final single line to bring himself back to earth, to re-anchor the mystical impulse of the last line of his triplet in the flesh.

It might be objected that the form of analysis undertaken in this chapter does violence to the 'organic wholeness' of the work of literature, that no separation should be practised at any stage or on any level between form and content, abstract pattern and verbal realisation, intention and achievement, device and expression. But the notion of 'organic wholeness' is either a useless or a dangerous assumption from which to work, because it is either logically *inevitable* that form is content, expression is device, and so on, and vice-versa, in which case the notion is analytically inoperable, or it is not logically inevitable, in which case the argument does need to be proved in each particular instance, and this can only be done by demonstrating the profound coherence of *separate parts*. Besides, quite apart from occasions on which the overt meaning of a stanza may be contradicted by the designs of a substructure, be it rhyme-scheme, rhythmic organisation, or any other prosodic system (e.g. 'M'introduire dans ton histoire'), we must affirm that our appreciation of a work is enriched when we can apprehend it as concert rather than as solo.

6

Fixed forms

This study does not seek to justify itself by the comprehensiveness of its definitions and historical accounts. It is certainly designed to provide necessary definitions, but it is more interested in discussion than description, and in the ways in which prosodic facts can be translated into interpretative observations. In a chapter, therefore, in which one might ordinarily expect to find a pretty exhaustive list of fixed forms – from ballade to virelai, from chant royal to pantoum – with definitions and potted histories, I would like to confine myself to comparative studies of only three forms – the villanelle, the rondeau and the sonnet – with a view not only to discovering the principal differences between French and English practice, but to deriving from comparison a more abstract notion of the particular forms' capabilities.

Historically, my treatment will, by and large, be limited to the period between 1850 and 1900, when fixed forms underwent a dramatic revival, thanks to the promotional energy of Théodore de Banville, and to the close ties that many late Victorian poets had with France. And it is considerations of history that lead me to choose some of my examples from the quiet backwaters of English verse; it would certainly be hard to justify the inclusion of poems by Austin Dobson and the Rev. Mr Wilton on the grounds of their literary merit alone. But Dobson's role in the re-adoption of these forms was crucial; the friendly rivalry between the group of poets working at the Board of Trade (Dobson, Gosse, Monkhouse) and the group at the British Museum (O'Shaughnessy, Marzials, Payne), the interchange of ideas and opinions about fixed forms between

Dobson, Edmund Gosse and Andrew Lang in the 1870s,
together with the pioneering work done by John Payne and
Robert Bridges, all conspired to create a fashion for these
forms which drew into its orbit most of the poets practising
in the last decades of the nineteenth century, either as pro-
ducers (Wilde, Stevenson, Hardy), or as critics (Hopkins).

And the work of Dobson and Wilton points to one of the
reasons for the popularity and transience of this fixed-form
revival: such forms were perhaps seen to their best, though
by no means their only, advantage in *vers de société*. Andrew
Lang (1891) was speaking for many when he wrote:
'Whether it is possible to go beyond this [*vers de société*], and
adapt the old French forms to serious modern poetry, it is
not for anyone but time to decide. . . . For my own part I
scarcely believe that the revival would serve the nobler ends
of English poetry' (p. 75). But the world of Victorian society verse has its charms; it is a world of half-measures:
half-comic, half-sad, half-cynical, half-affectionate. The
tones that this verse is most likely to court are the arch, the
wry, the urbane. Society verse, many would maintain, is the
luxury that goes with peaceful prosperity, and so promotes
an essentially uncritical complacency. But this is not
entirely true. It is not perhaps reformative or satirical, but its
grain of salt, its alertness, ensures that it is alive to social
vanities. Society verse is the point at which the purely
behavioural begins to take on moral colouring; and it is
precisely the art of the society poet to locate his poem where
the light-hearted and trivial engage the reader morally or
emotionally, without being pretentious or importunate.
Trollope's comment to Dobson in a letter of 19 May 1877,
gives some idea: '*Vers de société* are for me unalluring unless I
can sympathize with the feeling, and find a pathos even in
those which are nearest to the burlesque.'

Of course the sonnet was much too well established to
share the vulnerabilities of other fixed forms. But the sonnet
is perhaps still best defined in relation to these other forms,
simply because assumptions made about the sonnet on the
basis of its being a fixed form, and in ignorance of the lesser,

refrain forms (villanelle, triolet, rondel, rondeau), are likely
to exaggerate its rigour and misrepresent the functions of its
fixity.

(i) *The villanelle*
Standard definition: *A1 b A2/a b A1/a b A2/a b
A1/a b A2/a b A1 A2* (where the capital letters denote refrain
lines; like so many other fixed forms, the villanelle has only
two rhyme-sounds):

> When I saw you last, Rose,
> You were only so high; –
> How fast the time goes!
>
> Like a bud ere it blows,
> You just peeped at the sky,
> When I saw you last, Rose!
>
> Now your petals unclose,
> Now your May-time is nigh; –
> How fast the time goes!
>
> And a life, – how it grows!
> You were scarcely so shy,
> When I saw you last, Rose!
>
> In your bosom it shows
> There's a guest on the sly;
> (How fast the times goes!)
>
> Is it Cupid? Who knows!
> Yet you used not to sigh,
> When I saw you last, Rose; –
> How fast the time goes!
>> (Dobson, 'When I Saw You Last, Rose')

Along with other Romance forms, the villanelle is built
on the recurrence of a refrain. During the course of the
poem, the refrain may be subject to syntactical variations,
so that the fixed form becomes an exercise in the interpretation of a line, or, in the villanelle, of two lines. More often,

refrains in such poems have the haunting inexorability of a destiny which must have its way despite the poet's attempt to establish an alternative – of Ernest Dowson's villanelles, Ezra Pound (1915) writes: 'the refrains are an emotional fact which the intellect, in the various gyrations of the poem, tries in vain and in vain to escape' (p. xvii). Alternatively, a cherished idea or plea – e.g. 'In the clatter of the train/I shall see my love again' (W. E. Henley, 'Villanelle') – is housed in the refrain so that it shall be oft-repeated, kept in the front of the mind; but, paradoxically, because the refrain is the principal agent of the form, and thus of its 'endingness', this is a way of condemning the idea or plea to premature extinction; it may even be a form of perverse self-punishment.

The standard definition of the villanelle given above is in fact a definition of the English villanelle, the nineteen-line variety popularised by Joseph Boulmier (*Villanelles*, 1878) and based on the work of Jean Passerat (1534–1602). Obviously the villanelle is essentially stanzaic in nature, and there seem to be no structural reasons why it should not be longer or shorter than nineteen lines. This is the view that the French poets have taken, and they have extended or contracted the form at will. Even though Dobson, in his 'A Note on Some Foreign Forms of Verse' (1878), tried to transplant the French attitude, derived from Banville (1872) – 'The first and third line must form the final couplet, but there is no restriction as to the number of stanzas' (p. 344) – and even used Banville's example of the form, namely Philoxène Boyer's twenty-five-line 'La Marquise Aurore', the nineteen-line, usually octosyllabic, species became the unmistakably English possession; in the twentieth century, the octosyllable has given way to the decasyllable.

The difference between an extendable and a non-extendable form is crucial, because it makes the French version a stanza-type, rather like *terza rima*, while the English has more claim to being called a fixed form; put another way, the third stanza, say, of an English villanelle is a constituent part of a pre-ordained scheme of things, and

the third stanza of a French villanelle is an incident in a
sequence of incidents. The French villanellist with satirical
intentions, as Banville in his 'Villanelle des pauvres hous-
seurs' for instance, can use the fact that the refrain is more a
punctuation-mark than a formal device to make it into a
schoolboy taunt, a kind of heckling:

> Un tout petit pamphlétaire
> Voudrait se tenir debout
> Sur le fauteuil de Voltaire.
>
> Je vois sous ce mousquetaire,
> Dont le manteau se découd,
> Un tout petit pamphlétaire.
>
> Renvoyez au Finistère
> Le grain frelaté qu'il moud
> Sur le fauteuil de Voltaire.
>
> Il sera le caudataire
> Du fameux Taine, et, par goût,
> Un tout petit pamphlétaire.
>   etc.

And the final stanza is a guillotine resorted to in desperation
by the poet rather than a formal terminus arrived at by the
poem. Our reading of a nineteen-line villanelle, on the other
hand, is accompanied all along by a high degree of formal
interest. We do not see quite enough of the stanzaic principle to allow us to take it for granted; just as the refrains
reveal themselves as refrains and disclose their pattern of
alternation, they thrust upon the reader, in the final stanza, a
proof of their actual inseparability; oscillation between
apparent alternatives turns out to be a hidden singleness of
purpose. In the English villanelle, the refrain is altogether
more deliberate and severe; it is the germ of the poem and its
mortal disease, potentiality and potentiality's circumscrip-
tion, a pledge of imminent termination.

Let us look at a couple of examples in detail, first Austin
Dobson's already quoted 'When I Saw You Last, Rose'. In

this rather slight poem, the poet moves from a paternalistic 'What a big girl you suddenly are', in the first stanza, to a discovery, in the final stanza, which reveals a weakness of the flesh in the worldly wise, a submission to charms which he should be immune to by virtue of his age; presumably the poet is, in this final stanza, commenting on Rose's incipient love for an unspecified third party; but he perhaps half-fancies himself as the object of affection. As the first and third lines become refrains (*A1* and *A2*), so the more syntactically independent *A2* can become as much the insight of the reader commenting on the poet, as the poet's conclusion from his encounter with Rose. It is the poet's ability to respond to Rose as a female, it is his own subjection to the *A2* refrain, as desire awakens in one whom time puts beyond the fulfilment of desire, which gives this villanelle its pathos and at the same time acts as a guarantee of the continuing vitality of both Rose and the poet.

And it is a characteristic of the form that this vitality and responsiveness should be found in the *b* lines, which here resist the transition from the past of *A1* ('When I saw you last, Rose') to the ultimate futurity of *A2* ('How fast the time goes' reaches forward to 'How fast the time will be gone'). The *b* rhymes gamely set themselves against the unheeding forward movement of time by opposing to the restless change expressed in the verbal *a*/*A* rhymes ('goes', 'blows', 'unclose', 'grows', 'shows') their own permanences and qualities, nouns and adjectives ('high', 'sky', 'nigh', 'shy', 'sly'). But this resistance is broken, alas, in the final stanza where the *b* rhyme, the infinitive of 'sigh', has the beginnings of active verbality and captures so splendidly a pivotal point between longing and regret, anticipation and lost chances. If the refrains present the bland, analytic conclusion, it is the *b* rhymes which contain all the experiential turmoil; in 'nigh-shy-sly-sigh' is the whole history of an affair, a whole approach to a consummation which the poet must deny himself, as he remembers that he is sage rather than idolater, that the generation gap cannot be bridged by desire alone.

And with what effect is *A2* bracketed at the end of the fifth stanza? Does it express an attempt to suppress the knowledge of which Rose and the poet are the victims? Does it indicate how far sagacity has been set aside by instinctual behaviour? Is it a cruel, because illusory, respite offered, but only to make doubly peremptory and final the refrain's last appearance? Does the bracketing indicate that this line is the reader's comment, in mocking undertone, on the poet as he falls under Rose's spell, and where 'How fast the time goes!' means, in fact, 'Time has gone so fast that he's forgotten just how old he is'? It would deprive the poem unnecessarily if one were to decide.

It is thus the *b* lines which, by their vulnerability, endow the villanelle with its peculiar poignancy. While the minor *a* lines seem to serve only to call up the refrains, to urge the foregoneness of the conclusion, the *b* lines savour, wistfully perhaps, a unique, intimate drama which the refrains conspire against with an essentially insensitive truism. The delicacy of the *b* lines is presumably what Banville is referring to when he describes the villanelle's 'troisième fil': 'On dirait une tresse formée de fils d'argent et d'or, que traverse un troisième fil, couleur de rose' (*Petit Traité de poésie française*, p. 215). And this formal feature is indeed common to villanelles from both sides of the Channel, despite their other differences.

If the Dobson example has not already convinced us that the rustic character of the villanelle contained in the word itself (Lat. villa: farm – villanella: labourers' song) has quite disappeared, then Leconte de Lisle's contracted thirteen-line 'Villanelle' from *Poèmes tragiques*, with its serious, metaphysical subject, surely will:

> Le Temps, l'Étendue et le Nombre
> Sont tombés du noir firmament
> Dans la mer immobile et sombre.
>
> Suaire de silence et d'ombre,
> La nuit efface absolument
> Le Temps, l'Étendue et le Nombre.

Tel qu'un lourd et muet décombre,
L'esprit plonge au vide dormant,
Dans la mer immobile et sombre.

En lui-même, avec lui, tout sombre,
Souvenir, rêve, sentiment,
Le Temps, l'Étendue et le Nombre,
Dans la mer immobile et sombre.

Here the two refrains establish two contrary fields of interest, with contrary personalities: on the one hand is the
trinity of abstractions with their capital pretensions, brittle
concepts which discover their human relevance too late,
when they come face to face with their humble counterparts
'Souvenir, rêve, sentiment'; on the other hand is the duo of
adjectives 'immobile et sombre' – occurring in other guises
in the adjectival nouns 'de silence et d'ombre' and the adjectival pair 'lourd et muet' – bespeaking silence and opacity,
and the plain irreducibility of the common noun ('mer').
Leconte de Lisle is able to tie the whole structure of his
villanelle to this conflict between the refrains; ultimately the
A2 refrain engulfs the A1 refrain; in the last stanza, the two
groups of three nouns (b, A1) are but parenthetic clarifica-
tions of 'tout' (l. 10).

Unlike Dobson, Leconte de Lisle is not interested in
permanence in change as much as in the transition from one
permanence to another; thus all the verbal activity is in the b
lines, the lines between states, except in the final stanza
where the new permanence predominates, consolidating
itself in the poem's congealment. A progression paralleling
the gradual extinction of the old permanence is the movement of the verbs across the line, from first word in line two
to last word in line ten, so that the inner two stanzas are
experienced as fulcrum; the final verb has become part of
the new permanence insofar as it is now part of an a line, and
its effacement as a verb is made complete by its homonym-
ity with the adjectival 'sombre' of A2; the verb is now in
a very privileged way the instrument for summoning
the refrain, revealing a quite treacherous complicity; the

verbs we might say then, occur at increasing 'depths' in the line.

The final *b* line, therefore, is no longer verbal, but a glimpse caught of the human truth within the cosmic one. These abstractions are less weighty perhaps than those in the line following, but more crucial. The *b* lines, as in the Dobson example, contain the 'quick' of the poem. The last two enumerations –

> Souvenir, rêve, sentiment,   *b*
> Le Temps, l'Étendue et le Nombre   *A1*

– bear some study. To all intents and purposes, their syllabic groupings are opposite – 3-1-3 ('rêve' in the rhyme-position of 'Nombre' would count but one syllable) and 1-3-1 – for all their appositional relationship. The acoustic fullness of 'Souvenir' and 'sentiment' shows up the cerebral nudity of 'Temps' and 'Nombre'; on the other hand, while 'Étendue' has the syllabic extent of its extent, 'rêve' is infinity of imaginative reach within material diminutiveness, and stretches beyond these confines in the fully sounded *e atone*, which is part of the following measure (3 + 1 + 4). Furthermore, the singularity of the concepts in *A1*, with their sense of assigned role provided by the definite article, demonstrates at least a qualitative affinity with the sea into which they plunge. The wonderfully unconstrained, erratic, grammatically unharnessed nature of 'Souvenir, rêve, sentiment', on the other hand, opens up on to an absoluteness and indestructibility which, though only too human, is still somehow beyond the reach of *event* or *process*, however cosmic.

Boulmier's typification of the villanelle is perhaps as close as one can come to the truth: 'Les souvenirs aimés, les mirages du coeur, les divins enfantillages de l'amour, voilà son domaine. Cependant, comme elle est bonne fille, elle consent parfois à être sérieuse' (1878, p. 17); although it overlooks the satirical dimension supplied by Banville. And it has not been without its practitioners in this century, particularly in England. It is difficult to recognise any semblance of the fixed form we have just described, in Pound's 'Villanelle: The Psychological Hour'. But we find the standard nineteen-line variety in Auden's work ('My Dear One Is Mine', 'If I Could Tell You'), in Dylan Thomas's ('Do Not Go Gentle Into That Good Night') and in Empson's ('Villanelle', 'Missing Dates'). And in these modern examples, it is still the *b* lines which are concerned to withstand the tide, usually the tide of time, of the refrains, pitting against them the vivid particulars of human mortality:

> If we should weep when clowns put on their show,
> If we should stumble when musicians play,
> Time will say nothing but I told you so.
>
> There are no fortunes to be told, although,
> Because I love you more than I can say,
> If I could tell you I would let you know.
>
> (Auden, 'If I Could Tell You')

(ii) *The rondeau*
Standard definition: *a a b b a/a a b R/a a b b a R* (where *R* stands for *rentrement*, the special term for the rondeau's refrain which consists of the first word(-sound) or words(-sounds) of the first line). This form of the rondeau is the one popularised by Banville and derives from the practice of the seventeenth-century poet Vincent Voiture.

> In Flanders fields the poppies blow
> Between the crosses, row on row,
>   That mark our place; and in the sky
>   The larks, still bravely singing, fly
> Scarce heard amid the guns below.
>
> We are the Dead. Short days ago
> We lived, felt dawn, saw sunset glow,
>   Loved and were loved, and now we lie
> In Flanders fields.
>
> Take up our quarrel with the foe:
> To you from failing hands we throw

The torch; be yours to hold it high.
If ye break faith with us who die,
We shall not sleep, though poppies grow
        In Flanders fields.
        (MacCrae, 'In Flanders Fields')

'Rondeau' is the modern generical term for all three
forms (rondeau, rondel, triolet) originating in dance rounds
with singing accompaniment, in which the refrain was sung
by the chorus – the general body of dancers – and the
variable section by the dance leader. The *Ur*-rondeau was
what we know today as the triolet (*A B a A a b A B*).
'Rondel' itself is only the old form of 'rondeau'. During the
fourteenth century, the dance and music disappeared, as did
the distinction between soloist and chorus; the forms
became purely literary. The shortened final refrain of the
rondel (*A B b a/a b A B/a b b a A*) and the *rentrement* of the
rondeau were probably the result of copyists' abbrevia-
tions.

The most obvious idiosyncrasy of the rondeau is its
rentrement, a rhymeless element among forms which seem
to exist expressly for their rhymes. It would be idle to
discuss, at this stage, whether the *rentrement* is really a line or
not, but the common habit of not counting it as a line does
indicate a view that it is not a fully integrated structural
constitutent. But it can be maintained that the very way that
the *rentrement* resists integration is the source of the rondeau's lyric plausibility. Instead of becoming part of what
may appear to be an all-encompassing suavity, by slipping
into a pattern *dictated* by the rhyme, instead of partaking of
that air of unquestioning readiness so often assumed by a
line repeated in its totality, the *rentrement* comes quite without glamour, more as a thought that cannot be shaken off, a
momentary distraction by, or intimate communion with, a
phrase which turns out to be the irreducible nucleus of the
poem. In the MacCrae stanzas, the *rentrement* has indeed a
stylistic bluntness which is not shared by the remainder,
with its plaintive eloquence; the poet has no illusions in the

end; the *rentrement* stabilises, lends credibility to, the luxurious sentiments of the rhymed part.

And there is, too, something impenetrably private about the *rentrement*. Where, in the first line, 'In Flanders fields' is a geographically and topographically located site, it is, as *rentrement*, a place of privileged knowledge, a shorthand expression elliptically conveying an experiential fullness. The opening words are the source of a train of thought that is found not to transcend them, but merely to be a constituent part of them, possessed by them. What, at the outset, might have simply been a decorative way of saying 'Belgium', a neatly alliterative euphemism for a dull fact, turns out to be an access-point to a world beyond words. And if, despite its privacy, the *rentrement* does admit the reader, it does so by offering him an image of unpretentious, elementary humanity, and by inviting him to participate in its irreplaceability. That the rondeau is peculiarly suited to this investment of place with a sense of deeper inhabitation is, perhaps, borne out by the number of rondeaux whose *rentrements* are place-names – Henley's 'In Rotten Row', Dobson's 'On London Stones', Ashley Sterry's 'On Dover Pier', Hardy's 'The Roman Road' and 'On Beechen Cliff'.

The *rentrement* may resist the rhyme-structure's fastidiousness with its own unfussy self-sufficiency, but rarely in English examples does it resist the poem metrically – with the four-syllable *rentrement* of the MacCrae example, the continuity of the iambic rhythm is not interfered with. In English rondeaux we shall not find the fireworks and wittiness that so often characterise the French *rentrement*; we shall find an altogether quieter, but firmer, quality, the *rentrement* confirming what precedes it, while qualifying it with a sanity which comes from a thorough grasp of essentials.

On the other hand, Banville's rondeau to the actress 'Mademoiselle Page' uses the *rentrement* to give buoyancy and volatility rather than level-headedness:

Page blanche, allons, étincelle!
Car ce rondeau, je le cisèle
Pour la reine de la chanson,
Qui rit du céleste Enfançon
Et doucement vous le musèle.

Zéphyre l'évente avec zèle,
Et pour ne pas vivre sans elle,
Titania donnerait son
                    Page.

Le bataillon de la Moselle
A sa démarche de gazelle
Eût tout entier payé rançon.
Cette reine sans écusson,
C'est Cypris, ou Mademoiselle
                    Page.

Here the *rentrement* has much less, if any, rhythmical connection with the parent line, and it is by no means inevitable, though frequent, that the *rentrement*, in the French
rondeau, coincides with the divisions of *coupe* or caesura.
The first line of 'Mademoiselle Page' has its first *coupe* after
the third syllable, giving a pattern of 3 + 2 + 3. And this adds
to the independence of the *rentrement*, because it comes into
its own, rhythmically, only as it breaks its ties with the rest
of the stanza; 'Page', an unaccentuated ingredient of the
opening measure, becomes the terminal accentuated 'Páge'.
And this self-assertiveness, not to say cockiness, of the
rentrement is often supported by another factor, at least
where it concerns words with feminine endings. Only at
the end of the line is a word's femininity inviolable;
the feminine mute syllable is not counted, but at least
it is not elided, whereas the *e atone* within the line may be
counted, but equally it is vulnerable to elision. Banville's
'Mademoiselle Page' does not exemplify this, but another
of his rondeaux, 'Rolle n'est plus vertueux', does; its first
line runs:

Que l'Aurore ait à son corsage   4 + 4

so that, in the *rentrement* 'Que l'Aurore', 'Aurore' both receives an accent where it had not one previously, and recovers its femininity which it had lost to the verb-form 'ait'.

'Mademoiselle Page' testifies to another peculiarly French habit which has the result of disengaging the *rentrement* and making it, not the *ne plus ultra* that it is in English, but an entity whose very *raison d'être* is change and caprice. The habit I refer to is punning. This would seem to be the natural cause, or result, of the usually very brief French *rentrement* and is particularly characteristic of the rondeau which is built around the exploration of a proper noun. The *rentrement* that rhymes with itself is self-regarding; the punning *rentrement* not only outdoes the rest of the rondeau in rhyme – is not the pun the most perfect of rhymes? – but *uses* the rest of the rondeau to investigate its own sound-structure and parade its versatility. Banville's 'Page' is not only the actress's surname, it is also the page of a book and a page-boy. Léon Valade's 'Jean Aicard' has 'Écart' in its first line and 'Et quart' and 'Aicard' as *rentrements*, while his 'Tancrède Martel' moves from a first-line 'Tancrède' to the *rentrements* 'Temps, coeur, aide' and 'Tant que raide' (these rondeaux have the irregular scheme *a b b a b/a b a R/a b a b a R*); Coppée's 'Rondeau' sets out with 'Son or', which becomes, in the *rentrements*, 'Sonore' and 'S'honore'. So punning is no personal quirk, but a fundamental feature of French rondeaux, as even the conservative comments of A. Dorchain (1933) indicate: 'Le refrain ne compte pas comme vers; il ne rime pas avec le reste, et rien n'est plus piquant que de lui faire répéter les premiers mots de la pièce avec une acception différente, ou même de les rappeler seulement par une identité de son formant calembour' (p. 344).

This encouragement of pun and the equivocation about whether the *rentrement* is a line or not – Dorchain says not, but the modern analyst Henri Morier says it is; Banville says not, but guardedly – reveals perhaps a French neurosis about blank verse. A blank-verse line, many would like to think, is a contradiction in terms in French versification, hence the *rentrement* must be no line. Conversely, if the *rentrement* is a line, then it must rhyme, if need be with itself. Thus while a few French poets managed the unrhymed *rentrement* without discomfort (e.g. Maurice Rollinat), most felt the need to answer the imperatives of their national versification.

The *rentrement* that rhymes with itself must be distinguished from English practice in this direction, which takes us towards that exclusively English invention, the roundel *(a b a R (b)/b a b/a b a R (b)* – i.e. the *rentrement* rhymes with the *b* lines). If the English poet's *rentrement* rhymes with anything, it is not with itself, but with one of the other rhymes, *a* or *b* (an exceptional French instance is Valade's 'Tancrède Martel', where the *rentrement* rhymes both with itself and the *b* rhymes). In the Rev. Mr Wilton's 'Snowdrops and Aconites', the *rentrement* rhymes with the *b* lines:

> Ah, with how much more rare delight
> Upon my sense their colours smite
> Than if my fingers were to hold
> Silver and gold.

Instead of a word or phrase becoming a *rentrement*, a refrain, we have an internal rhyme becoming an external one, repeated. Instead of that which was introductory, circumstantial, becoming the *key* to an experience, a kind of private language, we have a latent rhyme/line becoming manifest, taking up its position within a scheme to which it is demonstrably subservient. And the shortness of the *rentrement* which might, in this particular example, have supplied the dismissive force which the sense seems to require, is countered by a rhyme which is, on the contrary, conciliatory and preserves the resonance of the phrase.

Another variation on *rentrement* usage is to be found in the work of Maurice Rollinat, perhaps the most prolific writer of rondeaux in the period. On several occasions, he builds into the rondeau – which, like all two-rhyme forms, is probably best suited to the presentation of a static, if deepening, experience – a dramatic dimension, a progression towards an abyss, the better to communicate his own peculiar and recurrent panic state. He does this by introducing prepositional variations into his *rentrements* – 'Devant ma porte' becomes, in the *rentrements*, 'De ma porte' and 'Derrière ma porte' ('Le Spectre'), and 'La tombe' becomes 'Dans la tombe' and 'Par-delà la tombe' ('Soliloque du rêve'). The *rentrement* thus acts as a threat, drawing the poet *into* his obsession. At the same time of course, by using the *fixed* form, Rollinat either commits himself to a perpetual brinkmanship, or saves himself from ever having to take the plunge, depending on how you look at it.

In the regular rondeau we are describing – unfortunately we have not the space to examine the several variations – the basic stanzaic structure is *a a b b a*, a pattern of juxtaposition (couplets) becoming a movement of encompassment with the final line. Once the *rentrement* has broken out of the first stanza, rather like a butterfly out of its chrysalis (an image which suits the French rondeau better than the English, perhaps), the stanza must either assimilate it or surrender all its own finality to it – and the last line in an encompassing scheme makes a point of its finality in a way that the last line of a set of couplets does not. Herein lies some of the structural drama of the rondeau, and not surprisingly, given the mere look of the form, the tercet is the area of greatest structural dispute. Is this *a a b R* pattern an incipient *a a b b a* which the *rentrement* interrupts, peremptorily, antagonistically? Or is the tercet a try-out, the last three lines of a notional quintet beginning with the *b b* pair, a dummy-run for the final lines of the third stanza, to see how the *rentrement* fits in and to accustom the reader to suspending his voice at the end of the last line of the quintet, in anticipation of the *rentrement*? The tercet is probably a combination of these things, the clash between the stanza's desire to reconcile and the *rentrement*'s desire to break free. But however we regard it, we must feel in the tercet something of the effort of parturition, of the quintet's search for a way to repeat itself *with* a *rentrement*, to remove some of the cocksureness of its own last line.

The last two stanzas of Jean Richepin's 'Rondeau' –

> J'ai bu les deux aromes précieux,
> Et jusqu'au jour dans mon lit soucieux
> Il m'a sonné des fanfares de cuivre,
>   Votre beau thé.
>
> Je vous voyais passer parmi les dieux,
> Dans un grand char aux flamboyants essieux;
> Et sous la roue en or, n'osant vous suivre,
> J'ai mis mon front, et j'ai cessé de vivre
> En bénissant, écrasé mais joyeux,
>   Votre beauté.

– should remind us again of the qualities easiest to associate with the French rondeau, its recourse to backdoor rhyming with the pun, its archness, its levity. The English rondeau tends to strike a graver, more meditative note; the English poet looks to the *rentrement* to provide a point of self-collection, of inescapable knowledge; the rhymelessness of the English *rentrement* falls more easily on the ear because the *rentrement*'s rhythmic recognisability allows it to extend the stanza without awkwardness. The French *rentrement*, too, may be a rhythmically recognisable part of the rondeau's basic verse-line – Richepin's *rentrement* is a 'natural' four-syllable constituent of his decasyllabic rondeau, the caesura falling after the fourth syllable in most of the lines – but as often it is not; at all events, it always gives the impression of having its own role to find, its own indispensability to impose.

(iii) *The sonnet*
    Standard definitions: Shakespearean (English) sonnet: *a b a b c d c d e f e f g g*
    Petrarchan (Continental) sonnet: *a b b a/a b b a/c c d/e d e* (+ other variations in the tercets)

Some distinction needs to be made between the refrain forms and the sonnet, as indeed one should distinguish between the fixed forms generally and various stanza-types like *terza rima*, rhyme royal and the French villanelle. The absence of refrain in the sonnet means that it has a more continuous and direct relationship with its end; the refrain in the other forms can act as a relay-station, a breathing-space, a short-term goal, is often even a digression. Of all the so-called fixed forms, the sonnet is perhaps the freest, and this is largely due to the length and continuity of its history. The other fixed forms have enjoyed revivals, and during these revivals certain versions of the forms have predominated sufficiently to be looked upon as impera-tives. This process of fixing has often been quite arbitrary, the result of the popularity or celebrity of single individuals – the Charles d'Orléans rondel, the Voiture/Banville ron-deau, the Passerat/Boulmier villanelle (for the English). The sonnet has never had a master in a similar way and its tenacious persistence through the centuries – with the not-able exception of the eighteenth – has meant that variations on the patterns given above, which have been manifold, have not so much been deviations from *the* sonnet as exten-sions of the sonnet's freedom, a freedom whose only qual-ifying limit is ultimate recognisability as a sonnet. Thus the quatrains of the Petrarchan sonnet may include the alternat-ing rhyme-scheme (*a b a b*), or the octave may be made up of alternating couplets *a a b b/a a b b* (Charles Cros's 'Croquis'), or the whole sonnet may be in couplets (Dobson's 'A Fancy from Fontenelle'). Other patterns we might briefly enum-erate are: *a b b a/a c c a/a d a d/e e* (Hardy's 'Barthélémon at Vauxhall'), *a b a b/a b a b/a c c/a c c* (Cazalis's 'A l'enfant blonde'), *a b a a/b a b b/c c d/e d e* (Ménard's 'Le Soir'), *a a b b/a b b a/c c d/e d e* (Moréas's 'Sous la rouille des temps'). As the standard definitions indicate, there are national and interna-tional traditions, which we shall further discuss, but these have increasingly interfered with each other and the struc-ture of the sonnet has acquired a peculiarly 'esperanto' flavour.

The reading of a sonnet is thus an experience fraught with uncertainty, an uncertainty which is particularly active at

the third line (enclosed or alternating scheme?), at the fifth
line (will the second quatrain repeat the rhymes of the first?),
at the seventh line (will the second quatrain repeat the rhyme-
scheme of the first?) and then more or less throughout
the tercets (will they have two or three rhymes? in which of
a large number of possible combinations?). The sonneteer
must capitalise upon this anxiety, but at the same time must
create in the reader, as the poem comes to a close, a strong
sense of the inescapability of the chosen scheme, so that the
most eccentric variation will still have the feel of a *fixed
form*. The sonneteer's art might be described as a fourteen-
line postponement of the reconciliation between projective
unpredictability and retrospective fittingness. While the
other Romance fixed forms have capriciousness built into
their structures as *known* quantities – we may think of the
rondeau's *rentrement* or the arbitrariness of the villanelle's
ending – the sonnet has capriciousness, admittedly of a
circumscribed kind, at its constant disposal; the other fixed
forms have been fixed by historical accident if anything,
while the sonnet is fixed, not in fact, but by general consent
and supposition.

We have already looked at some of the capabilities of the
enclosed and alternating schemes, and what we have said
applies broadly to the quatrains of the Petrarchan and
Shakespearean sonnets. The self-engrossment of the
enclosed scheme, its cyclical nature, give the Petrarchan
octave a peculiar structural stability and deliberateness; the
second quatrain tends to complement the first in relationships of apposition, development, even counteraction. On
this solid foundation is built something very different, the
nervous disequilibriating acceleration of the tercets, often
using three rhymes in their six lines against the octave's
customary two, each tercet being structurally incomplete,
unstable. The fact that the stanzas of the continental Petrarchan sonnet are usually separated typographically means
that they can relate to each other in a number of ways – first
quatrain with first tercet, first quatrain with second tercet,
and so on – and their relative autonomy helps to project

their images as realities in their own right, making their own demands. Thus we can call the Petrarchan sonnet a supremely *dramatic* form, engendering complexity from the tensions within it, between symmetry and asymmetry, the static and the dynamic, the restful and the nervous; and often the sestet strikes one as an assault on the bland patentness of the octave, an attempt to surprise the essential detail or uncover a spiritual significance:

> Et tandis que l'essaim brillant des Cavaliers
> Traîne la pourpre et l'or par les blancs escaliers
> Joyeusement baignés d'une lumière bleue,
>
> Indolente et superbe, une Dame à l'écart,
> Se tournant à demi dans un flot de brocart,
> Sourit au négrillon qui lui porte la queue.
>
> (Heredia, 'La Dogaresse')

If the Petrarchan sonnet's dramatic nature depends, to a large extent, on the separateness of its stanzas, the more discursive character of the Shakespearean sonnet derives from its being more a quatorzain than a sonnet, that is to say, more a single unit of fourteen lines than a combination of four stanzas. And most frequently it is, of course, printed as continuous verse. Because of this continuity, because of the give and take of its non-committal alternating scheme, minimised as *scheme* by its repetition, the Shakespearean sonnet will strike us as expatiatory and its effect cumulative. There is no discernible interaction among its parts because it has no discernible parts. For this reason, the two unchallenged thrusts of the final couplet may appear to have a contrived or factitious finality, or the first twelve lines may seem to be a mere preamble for the couplet – these are the two principal dangers. It is much easier for the Petrarchan sonneteer to yield the initiative to images because, in the Shakespearean sonnet, all images are part of the poet's *discourse*, their function is more expressive and illustrative than self-generating. The Shakespearean sonnet is more essentially a poem of *address*, a pondered *causerie*; it looks like a way of making up one's mind. And the terminal couplet provides 'a logical, critical note' (Lever, 1956, p. 16); it is a consolidating crystallisation of circumstantial perception, and this crystallisation takes many forms, perhaps the reduction of self to example, to part of an axiom –

> Pleasure's not theirs, nor pain. They doubt, and sigh
> And do not love at all. Of these am I.
>
> (Brooke, 'Sonnet')

– or the reduction of others, to satisfy social snobberies or to convince oneself of one's penetrative powers:

> Withal, outside the gay and giddy whirl,
> Liza's a stupid, straight, hard-working girl.
>
> (Henley, 'Liza')

It is in translation that we perhaps see most clearly the clash of wills between national traditions, the operation of innate prosodic reflexes. Take Shakespeare's sonnet CXLVI –

> Pour soul, the centre of my sinful earth,
> Fool'd by these rebel powers that thee array,
> Why dost thou pine within and suffer dearth,
> Painting thy outward walls so costly gay?
> Why so large cost, having so short a lease,
> Dost thou upon thy fading mansion spend?
> Shall worms, inheritors of this excess,
> Eat up thy charge? Is this thy body's end?
> Then, soul, live thou upon they servant's loss,
> And let that pine to aggravate thy store;
> Buy terms divine in selling hours of dross;
> Within be fed, without be rich no more:
>   So shalt thou feed on Death, that feeds on men,
>   And Death once dead, there's no more dying
>   then.

Now take its petrarchised translation by Alfred des Essarts:

> Toi qui vis au dedans d'une chair vulnérable,
> En butte à l'ennemi que tu veux protéger,

O pauvre âme, pourquoi rechercher le danger
Et te rendre toi-même abjecte et misérable?

Ayant avec la vie un bail si peu durable,
Pourquoi parer un corps qui n'est qu'un étranger?
De riches ornements à quoi bon surcharger
Ta fragile demeure assise sur le sable?

Crois-tu qu'avec le corps il te faille finir?
Sa ruine est ta vie et sa douleur ta gloire;
Au prix du temps impur gagne un saint avenir.

Fais-toi de vrais trésors: le reste est illusoire.
Nourris-toi de la mort; que ce soit ta victoire:
Car, la mort étant morte, on ne doit plus mourir.

In such an exercise of comparison, we are as likely to uncover the difference in quality between the poets as much as the difference between forms. Be that as it may, it might be argued that, being the only sonnet in which, Leishman (1961) tells us, 'the distinction between body and soul, terrestrial and celestial, finds clear and memorable expression' (p. 119), Shakespeare's piece admirably suits the Petrarchan sonnet's, and classical alexandrine's, appetite for antithesis; were it not for the rhyme-scheme, Des Essarts's first tercet might be lines from *Polyeucte*.

Des Essarts's scheme (*a b b a/a b b a/c d c/d d c*) draws into the two-rhyme nexus of the octave those rhetorical questions which had four rhymes to play with in Shakespeare's first eight lines; this may seem to nullify somewhat the real individuality, or individual urgency, of questions which are admittedly reformulations of the same basic idea, but which seek to convince by their multiplicity, by their 'well-let's-look-at-it-from-another-angle' technique. Des Essarts's version accepts the basic similarity of the questions and seeks to convince, not by the accumulated weight of each graphic image, but by the weightiness of a rhetorical structure; here the postponed return of the final *a* line in each of these complacently solid quatrains serves to create the sense of an open-and-shut case, a patentness which allows the

poet to indulge in a broad rhyme gesture. While Shakespeare's alternating scheme, with its greater forward impetus,
works by a saturation technique, a persistent remonstration
which has the haphazardness of random conversation, the
greater finality of the enclosed scheme gives Des Essarts's
quatrains an implied 'just-you-think-about-it' tone. True,
there are obvious rhetorical devices in Shakespeare's sonnet, the straightforward 'Why' clause of line three (normal
word-order) being followed, in line five, by a 'Why' clause
with inversion. But the change of rhyme and the alternating
scheme mask this chiasmus, while the chiastic structure of
the Petrarchan quatrain serves to *concentrate* the rhetoric of a
similar construction used by Des Essarts in his second
stanza, where, in the question of lines 7–8, there is a pre-
positioning of an adverbial phrase, in contrast to the normal
word-order of lines 5–6.

Having omitted Shakespeare's characteristic reference to
worms, Des Essarts takes up, while smoothing out, Shakespeare's blunt: 'Is this thy body's end?' transferring it from
line eight to line nine, so that the final interrogative acts as a
bridge between quatrains and tercets. But in so doing, he
totally disregards the structurally crucial break between the
octave and the sestet, crucial because it is not signalled by
the rhyme-scheme and acts, perhaps, as an allusion to Petrarchan practice. Shakespeare's line nine has already moved
from the interrogative to the imperative, and his poem
proceeds speedily to the final couplet. In this final couplet,
the conceit, the abruptness of the syllogism, exude a kind of
delight in argument which is argument itself; the poet
seems to arrive at a point where the practical effect of
argument is no longer relevant, where argument no longer
seeks to obtain a result; it has been instrumental in releasing
enough intellectual energy for the mind to thrive on itself,
to engender its own cosmos, its own natural laws, so that it
can, with consummate ease and *panache*, vindicate its own
convictions and desires. There is not much suggestion of
this in Des Essarts; there is only a wary indulgence in syllogism, and recourse to the cut-and-driedness of antithesis, to

the heavily logical conjunction 'Car'; there is, too, a return, in the last four lines, to an enclosed scheme, with a consequent return to the argumentative techniques of the quatrains, that is to say, to a measured insistence, to an appeal, not to the dazzling, if doubtful, Q.E.D., but to manifest moral and intellectual certitudes.

We have referred to, and seen something of, the great variety of rhyme-schemes available to the sonneteer. There are also many stanzaic organisations available to him. He may add a final one-line stanza, write a fifteen-line sonnet, the so-called 'tailed' sonnet, as the Symbolist poet Albert Samain occasionally does (e.g. 'Keepsake', 'Galswinte'). He may enclose his tercets within the two quatrains (e.g. Yvanhoé Rambosson's 'Instincts', Baudelaire's 'L'Avertisseur'). He may turn his sonnet upside down in a *sonnet renversé* or *sonetessa*, so that the tercets precede the quatrains (e.g. Verlaine's 'Sappho'; Rupert Brooke's 'Sonnet Reversed' is an example of a reversed Shakespearean sonnet). It is an instance of this last species, Baudelaire's 'Bien loin d'ici', which I wish to consider in closing, because of the fascinating structural problems it poses and because it takes us back to a stanza we have already examined, the monorhymed triplet:

> C'est ici la case sacrée
> Où cette fille très parée,
> Tranquille et toujours préparée,
>
> D'une main éventant ses seins,
> Et son coude dans les coussins,
> Écoute pleurer les bassins;
>
> C'est la chambre de Dorothée.
> – La brise et l'eau chantent au loin
> Leur chanson de sanglots heurtée
> Pour bercer cette enfant gâtée.
>
> Du haut en bas, avec grand soin,
> Sa peau délicate est frottée
> D'huile odorante et de benjoin.
> – Des fleurs se pâment dans un coin.

Is this in fact a *sonnet renversé* or a set of four tercets, or rather of monorhymed triplets, which find themselves to be, to add up to, a *sonnet renversé* because of the intervention of two 'foreign' lines (8 and 12)? What helps to suggest the intention of maintaining some stanzaic consistency is the alternation of rhyme by stanza – the e (phonetic) of stanzas one and three, the ẽ of stanzas two and four. The rhymes between stanzas (i.e. between one and three, two and four) are *pauvres*, but within stanzas *suffisantes*, except in the fourth stanza.

The stanzaic autonomy of the first two triplets – we can hardly call them tercets since they do not have the customary interdependence of tercets, the desire to become a sestet, other than syntactically – breaks down, so that, in the final eight lines, there is some inter-stanzaic contamination. The pattern *a b a a/b a b b* is certainly not unknown for quatrains – we have already mentioned Louis Ménard's 'Le Soir'. But the real structural intention is, I think, to allude both to triplets, as we have said, and beyond that, and more intricately, also to the classic two-rhyme sestet *c d d/c d c*. In other words, while there is a sense in which lines eight and twelve are interpolations, there is another sense in which lines seven and fourteen are also trespassers, and indeed they are isolated, by a dash and by their syntactic completeness, from the body of the stanzas. If we take this latter view, we can say that while the opening triplets are, in terms of rhyme, self-sufficient, but syntactically interdependent, the final quatrain-tercets are the reverse.

This structural complexity has to do with the mixture of mockery and compassion which the poet's attitude towards Dorothée seems to contain. The mocking hyperbole of the first line, with its almost oxymoronical collision of 'case' and 'sacrée', leads into triplets which convey not only the apparent self-possession of the girl, but also the monotony of her preparations (this is all she ever does) and their excess. But against the easy, even facile, continuity of the syntax in the triplets, we must set the comparative brokenness of the syntax and rhyme in the 'quatrains'. A new relationship between poet and subject is inaugurated with line seven:

C'est la chambre de Dorothée

a statement of plain fact, uttered with familiarity, even
affection, in answer to line one. 'Cette fille' becomes 'cette
enfant' (l. 10), as the poet lets his compassion have its way
and reveal a pathos, the pathos of an innocence that female
guile cannot, despite its efforts, erase, the pathos of a loneli-
ness that no physical gifts can alleviate. Why has she prepared herself? So that the flowers can swoon in the corner?
And is not this last line already a kindness of the poet's, an
hyperbole to answer her hyperbolic preparations? Or is it
perhaps a mercy, leading the reader's attention away from
the carefully adorned girl now embarrassed by her adorn-
ment? Or does it signify the inevitable loss of interest, there
being no depths to plumb in dear Dorothée, only a surface
to cover? All these possibilities are caught by the break-
down of the triplets and the sonnet-tercets into false quatrains. One form, the triplet, deviates into a muddled view of
itself; the lines inserted into it (lines eight and twelve) are the
carriers of the principal main verbs, as if much of the life,
much of the ability to animate and control an existence,
were leaking out of the triplet. And the lines inserted into
the tercet (lines seven and fourteen) are acts of special
condolence and sympathy, personal additions to alleviate
a predicament (Baudelaire actually instructed Catulle
Mendès that the fourteenth line should be 'précédé d'un
tiret (–), pour lui donner une forme d'isolement, de distraction'). And so in the end, and paradoxically, the hybrid
quatrains *do* create structural interdependence between
stanzas and *do* reconcile tercet and triplet, however prob-
lematically.

It is in dealing with fixed forms that we begin to understand how vital rhyme's part has been in the diversification
of stanza and fixed form, and how durable and cosmopolitan it has made them. While those antique forms which are
purely metrical in foundation (e.g. elegy, satire, ode) have
survived only as the poetic postures of their dominant

themes, because of national prosodic dissimilarities, the Romance forms, with their basis in rhyme and refrain, have enjoyed prolonged international favour because of the transferability of rhyme-schemes; they are threatened, periodically, only by over-use. In fact, if anything, these Romance forms have moved in the opposite direction to the antique ones; their hardening into definite and perhaps more arbitrary structures seems to be the natural outcome of the loss of peculiar function (e.g. the villanelle's originally rustic character, the rondeau as dance accompaniment). Such a development has, of course, increased their formal reliability and has permitted the poet to capitalise upon the reader's recognition of the end in the beginning, upon the forms' protracted atmosphere of imminence.

7

Free verse

In isolating free verse in a separate chapter, we are doing an injustice to the continuity of verse's evolution. It would, of course, be easy to argue that historically, in France at least, the introduction of free verse was a radical, not to say revolutionary, departure; certainly its early adherents took a strongly polemical stance and found that the only way to promote free verse was to disparage regular verse, so that for some years it seemed that the existence of the one presupposed the abandonment of the other; but as free verse established itself, the real coextensiveness of regular verse, and particularly regular verse of a liberated kind, and free verse became apparent, not only because certain poets – Maeterlinck and Apollinaire, for example – found it easy to shift between the two worlds without undergoing a rupture of poetic personality, but also because analysts themselves have not been slow to demonstrate the persistence of traditional features in free verse – see, for example, Jean Mazaleyrat's 'La tradition métrique dans la poésie d'Éluard' (1967, ed. Parent) and Frédéric Deloffre's 'Versification traditionnelle et versification libérée d'après un recueil d'Yves Bonnefoy' (1967, ed. Parent). There are nonetheless some justifications for dealing with free verse separately; it gives one an opportunity to underline its essential coherence, and it does maintain a sense of historical proportion, for let us not forget that while we can look back over three and a half centuries of regular verse, French free verse dates only from 1886. There is still some controversy about who should be credited with the introduction of free verse, but 1886 was certainly the watershed year, the year in which *La Vogue* published Laforgue's translation of some Whitman poems and some of his own free verse, and other free verse poems by Rimbaud ('Marine' and 'Mouvement' from *Illuminations*), Gustave Kahn, and by Jean Moréas and Paul Adam in conjunction; 1887 saw the publication of the first free-verse collection, Gustave Kahn's *Palais nomades*.

It is difficult to speak of the causes of free verse, so manifold may they be. But as a beginning, we can draw attention to two closely allied phenomena. First, as we saw in our treatment of accents in Chapter 2, the gradual loosening of verse creates an increase in the number of possible readings of a particular line, and tends to highlight the expressive, recitational considerations at the expense of the purely prosodic ones. This trend has been aided by the development of apparatus, the oscillograph in particular, able to measure very finely the data of 'live' recitation, and by a concomitant emphasis, in modern verse analysis, on the accidents of the spoken poem; that is to say, the prosody of free verse is often regarded as a prosody of the voice, centring on the duration of syllable and patterns of cadence. Secondly, the pursuit of *expression*, as against a submission to the interpretative powers exercised by conventional prosody itself, has given a special prominence to tone, as against prosodic structure, as the multiplier and compounder of meaning. It is perhaps significant that one of the more potent strains of early free verse was one which explored modes of irony (Laforgue, Pound, Eliot) (this is not to forget an equally influential *rhapsodic* strain connected with Whitman, Maeterlinck, Claudel, Lawrence) and that French free verse grew out of Symbolism, out of a movement which might be said to have overtaxed the purely lexical and syntactic sources of semantic multiplicty. Would it be going too far to maintain that free verse arose from an exasperation with traditional Symbolism, that it nonetheless sought to develop the acutely critical attitude to language and the exploitation of semantic multivalence which Symbolism had fostered, even as it deflated Symbolism? Be that as it may, free verse, for the foregoing reasons, implicated the reader in the construction of the poem's

prosody, in a way that regular verse never had; the reader
had to, has to, search his own prosodic conscience, commit
himself constantly to a particular interpretative stance, in
order to arrive at the poem, in a way that regular verse had
never required of him.

This already uncovers a potential contradiction in free
verse, for one of the justifications for its existence is its
ability to register the psychic, emotional and intellectual
irregularities of a unique, inimitable existence, that of the
poet himself; as Gustave Kahn (1897) writes: 'Depuis long-
temps je cherchais à trouver en moi un rythme personnel
suffisant pour interpréter mes lyrismes avec l'allure et
l'accent que je leur jugeais indispensables' (p. 16). We might
equally cite Pound (1918): 'I think one should write vers
libre only when one "must", that is to say, only when the
"thing" builds up a rhythm more beautiful than that of set
metres, or more real, more a part of the emotion of the
"thing", more germane, intimate, interpretative than the
measure of regular accentual verse' ('A Retrospect', p. 12).
But how can we reconcile these assertions with the notion
of the reader as prosodic creator, using the written poem as
a scenario for his own recited poem?

But there are other, more specific and technical reasons
for the emergence of free verse. Let us return for a moment
to English verse. The foot-division in English verse, like the
coupe in French, is a fiction, a tool of scansion, used to
investigate rhythm; it has no necessary existence in language. Unfortunately, foot-scansion has a way of engendering foot-composition, and of exaggerating the importance
of beat; in the end, almost without knowing it, the poet
finds himself a slave to short-winded pre-fabricated units,
occurring with such regularity that his verse can only patter
or lilt. *The* foot, in English verse, is the iamb, and for that
reason called upon itself all the crimes of over-regularised
metre; Pound never tired of ascribing to it all the sins of
rhythmic simplification: 'Don't chop your stuff into separate *iambs*. Don't make each line stop dead at the end, and
then begin every next line with a heave. Let the beginning of

the next line catch the rise of the rhythm wave, unless you want a definite longish pause' ('A Retrospect', p. 6). It was 'politically' necessary to attack the iamb; if tonal variety was to be installed, if the ruminative was to rub shoulders with the colloquial, the ironic, the dithyrambic, feet had to be opened up or dissolved, so that voice-quality could be let in, so that beat could yield to 'rhythm wave'.

For the poet seeking to escape the tyranny of syllable-stress metre, several avenues were open. He could turn to those English metres in which the foot has no real, because no stipulated, existence, the pure-stress and the syllabic (for a definition, see Chapter 1). Alternatively, the poet could continue to write a poetry whose metric was still basically syllable-stress, but in which feet were lengthened, essentially phrasal, and not used with any regularity, but recurred intermittently as vertebral *leitmotifs*; Eliot's 'Gerontion' is one of the classic examples:

1	Here I am, an old man in a dry month,
2	Being read to by a boy, waiting for rain.
3	I was neither at the hot gates
4	Nor fought in the warm rain
5	Nor knee deep in the salt marsh, heaving a cutlass,
6	Bitten by flies, fought.
7	My house is a decayed house,
8	And the jew squats on the window sill, the owner,
9	Spawned in some estaminet of Antwerp,
10	Blistered in Brussels, patched and peeled in London.
11	The goat coughs at night in the field over-head;
12	Rocks, moss, stonecrop, iron, merds.
13	The woman keeps the kitchen, makes tea,
14	Sneezes at evening, poking the peevish gutter.
15	I an old man,
16	A dull head among windy spaces.

These opening lines indicate the predominance of the ionic foot (ᴗᴗ//), which I have underlined. This foot – measure might now be a more accurate description – coincides in most instances with a unified grammatical group, that is to say, is properly phrasal in the French manner. But its predominance is challenged by a recurrent choriambic foot (/ᴗᴗ/) – 'héavĭng ă cút/lass', 'Bĭttĕn bў flíes', 'Blĭstĕred ĭn Brú/ssels', 'Snéezĕs ăt éve/ning', 'pókĭng thĕ pée/vish. . ' – and there are two instances where the conflict is particularly acute, because the two kinds of foot overlap, challenge each other, in line two – '(bў ă bóy, (wái)tĭng fŏr ráin)' – where the choriamb has the greater syntactical claims, and in the eighth line – '(Ănd thĕ jéw (squáts) ŏn thĕ wĭn)dow sill' – where the ionic has the greater syntactical plausibility. If the ionic carries the overall victory as the 'bearing' *leitmotif*, it is because of the support it gets from a foot which is very like a shortened ionic, the bacchic (ᴗ//) – 'ăn óld mán' (l. 1), 'Nŏr knée déep' (l. 5), 'Thĕ góat cóughs (l. 11), 'kit/chĕn, mákes téa' (l.13), 'Ă dúll héad' (l.16). What is noticeable about the choriambs and bacchics is that while they are sometimes made up of complete syntactical units, sometimes they are not; and this may be a further argument for the ionic's pre-eminence. And let it be said that the pleasure the metrist finds in these lines derives not only from the conflict between the different kinds of extended foot, but also from the tension between an essentially phrasal prosody on the one hand and traditional syllable-stress metre, which does not actively relate to the phrase, but often cuts across it, on the other. And this should alert us to a feature of free verse which current analysis does not sufficiently respond to, namely that within the course of a single free-verse poem, different scansional approaches may be required, applied serially or simultaneously. In a short quotation from Arthur Symons's 'Intermezzo', in Chapter 1:

> The insinuations indiscreet
> Of pirouetting draperies

we have already seen how prosodic consciousness may drift

from syllable-stress to pure-stress metre. Cannot free-verse poets create and exploit such shifts of consciousness for the purposes of texturing their verse, of engineering corresponding shifts in tone, since prosodies and metres themselves are associated with different attitudes, periods, traditions of utterance, and so on?

With our mention of phrasal prosody we have touched on what is perhaps, for our purposes, the most significant alternative to syllable-stress, namely a verse which inclines towards the French tradition, towards a prosody governed by cadence rather than beat, by the varying length of measures rather than by their accentual constitution. In a letter to Edward Marsh of 19 November 1913, D. H. Lawrence wrote: 'I think I read my poetry more by length than by stress – as a matter of movements in space than footsteps hitting the earth.' The American poetess Amy Lowell was perhaps the chief proponent of this trend and was glad to admit French influence. She calls her *Sword Blades and Poppy Seed* (1914): 'poems in "unrhymed cadence". . . . They are built on "organic rhythm" or the rhythm of the speaking voice with its necessity for breathing, rather than upon a strict metrical system' (pp. x–xi). 'Cadence' means several things for Amy Lowell, but essentially it refers to a French-style phrasal prosody, which incorporates into its stresses/accents the changing pitch of the reciting voice; one of the functions of typographical lay-out in free verse is to reveal the intonation-patterns inhering in a piece of prose read expressively. In a similar way to Eliot in 'Gerontion', Lowell constructs her poems on the 'returning cadence unit of *vers libre*' ('The Rhythms of Free Verse', 1918, p. 52), that is, a dominant *leitmotif*-measure which creates an overall, stanzaic rhythm, rather than engaging with an abstract metrical pattern governing each individual line. Not surprisingly, Lowell makes the reading aloud of her poems a virtual condition of their existence.

'Cadence' is too loose a notion to lend itself to easy analytic application. It has tended to have a syntactical, rather than an intonational, focus, although its inevitable

connection with intonation is tacitly acknowledged. For
Joseph Malof (1970), 'cadence' both denotes the more complex varieties of foot (amphibrach, bacchic, choriamb, etc.)
and is, in free verse, 'the rhythmic shape of the span of
language between natural voice pauses (not metrical
pauses), measured or described impressionistically' (p. 154).
But can we afford to overlook the metrical pauses which no
verse, however free, can do without, and can any prosody be
built on impression? John Nist (1964) argues that word-
group cadences have always been a primary consideration
for English poets and defines cadence as *'that rhythmical
pattern or accentual collocation which occurs between two actualised major junctures'* (p. 77). This definition, but for terminological differences, has much in common with
Malof's; word-groups are the basic units of *syntactical* structure, but they are presumably to be related in a rather
traditional metrical way, according to similarities and differences of 'accentual collocation' and syllable-number.

If properly intonational considerations have taken so
long to graft themselves on to cadence, it is understandable:
while we may confidently identify tone-groups, the charac-
terisation of tones themselves may lead us into the domain of
paralanguage. Even if we can accept the linguistic normality
of, say, Halliday's (1970) five primary tones – falling, high
rising or falling-rising (pointed), low rising, falling-rising
(rounded), rising-falling (rounded) – and if we accept that
all forms of utterance (declarative, interrogative, enumerative, imperative, exclamatory, hortatory, etc.) can be classified satisfactorily and consistently on this scale of tones,
we must remember that such tones are designed to describe
standard spoken English; verse-structure makes its own
peculiar intonational demands, will tend to ritualise the
voice, will frequently distort normal tone-curves. So far, an
adequate description of verse-tones seems to be lacking, as
Maciej Pakosz (1973) points out: 'The traditional terminology pertaining to intonation . . . cannot be applied to
verse-lines which are purely formal units of discourse as
opposed to speech segmentation where these terms reflect

prosodic phenomena satisfactorily. The formulation of
terminology adequate to the description of metrical intonation appears to be imperative for future research in the field'
(p. 163).

In the following scansion of an example of cadenced free
verse, therefore, I am only too aware how tentative and
embryonic my approach must be; my references to intonation are crude in the extreme and I adopt Malof's very blunt
notational system. The example is a stanza from Amy
Lowell's 'The Captured Goddess', a poem reminiscent in
many respects of Rimbaud's 'Aube':

1	I followed her for long,	A
2	With gazing eyes/ and stum- bling feet,	B/B
3	I cared not where she led me,	A
4	My eyes were full of colours:	A
5	Saffrons, rubies,/the yellows of beryls,	C/C(D)
6	And the indigo-blue of quartz;	D
7	Flights of rose,/layers of chrysoprase,	C/C
8	Points of orange,/spirals of vermilion,	C/C
9	The spotted gold of tiger-lily petals,	D
10	The loud pink of bursting hydrangeas.	D
11	I followed,	A
12	And watched for the flashing of her wings.	A(D)

The letters sketch out the pattern of recurrent cadences. The
A's are, with the exception of the last line, impulsive,
declarative cadences connected with narration and the
first-person perspective. The isolated B's are adverbial
groups, dipping in intonation, but not sufficiently allied to a
larger syntactical pattern to have a very positive cadence

direction. The C measures are enumerations of phenomena, where the absence of article and the plurality betray wonderment, lack of specificity, the sense of being enveloped; these measures are intonationally level or slightly rising. The D measures are falling measures of closure, focussed and given control by the definite article and the singular; they are lexically fulsome. There are two equivocal measures, or measures where different cadence principles are amalgamated, in the fifth and twelfth lines. The second measure of the fifth line has the characteristic article of D, but the plurality and intonational hesitancy of C. Line twelve, connected with the eleventh line by coordination, by the impetus of a main verb, veers nonetheless into the nominal pattern of the D lines, and into closure. This reading has little sophistication, but it may serve as a beginning. However, other scansions may serve equally well. If we applied a pure-stress approach, we would relate lines 2, 5, 7, 8, 9, 10 with their four stresses, and lines 3, 4, 6 and 12 with their three-stress quota and perhaps note how this structure counterpoints the pattern of cadences. Or perhaps we would see what a syllable-stress reading would give. Traditional methods of scansion are still eminently applicable to free verse, and should still constitute our point of departure; but they may prove to be insufficiently wide-ranging. Certainly we should approach free verse without scansional prejudice, alive to the fact that any method we use may be missing the mark or may need qualifying by another method. The prosodic richness of free verse may derive precisely from the tension between different scansions.

If we now turn to Gustave Kahn's 'Préface sur le vers libre', which serves as a prologue to his *Premiers Poèmes* (1897), we shall find much that harmonises with Lowell's views: an insistence on the recitation of the poem, on the centrality to free verse of a cohesive recurrent measure, the *leitmotif*, which Kahn calls the 'accent d'impulsion' and which might, with more clarity, be called, after the manner of Duhamel and Vildrac (1910), the 'constante rythmique'. Lines from André Fontainas's 'Fraîcheur des herbes', with

their four-syllable constant, recurring as the initial, and
often as the final, measure, will exemplify this last notion:

Et, loin des foules et des villes   4+4
Et des vains bruits et des secousses stériles4+4+3
Où toute ma vie apparaît en exil,   5+3+3
Je me libère vers les îles du silence!   4+4+4
Ardente proue, une âme s'élance   4+5
Fière vers les conquêtes plus superbes   1+5+4
De mer en mer où le mirage   4+4
Féconde d'inconnu les anses et les plages.
                                                     2+4+2+4

In poems using repetition of whole phrases or of the syntactic structure underlying them, the rhythmic constant would
obviously impinge on the reader's consciousness much
more forcibly. Kahn is also anxious to emphasise the
stanza's ascendancy, in the free-verse poem, over the line, as
the controlling rhythmic perspective ('Je crois que dès ce
moment, et à ce moment (surtout), mes efforts porteront
surtout sur la construction de la strophe', p. 17).

We shall have occasion to return to Kahn's preface, but
before leaving it, we should glance at his treatment of two
lines from Racine's *Athalie*, a treatment which has broader
implications for our approach to free verse. The couplet
Kahn busies himself with is:

Oui, je viens dans son temple adorer l'Éternel,
Je viens selon l'usage antique et solennel.

Of these lines Kahn writes:

le premier vers se compose de deux vers de six pieds
dont le premier est un vers blanc

Oui, je viens dans son temple

et dont l'autre

adorer l'Éternel

serait également blanc, si, par habitude, on n'était
sûr de trouver la rime au vers suivant . . . Donc à

premier examen ce distique se compose de quatre vers de six pieds dont deux seulement riment. Si l'on pousse plus loin l'investigation on découvre que les vers sont ainsi scandés

$$\overset{3}{\text{Oui je viens}} - \overset{3}{\text{dans son temple}} - \overset{3}{\text{adorer}} -$$
$$\overset{3}{\text{l'Éternel}}$$
$$\overset{2}{\text{Je viens}} - \overset{4}{\text{selon l'usage}} - \overset{2}{\text{antique}} - \overset{4}{\text{et solennel}}$$

soit un premier vers composé de quatre éléments de trois pieds ternaires, et un second vers scandé 2,4,2,4. – Il est évident que tout grand poète ayant perçu d'une façon plus ou moins théorique les conditions élémentaires du vers, Racine a empiriquement ou instinctivement appliqué les règles fondamentales et nécessaires de la poésie et que c'est selon notre théorie que ses vers doivent se scander. La question de césure, chez les maîtres de la poésie classique, ne se pose même pas (pp. 24–6).

The implication of Kahn's comments is that Racine composed his verse along the same lines as Kahn himself; Racine writes regular verse, by historical accident almost, only because he arranges his measures according to a totally arbitrary, therefore ultimately meaningless, set of conventions which constitute the line of verse.

Here we must briefly digress. The standard arguments for minimising the differences between regular and free verse, either to underline how far free verse is a rationalisation of regular verse and in no sense a reaction against it – it is, if anything, a reaction only against the 'rules' which prevented verse from rationalising itself earlier – or to deride free verse as a factitious creation dependent on the purely cosmetic and mystificatory art of lay-out, are: on the one hand to discover embryonic free verse in regular verse, as Kahn does, and on the other to reconstitute free verse as acceptable regular verse. The reconstitution of free verse takes two forms: the re-assembly of short free-verse lines

into familiar larger units (decasyllable, alexandrine), a procedure practised, for example, by Rémy de Gourmont
(1955) on some lines by Henri de Régnier (on this basis,
these short lines can be called *vers démontés*); alternatively,
the de-constitution of long free-verse lines into conventional shorter units; Graham Hough (1960) de-constitutes
three long lines from Eliot's 'Love Song of J. Alfred Pruf-
rock':

> The yellow fog that rubs its back upon the
>   window-panes,
> The yellow smoke that rubs its muzzle on the
>   window-panes
> Licked its tongue into the corners of the evening

into blank verse (unrhymed iambic pentameter):

> The yellow fog that rubs its back upon
> The window-panes, the yellow smoke that rubs
> Its muzzle on the window-panes, licked
> Its tongue into the corners of the evening.

Another manifestation of this compound long line is the
so-called *vers emboîté*, that is, a line which comprises two
overlapping conventional lines – thus a line of eighteen syllables might be read as two dovetailed alexandrines, thus
(6//(6)//6) (see Mazaleyrat, 1974, pp. 162–3). Such scansional practices are understandable when called upon to
serve polemic; but otherwise they should, in my view, be
discouraged. We cannot do justice to free verse if we come
to it with the intention of turning it into something else; we
shall never grasp the peculiar resources of free verse if our
scansional methods make it, willy-nilly, a confidence-trick.
   The long line, as we see it in the Eliot example, de-
intensifies experience and in so doing encourages the voice
to shift from a stress reading to a cadence/phrasal one; and
this shift must be made anyway, if we are to apprehend the
line as a totality; in other words, the longer a line becomes,
the more we have to reduce the number of its structuring
units. In fact, a free-verse poet can use the variation of

line-length to vary the kind of scansional attention we bring
to his poem. The slack quality of the long line, which in
Whitman often looks like complacency but is confident
equanimity, and which in Eliot exudes existential fatigue,
ineffectuality, here provides a perfect cover for the fog's/
smoke's insidiousness. And because the long line does not
relate itself to some abstract metrical norm, because of the
recalcitrance of its extra syllables, so it actually makes itself
scansionally more available and equally, as should happen
with a poetry which is increasingly the voice's possession,
scansionally more impenetrable. More obviously, of
course, the re-writing of these lines as iambic pentameters
obscures the syntactical and lexical parallelism of the first
two lines, the parallelism of the tri-phrasal structure in all
three lines, and the progressive pattern of phrase-endings:

> The yellow fog/that rubs its back/upon the
> window-panes,   4+4+6
> The yellow smoke/that rubs its muzzle/on the
> window-panes   4+5+5
> Licked its tongue/into the corners/of the evening.
> 3+5+4

All phrases in the first line end with a stressed syllable,
giving the line a certain matter-of-fact starkness, a certain
resistance to pressure, backed up by the predominant
monosyllables. The feminine ending of the second 'measure' of the second line introduces an element of concession
or self-insinuation; what was descriptive metaphor in the
first line (fog as cat), develops in the second line into a
metaphor of incipient relationship. And in the third line,
where both the second and third measures have a feminine
ending, the metaphor is one of familiarity enjoyed,
exploited; the feminine endings act as indices of intimacy, of
resistance broken down.

And even where there is manuscript evidence of *démon-
tage*, as in the second and third lines of Apollinaire's 'Les
Colchiques', which in the first draft formed a single alexandrine:

Le pré est vénéneux mais joli en automne
Les vaches y paissant   2+4
Lentement s'empoisonnent   3+3

we should avoid reconstructing the manuscript version and
basing our interpretation on that. In this instance, it is easy
to say that Apollinaire wished to give greater prominence to
the caesural accent and pause, and that he used a disposi-
tional device to do so, and that thereby he manages to slow
down the movement of the poem, the better to give a
sudden and inexplicable depth to apparently innocent
actions and to imitate the deliberateness of the grazing
cows. But all this is as much to ease our minds about an
anomaly as to congratulate Apollinaire on a happy effect. A
glance at the overall structure of the poem will show that
the second line has an important part to play *as a line*. Its
temporary rhymelessness helps increase the sense that the
cows are sublimely unaware of being poisoned, while the
poet is only too conscious of the fatal process taking place in
himself; the cows do not at first, while they still enjoy a full
literalness, fit into the design of malignant influence repre-
sented by the rhymes; they are not poisoned by enthral-
ment, which rhyme is, but by dietary accident, and
ultimately are able to leave the field. But in the last line of
the second stanza, and in the final stanza, the ã ending is
taken up:

Qui battent comme les fleurs battent au vent
dément

Le gardien du troupeau chante tout doucement
Tandis que lentes et meuglant les vaches abandon-
nent
Pour toujours ce grand pré mal fleuri par l'automne.

'Paissant' becomes retrospectively a subliminal rhyme – we
shall have more to say on the function of rhyme-interval in
free verse later, but this is an extreme example, for there are
nine lines between 'paissant' and 'dément' – and the contiguity of its ã and the surrounding ɔn sounds is shown by

these last lines to be peculiarly preordained; in other words,
as the cows themselves become metaphors of lovers who
have escaped their condition, never to backslide ('pour toujours'), they become participants in the intention of the
poem which is to isolate the poet beyond salvation, to leave
him to his destiny.

But it is time we returned to Kahn's preface. Using
Racine as his example, Kahn re-affirms one of the basic
tenets of all classical prosodic thinking, namely that the
measure should be governed by the syntax, should have
syntactical integrity: 'Dans les vers précités, l'unité vraie
n'est pas le *nombre* conventionnel du vers, mais un arrêt
simultané du sens et du rythme sur toute fraction organique
du vers et de la pensée' (p. 26). With this reference to the
'fraction organique', we are perhaps reminded of Amy
Lowell's 'organic rhythm'; but whereas Lowell is looking
to push English verse in a new direction and break the
stranglehold of the deeply-entrenched foot-metric, Kahn is
essentially verifying what has always been fundamental to
French verse-making; indeed, as we intimated much earlier,
Kahn's theory often seems more backward-looking, more
hidebound by intolerant principle, than it should: we have
mentioned his rejection of *enjambement*; we shall also meet a
view of the *e atone* which radically curbs its versatility; his
opinion of the liberties taken by Romantic and Symbolist
poets with the classical lines is that they are either mis-
guided, because they divorce eye and ear, prosodic break
and syntactic break, or that they are merely an expression of
a frustration with verse-forms which will not allow them to
write in the way they want to. He does not seem able to
imagine that tradition itself ends by condoning freedom and
deviation, because the weight of tradition, the force of
fundamental principles, is a necessary presupposition of all
liberty; tradition develops towards a freedom from its own
inertia.

What also emerges from Kahn's treatment of the Racinian lines is that his quarrel is not with the measure but with
the line. As we have already remarked, while the foot is the

basic English rhythmic unit, in French verse the measure
may be the basic constituent of rhythms, but it is not itself
an indicator of rhythm; the basic *rhythmic* unit, and by that I
mean the lowest *common* denominator of rhythmic *structure*,
is the line, because French rhythms grow not from a principle of *repetition* but from a principle of *combination*. Kahn
wanted to establish the ascendancy of the measure, to introduce a notion of *repetition* (precisely the *leitmotif*-measure) to
set against combination, or at least to release combination
from the constraint of being answerable to a fixed rhythmic
perspective (the line). Kahn sought to achieve his end by
increasing the directness of the relationship between measure and stanza, so that the structure of the stanza was
actually referable to a significant pattern of measures, and
not to the grouping of lines or a rhyme-scheme. In other
words, the line had to be minimised, if not eradicated, as a
mediator between measure and stanza, as that which determined both the possible combination of measures *and* the
nature of the stanza; to do this, Kahn needed to suggest, in a
rather English way, that the line was not so much the key to,
as the accidental result of, the arrangement of measures
within it, that it had no stipulative function. This is how he
expresses these ideas: 'Comment l'[le vers] apparenter à
d'autres vers? par la construction logique de la strophe se
constituant d'après les mesures intérieures du vers qui dans
cette strophe contient la pensée principale ou le point essen-
tiel de la pensée' (p. 27). He consequently attacked, as we
shall see, the regularity of rhyme, which ties the hands of the
stanza and gives authority, identity, definition, to the line of
verse. And, more fundamentally, he attempted to undo the
notion of number, of syllabic count, as a principle of line
organisation; what this involves is the establishment of a
new principle for combining measures which is not numer-
ical, but musical: 'Pour assembler ces unités et leur donner la
cohésion de façon qu'elles forment un vers il les faut apparenter. Les parentés s'appellent allitérations, soit union
de consonnes parentes ou assonances par des voyelles
similaires' (p. 27). It equally involves not counting syllables

beyond the boundaries of the measure. By this latter I mean that while Kahn *must* count, must use number, to distinguish his measures, and particularly his dominant measures, he wishes the reader to forgo the process of aggregation; in the first line of the Racinian couplet, for instance, we should see the line as four trisyllabic measures rather than as an alexandrine; we can draw consequences from the 3s of the measures themselves, but we should not draw consequences from the 12 they add up to; put another way, a measure of three syllables in a twelve-syllable line is of exactly the same nature as a measure of three syllables in a decasyllable, or octosyllable, or pentasyllable; it does not owe its significance to the measures it is combined with and what they add up to.

This system of accounting seems awkward, particularly where *coupes enjambantes* or *césures enjambantes* may still be involved, and, besides, it is difficult to believe that any theorist, by the power of his word alone, can change reading habits, or get the reader to overlook undeniable facts. If the number of syllables in a line does add up to twelve, can we blind ourselves to that fact, and on what grounds would Kahn be able to argue that it is not an alexandrine, what evidence could he call upon to *demonstrate* that it is not? But we can assume that the underlying positions adopted by Kahn are common to other initiators, Francis Vielé-Griffin, Henri de Régnier, Albert Mockel, Édouard Dujardin.

It is this attack on the line, and on those factors which maintain the line, number and rhyme, which clearly distinguishes *vers libre* from the *vers libéré* of Verlaine, Rimbaud and Mallarmé. *Vers libéré* was for a long time stigmatised as 'decadent', anarchic, careless; and yet Verlaine himself, who in his 'Ariettes oubliées' (*Romances sans paroles*) ritualised the liberation of verse by punctiliously presenting a different novelty in each one of them, stubbornly refused to practise free verse, and indeed mocked those who did:

Que l'ambition du Vers Libre hante

De jeunes cerveaux épris de hasards!
C'est l'ardeur d'une illusion touchante.
On ne peut que sourire à leurs écarts.

('Épigrammes')

To the foreign eye, the distance between *vers libéré* and *vers libre* seems very small. The practitioners of *vers libre* cast in doubt the prosodic value and validity of the *e atone*, consciously capitalised on the confusions surrounding synaeresis and diaeresis, abandoned the distinction between masculine and feminine rhymes and disregarded the principle of rhyme alternation. They used rhyme frequently, but allowed assonance, consonance and rhymelessness with equal ease. They rejected isosyllabism (the repetition of lines of equal length) and isostrophism (repetition of stanzas of identical construction) in favour of a free grouping of lines of any length. But the poets of *vers libéré* had already made free with the notion of the alternation of rhymes, had ignored other rhyming conventions (masculine with masculine, no plural with a singular, etc.) and taken rhyme as far as assonance. They, like many of the *verslibristes*, practised bold *enjambements*, mobilised the caesura, exploited hiatus and the *impair* (line containing an odd number of syllables). And yet the differences, fine as they appear, were crucial, precisely because they bore on those elements in French verse which had for so long seemed indispensable to its very existence, as dykes against the incursions of prose, syllabism and rhyme.

But a further distinction should be made, between modern *vers libre* and the *vers libres* (or *vers mêlés*, or *vers libres classiques*, or *vers irréguliers*) of the seventeenth and eighteenth centuries. This latter heterosyllabic and irregularly rhyming species of verse was characteristic only of certain verse-forms like the madrigal, the fable, the elegy, the idyll – the eighteenth-century Desforges-Maillard's madrigal 'La Belle Chasseuse', for example, is a fifteen-line poem rhyming ababcbcdeeddfdf, whose line-lengths run in a counterpointing sequence 12,12,8,8,12,12,8,12,8,8,12,12,8,12,12.

These earlier *vers libres* are best expressed in the plural, because the plural helps to suggest that they are *libres* only by virtue of their grouping, by virtue of the irregular way in which standard regular lines – not excluding, however, the odd *impair*, particularly the heptasyllable – are put together; they rhyme, and observe the alternation of masculine and feminine rhymes and the other rhyming conventions (singular with singular, masculine, with masculine, etc.). Each line of Symbolist and post-Symbolist *vers libre*, on the other hand, is *libre*, both internally (with regard to caesura, hiatus, treatment of the *e atone*) and in terms of its syllabic outline (i.e. any regularity is either accidental or for some special effect); thus we may say that *vers libre* is *libre* as *substance*, and therefore in each single embodiment, while *vers libres* are *libres* solely as *arrangement*.

Having sketched out a broad context, part historical and part theoretical, we need now to fill in some of the details and in so doing to discover what effect free verse has had on the mechanics of the poem and the business of scansion.

(i) *Accent and syllable*

(a) *Accent*. All that was said about the accent in Chapters 1 and 2 is applicable to free verse; as is hardly surprising, free verse has brought no radical change in the accent-structure of French. What free verse has been able to do, however, is to use line-length to distribute accent in a rather different way, more unevenly.

Whatever Kahn has written about the desirability of masking the line, of undermining its control, in favour of the measure-module, the reader will still feel the need, most probably, to make sense of lineation in free verse by comprehending each line as a rhythmic totality. Certainly the reader may cease to embrace the line as a *syllabic*, mathematical whole, but he may still respond to the line as a combination of a certain number of measures. This tendency is especially encouraged by the long line, where the very density of syllables makes it difficult to keep track of syllabic outline. But not only will the reader thus resort to a reading

by measure-number, he will probably find himself lengthening measure the longer the line is, the better to keep the
number of measures within manageable proportions. This
will naturally lead him to reduce the number of principal
accents within the line, to glide over some of the accentuable
syllables. He will therefore tend to read over what would be
natural *coupes* in regular verse and to endow those accents
which would, in regular verse, have a full prosodic existence
with a minor status, transforming them into something
more like *accents contre-toniques*. The following line from
Supervielle's 'Saisir', for example:

> Il faudra bien l'étendre dans le lit blanc de la
> mémoire, aux rideaux tirés

would, in a 'regular' reading, be a twenty-syllable line with
a 4+2+5+4+3+2 disposition. But would such a reading
allow us to apprehend the line as a total structure? Are there
not just too many elements for us to combine them meaningfully in our minds? Is it not, in fact, more probable that
we would respond to the line as an essentially trimetric,
three-phrase structure with 6+9+5 divisions and consequently give support status to the accents on the fourth,
eleventh and eighteenth syllables?

> Il faudra bìen l'éten/dre dans le lit blànc de la
> mémóire,/aux rideàux tirés

Another way of expressing this would obviously be to
say that the *coupes* at the sixth and fifteenth syllables are in
fact caesuras, while there are normal *coupes* at the fourth,
eleventh and eighteenth syllables, and that we read this line
using the caesuras as our principal prosodic *points de repère*.
But what we should remember, if we adopt this latter
approach, is that the caesura in regular verse is a break (of
whatever kind) within a line which can, *despite* the caesura,
still be perceived as a totality; in the above example, we are
suggesting that the line cannot be perceived as a totality
without caesuras, and that the function of the caesuras is
precisely to make it perceptible. This is to imply that free

verse, or perhaps merely the long line, changes the caesura's role, deprives it of all but a prosodic significance; and lurking round the corner is the danger that we shall make the caesura the equivalent of a line-ending, and this line a compound of three separate lines.

Each man to his own manner of reading, as long as it is plausible. But however we approach this line, we are bound to affirm, I think, that long lines involve us in a different kind of reading from shorter ones, and if we use the caesura in the way we have, we can add that the function of the caesura changes, depending on whether it occurs in a long line or a shorter one. And obviously, as we read a free-verse poem, as we variously encounter long lines and short ones, so our scansional responses will change.

The line we have just quoted is immediately followed by:

> Et le regarder avec attention

an eleven-syllable line – supposing 'attenti-on' – $5//(2+4)$ which restores a traditional kind of reading and a traditional caesura, that is to say, a caesura which *relates* two halves of a line, rather than *separating* a line into manageable components.

But all we have said should be qualified by the reminder that context, too, may play a large part in determining the way we read. If the poem 'Saisir' has established a dominant tetrasyllabic, or dissyllabic, measure, then a more traditional account of the long line may be justified on those grounds alone. A free-verse poem may derive its rhythmic complexity from the contradiction between a desire to give relief to Kahnian measure-modules and a desire to sustain the coherence of the line. And the longer the line, the more complicated the contradiction, because the greater the number of possible levels of organisation. In the following *verset* (the Biblical 'verse', the short, rhythmically whole, intoned paragraph) by Claudel, for example:

> Mon Dieu, qui au commencement avez séparé les
> eaux supérieures des eaux inférieures
>
> > ('L'Esprit et l'eau')

may be seen, supposing the suppression of the terminal atonic e's and that -ieu- is but one syllable, as 8//15, 2//6//15, 2//6//5+5+5, 2+6+5+2+3+2+3.

The converse of accent-reduction in the long line is the accentual increase brought about by a series of short lines. Whether the short line (three syllables or less) constitutes a line of verse, whether indeed a very long line constitutes a line of verse, are not questions I wish here to confront. They exist in free verse. They may be poles of prose between which free verse vibrates. They may be oddities which compel us to redefine the line in terms of margin, i.e. any word or words using a poetic rather than a prose margin should be regarded as a line of verse. Be that as it may. Mazaleyrat (1974) calls such short lines 'des segments du discours poétique que ne vient organiser métriquement aucun système ni extérieur à eux, ni intérieur' (p. 26). He may well be right, but he may also be a little beside the point. If we look upon the variation of line-length as a way of manipulating accent, its frequency and nature, then the short line can be understood. Let us remember that the stanza, rather than the line, may well be the proper point of rhythmic reference in free verse; lines exist to create the accentual constitution of the stanza; if the poet wishes to increase accentual density within the stanza, the short line may be a helpful resource.

> Il pleut les globes électriques
> Montrouge Gare de l'Est Métro Nord–Sud bateaux-
>   mouches monde
> Tout est halo
> Profondeur
> Rue de Buci on crie *L'Intransigeant* et *Paris-Sports*
> L'aérodrome du ciel est maintenant, embrasé, un
>   tableau de Cimabue
> Quand par devant
> Les hommes sont
> Longs
> Noirs

Tristes
Et fument, cheminées d'usine.

This is the final stanza of 'Contrastes', the third of Blaise
Cendrars's *Dix-Neuf Poèmes élastiques* (1919). Like the Apollinaire of 'Zone', Cendrars seeks the fusion in imagery of
the Christian tradition and the often exhilarating, often
dispiriting, always sensorily unmitigated modern city. The
men of the stanza's final lines, and the factory chimneys, are
like those figures who so often crowd out the foreground of
Cimabue's work, stiff, dark, distant, melancholy. The
single-word monosyllabic lines here not only calligram-
matically imitate the elongation and starkness of men and
chimneys, but create an accentual density in the stanza
which would be difficult to achieve otherwise. Cendrars is a
poet of perceptual shock and of radical ellipsis. It is obvious
that in doing away with grammatical tools, particles, modal
elements and so on, one naturally condenses the recurrence
of accents. By using the short line, Cendrars is able to
produce the effect of ellipsis even where none exists and to
give his adjectives a peculiar grammatical absoluteness. As a
result of our investigation, in Chapter 2, of the non-
coincidence of accentuable syllables and available conventional accents in the alexandrine, we can see how a regular
line would counteract ellipsis precisely by resisting closely
recurrent accents; it is worth noting that Mallarmé's syntax,
for all its outlandishness, is still discursive, full of grammatical detail, and thus still fits comfortably into a regular-verse
frame. Inasmuch as ellipsis is characteristic of the modernist
poet, free verse, and the short line, must inevitably be
characteristic also.

(b) *Syllable*. If we have argued for the long line's tendency
to encourage a phrase/measure reading of the line, rather
than a syllabic one, we might point for justification not only
to the difficulty of mentally encompassing the long line as a
number of syllables, but also to the uncertainty attached to
syllable-counting in free verse. This uncertainty belongs to

lines of every length and centres on two factors, the *e atone* and the synaeresis/diaeresis question.

Towards the end of the nineteenth century, poets were becoming increasingly disturbed by the phonological anachronism that the *e atone* had long been – it had not been pronounced in 'ordinary' speech since the end of the sixteenth century – and the insistence on the counting of the *e atone* was symptomatic, in the eyes of the *verslibristes*, of the anachronism that regular verse itself had become. The lobby against the sounding and counting of the *e atone* sought evidence for its case in popular songs, which, it was felt, reflected more faithfully the reality of contemporary speech and which made short shrift of the *e atone* by simply disregarding it. This recourse to the popular song was not without its potential pitfalls, however, for, as Rémy de Gourmont (1955) points out, the singer is as likely to add an *e atone* where none exists, merely to make up his numbers:

> J'irai me plaindre
> J'irai me plaindre
> Au duc de Bourbon.   (duque)

Anyway, when we turn to free verse, we shall find ourselves in a fairly persistent quandary, whether to count, or not to count, the *e atone*.

By way of introducing the terminology of this problem and of showing what kind of considerations may govern our resolution of it, I would like to quote at some length from an article by Jean Mazaleyrat (1969) on Apollinaire's 'Les Colchiques', an admirable introduction to the treatment of the *e atone* in free verse. The subject of the quotation is the third of the following lines:

> Ils cueillent les colchiques qui sont comme des
> mères
> Filles de leurs filles et sont couleur de tes paupières
> Qui battent comme les fleurs battent au vent
> dément.

Mazaleyrat comments:

Ici encore un second hémistiche sans problèmes prosodiques:

//ba/ttent au vent dément

La difficulté réside à nouveau dans le choix à faire dans le premier: apocope du premier *battent* ou, une fois de plus, de *comme*:

Qui batt(ent)/comme les fleurs//

ou:

Qui ba/ttent comm(e) les fleurs//

Et c'est encore ici la réflexion poétique qui doit commander, faute d'indications claires du poète. Ou bien en effet c'est l'impression de mouvement répété qui domine, et les deux verbes doivent être syllabés de la même façon pour que cette répétition produise son effet:

Qui ba/ttent comm(e) les fleurs//ba/ttent au vent dément

Scansion un peu raide, mais toujours possible. Ou bien – interprétation plus nuancée peut-être – la charnière de la comparaison, l'instrument comparatif, garde son volume maximal, comme il est normal dans un poème fondé sur cette comparaison même, et les deux *battent* se diversifient: le premier isolé par l'apocope et la coupe 'épique' (isolement possible sur le plan de la grammaire, puisqu'on change de proposition); le second normalement syllabé et ainsi, la liaison phonétique aidant, non isolé de la suite (rapprochement légitime puisque la fin de l'hémistiche est constituée par son complément déterminatif). Ainsi seraient figurés comme deux mouvements: l'un rapide, brusque et idéalement suivi d'un instant de contemplation (celui des paupières); l'autre élargi et amplifié par son syllabisme plein et son prolongement sur tout l'hémistiche (celui du vent sur le pré). D'où une scansion sans doute plus riche, plus délicate et plus expressive:

> Qui batt(ent)/comme les fleurs//ba/ttent
>   au vent dément

Ou, autrement dit, rythme alexandrin, avec effet de coupe 'épique', différenciant les deux verbes au sein de leur similitude lexicale, l'un traduit en sensation vive, l'autre converti en vaste tableau (p. 146).

The term 'apocope' refers to the full muting of the e *at the end of a word*; the muting or dropping of the e *within a word* is called 'syncope' (e.g. 'seul'ment', 'bouch'rie'); under no circumstances should apocope be confused with 'lawful' elision. *Coupe épique* derives from *césure épique*, which in turn relates to medieval practice in the epic *chansons de geste*, where the hemistich was treated much as a line and the hemistich-ending as a line-ending, so that the e *atone* at the hemistich was not counted (apocope and syncope are common in medieval versification); the *coupe épique* is merely an extension of this principle to measures within the hemistich. This extension of the end-of-line treatment of mute e's to all terminal mute e's within the line is very much what Kahn had in mind:

> Le vers régulier compte l'*e* à valeur entière quoiqu'il ne s'y prononce point tout à fait, sauf à la fin d'un vers. Pour nous, qui considérons, non la finale rimée, mais les divers éléments assonancés et allitérés qui constituent le vers, nous n'avons aucune raison de ne pas le considérer comme final de chaque élément et de le scander alors, comme à la fin d'un vers régulier (pp. 30–1).

So in Kahn's view the e *atone* has no syllabic existence but is to be regarded as 'un simple intervalle'. The first line of André Fontainas's 'Fraîcheur des herbes':

> Fraîcheur des herbes! un matin de clarté pure
>   4//3+4

has such a *césure épique*, establishing the initial tetrasyllabic *constante rythmique* emphatically, and looking forward to the first hemistich's appearance as a full line at the end of the poem.

But how can we ultimately decide whether to drop or count the *e atone*? We must remember that Mazaleyrat had a great advantage, for he was asking himself not so much 'Shall I count or not?' but 'Shall I count this one or that one?' In other words, he was working within a stable frame of reference, the alexandrine, and cutting his cloth to suit his coat; Apollinaire's lines are *vers libre* pre-scansionally, and liberated regular verse post-scansionally. But how horrifyingly unresilient it would be for the reader always to use the 'nearest' regular line as the goal of his reading of a free-verse line, and to use the freedom given him in the treatment of the *e atone* to make a Procrustean bed for the line. We might take Cendrars's enumerative line:

> Montrouge Gare de l'Est Métro Nord-Sud bateaux-
> mouches monde

and argue that this is a regular *alexandrin trimètre*, by grouping the items and practising apocopes, thus:

> Montroug(e) Gar(e) d(e) l'Est/Métro Nord-Sud/
> bateaux-mouch(es) monde.

But to what end? Have we not merely used the *trimètre* to make a decision for us? Why create a freedom in the *e atone* if it is only to be used as a freedom to fix arbitrarily and to produce concatenations of consonants into the bargain?

Of course I am not suggesting that free-verse poets do not often sidle alongside regular lines and invite us to recognise them, as Laforgue does, in 'L'Hiver qui vient', for instance:

> Non, non! c'est la saison et la planète falote!
> $\qquad\qquad\qquad\qquad\qquad$ 2+4+4+2
> Que l'autan, que l'autan $\qquad\qquad\qquad$ 3+3
> Effiloche les savates que le Temps se tricote!
> $\qquad\qquad\qquad\qquad\qquad$ 3+3+3+3

C'est la saison, oh déchirements! c'est la saison!

4+4+4

Tous les ans, tous les ans,   3+3

J'essaierai en chœur d'en donner la note.

3+2+3+2

In order to bring these lines round, we have introduced a *coupe épique* at 'planète' in the first line, a *coupe épique* and a *césure épique* in the first hemistich of the third line, and a syncope into the medial measure of the following *trimètre* ('déchir'ments'). These rather down-at-heel regular lines, salvaged as it were, capture the contradictoriness of the poet's intention, the *tentative* approach ('J'essaierai') to *confident* unison ('en chœur'). And it is important that the stanza should find its almost mindless regularity, supporting and supported by the recurrent nasals (ã, ɔ̃), the internal rhymes, the senseless, unchanging circularity of time and the seasons; but it is important, too, that it should bear traces of pitiful wear and tear, or incipient deviation, to harmonise with the after all wretched footwear ('savates') that Time needs to move forward in, and with the poet's attempts to sabotage Time's unremitting progress. And the combination of the plangently regular and the slightly sorry-looking is the quality of the word 'falote', a mixture of the comically stupid and the pathetic.

But this Laforgue example will not help us to solve the Cendrars problem. With Cendrars, it seems, we shall have to settle for a line situated *between* certain limits (12 and 16 syllables), occupying a prosodic area, though not prosodically defined. We can pair its constituents, or leave them separate; we can argue for a caesura, or two, or none at all. No longer does a prosodic structure obtrude and interpret the line for us, help us to read it; instead we must do prosodic justice to the line on the basis of our own will to make the poem work as efficiently as it can; and if we do this, there is no sense in which reading ceases to be a rigorous discipline, no sense in which verse suddenly becomes formless and incoherent. But the quality of the verse will depend, in a way it does not in regular verse, on the quality of the analytical attention we bring to it. If free verse lays more store by the recitational reality of verse, than regular verse does, we should add that recitation has a slightly different role. It is still an act of interpretation, of course, but it is no longer an exercise of freedom and an affirmation of personality in the realisation of a given prosodic structure; it is, rather, an effort to give a lasting prosodic identity to a structure asking to be discovered.

Of course there are factors which help us come to a reasonable decision about the *e atone* in free verse. We know that poets allow themselves to use unelided mute syllables after a vowel at the end of words (pluie, rue, etc.) on the understanding that they are treated as mute, as such syllables have always been treated within words – Valery Larbaud's line:

> On glissait à travers des prairies où des bergers
> ('Ode')

undoubtedly contains thirteen syllables. And we can refer ourselves to those principles of pronunciation which we outlined in Chapter 1, where the *e atone* is 'naturally' sounded, in liaison, between identical consonants, after two or more preceding consonants, or where its disappearance would bring three consonants together (exactement). And we can seek the help of stylistic considerations, of the kind that Mazaleyrat appeals to in his analysis of 'Les Colchiques', or that we have used in our reading of Laforgue. We can also propose that the more conversational, or prosaic, or flat, the informing tone of the poem, the more ready we should be to practise apocope and syncope. But even with these aids, there will still be plenty of cases of reasonable doubt, where intuition is likely to be the only resource. Henri Meschonnic (1974) draws the following conclusion about the loss of syllabic specificity in free verse: 'Le passage à une prosodie proche de celle du langage véhiculaire, sinon à celle-là même . . . réduit le principe syllabique. On ne sait plus ce qu'il faut compter exactement. Ainsi s'accroîtrait le caractère accentuel du langage versifié, avec modification de la notion d'intervalle entre les accents' (p. 18).

In view of all we have said about the *e atone*, we need not delay long over the problem of synaeresis and diaeresis (should contiguous vowels be read as one or two syllables?), because it is so similar. In regular verse, any doubts can be resolved, as we have pointed out, simply by counting backwards from the known quantity, the number of syllables in the line or hemistich. But this expedient is not available in free verse, unless we are dealing with lines like those of Laforgue, set purposely close to a regular norm. We can, of course, apply the classical rules for counting double vowels as a working basis, as long as we are aware that the maintenance of traditional diaereses may itself be a stylistically positive act, a resistance to the encompassing trend of colloquial pronunciation towards synaeresis. In these lines from Pierre Reverdy's 'X':

> Loin dans le désespoir
> J'aurai le visage enfoui dans la glace
> La cœur percé des mille feux du souvenir

we may feel inclined to count 'enfoui' as two syllables, in order to realise the potential decasyllable. But if we are to invest 'enfoui' with the effort needed to bury the face, the keen desire to bury the face, in something totally resistant, something which compels the poet to look over his shoulder, because of its reflecting surface, then we must let the decasyllable go and opt for a more expressive eleven-syllable line (thus 'en-fou-i').

And the diaereses seem in order in these lines from Aragon's 'La Rose':
. . . l'éclatement

> De paupières cette conspiration fraîche
> Cette respiration de couleurs qui sera
> La rose

at least in the first line, where, with the support of sounded atonic e's, 'conspirati-on' captures the delicate unfolding of the rose, its careful concertedness, like the very gradual opening of many eyelids. But if we are to maintain the twelve-syllable outline of the first line in the second, we must either jettison the e of 'Cette' (apocope) or read 'respiration' with a final synaeresis. But can we afford to break the spell, the concentration, the absorption, the deliberateness, of parturition, the growing definition of colour? Better to maintain both the e and the diaeresis and take the consequences of a thirteen-syllable line.

Once again, as with so many verse-principles in free verse, we discover that our decisions regarding double vowels rest entirely on our convictions about the most expressive reading and in no sense follow the dictates of a body of shared conventions. In many respects, as we have already suggested, this is beneficial. There can be no such thing as a 'lazy' reading of free verse because the verse no longer obligingly makes sense of itself; if anything, free verse necessitates a firmer grasp of the essentials of verse than regular verse does, or, put another way, it repays ignorance less than regular verse which tends to implant knowledge by its very functioning. But let us not overlook at least one potential drawback, namely that verse should become intolerably, because unremittingly, expressive. Both meaning and involvement must have a *regulated* tempo, because, after all, we are *readers* of poetry, not reciters or writers. In regular verse, certain things apparently happen because conventions say they will, and this is good because we must not be constantly oppressed by the burden of justification, and because poetry must always seem to be greater than any of its time-bound practitioners, with its own laws and demands. Conventions train the mind to understand, and also, of course, act as platforms for the unconventional. If all decisions are left to the reader, if expressiveness is the only yardstick, then the poet will become a pitiful prey to all kinds of emotional and psychological usurpation, to all shades of sentiment and vulgarity. The contract between reader and writer is one of *shared* work.

(ii) *Rhymeless free verse*
    (a) *With enjambement.* *Enjambement* in regular verse
has many expressive functions to perform, but is always
prosodically explicable ('the line must end here, even though
the sense is incomplete, because it has the requisite number
of syllables and because the final syllable rhymes'); however
much positive force the poet has endowed *enjambement* with,
there will always be an adequate negative justification. In free
verse, the prosodic justification would no longer seem to hold,
and this is why we have found Kahn arguing against it, as
others do:

> Le vers libre n'étant soumis à aucune obligation
> imposant un cadre rigide et préétabli, son rythme, sa
> courbe mélodique et son contenu sensible sont en
> concordance constante et absolue avec son étendue
> et son unité.
> Il en résulte que le vers libre ignore l'enjambement
> (L.-P. Thomas, 1943, p. 75).

But arguments like this overlook not only the continuing
stylistic usefulness of *enjambement*, but also the psychological benefits it provides for the free-verse poet. By retaining
enjambement, the free-verse poet both safeguards his own
right of summary decision and promotes the line as a self-
imposing entity, an entity whose ungainsayable existence
depends on an element of the arbitary, here not the evident
arbitrariness of syllable-number, but of a perhaps hidden
principle whose only visible manifestation is the arbitrary
treatment of syntax. The richness of so much regular verse
derives from the fact that both the poet and the reader have
to make sense of, and vindicate, the dictates of inexplicable
conventions; the use of *enjambement* in free verse is a restoration to the line of this inexplicability and thus of its independence. It is no wonder, therefore, that those free-verse
theorists, Kahn among them, who felt threatened by the
line, who felt that the liberation of verse depended on the
destruction of the line, should attack *enjambement*.
    Enjambement, in free verse, can have a structural function

that it does not enjoy in regular verse, where rhyme and
rhythm are accepted as the unquestioned structural principles; in rhymeless free verse, it can point up the organisation of the whole poem. In Valery Larbaud's 'Ode', for
example, *enjambement* is an integral part of the poem's bipar-
tite arrangement and a natural concomitant of the mood of
the poem's last two stanzas.

The first two stanzas are each addressed to a European
express (the Orient Express and the Nord-Express) separately, so that the poem opens with a singular plea ('Prête-
moi'). These stanzas collect physical data and deal in lines
which are predominantly endstopped, or if not endstopped,
composed of complete grammatical units. The last two
(third and fourth) stanzas are addressed to two expresses
(the Orient Express again and the Sud-Brenner-Bahn) col-
lectively, and thus open with a plural plea:

> Prêtez-moi, ô Orient-Express, Sud-Brenner-Bahn,
>   prêtez-moi
> Vos miraculeux bruits sourds et
> Vos vibrantes voix de chanterelle;
> Prêtez-moi la respiration légère et facile
> Des locomotives hautes et minces, aux mouve-
>   ments
> Si aisés, les locomotives des rapides.

The plea has intensified (the *threefold* occurrence of the
imperative) and at the same time generalised itself, demanding a much vaguer experience of music and movement,
rather than particular sensations associated with particular
places (as in the first and second stanzas). And *enjambement*
has become a permanent feature of the verse, as the poet
identifies himself, or his hopes, with the trains' constant
forward motion rather than with the scenes in their corridors or through their windows. And it is the *enjambement*
which organises the wealth of these hopes by syncopating
the rhythm of the syntax and thus re-deploying emphasis:

> Ah! il faut que ces bruits et ce mouvement
> Entrent dans mes poèmes et disent

> Pour moi ma vie indicible, ma vie
> D'enfant . . .

In the first two lines here, the rising, line-terminal accent shifts from the subject ('ces bruits et ce mouvement') to the verb ('disent'), and it does this via the intonationally falling, less accentuated, line-initial 'Éntrent'. The different rhythmic and intonational definition of the verbs produces an effect of syncopation which, coupled with the syncopation of nouns in the following line ('ma vie indicible, ma vie'), where the accent shifts from the adjective 'indicible' to the repeated noun, now line-terminal, creates a sense of dynamic growth that matches well the poet's absorption of the trains' ease and gathering momentum. It is noticeable how, in our quotation, 'vie', in disengaging itself from the weight of the descriptive 'indicible', is able to *express* its own ineffability by its suspension as a *contre-rejet*, by its accentual, and corresponding spiritual, fullness; and the line-ending it forms becomes the object of the previous line-ending 'disent', itself no longer frustrated by the paradox 'disent/. . . ma vie indicible'. Lines are used to energise words and to launch them, by *enjambement*, into utter potency.

And just to underline the structural coherence of these enjambing lines, we should notice the following: *enjambement* is established from the very first line of the third stanza and is then sustained, with odd interruptions, until, in the final stanza, it seems to be a verse-principle occurring in every line. It is established in the first line of the third stanza in a pattern which reappears twice, as we have seen, in the fourth stanza, that is, the pattern in which a word or part of speech is used in an initial and/or medial position in the line and then is repeated as part of an *enjambement* at the line-ending. And the enjambing 'aux mouvements' of the third stanza is answered by the enjambing 'ce mouvement', singular and synthesising, in the final stanza.

Enjambement used exceptionally, particularly in lines as long and as prose-related as Claudel's *versets*, has more dramatic functions, is a bringing into question of the governing endstopped form by sudden outbursts of anarchy, impetuosity, enthusiasm.

One of the most frequent types of *enjambement* used by Claudel in his *Cinq Grandes Odes* (1910) is that singled out by Leo Spitzer (1962) in his analysis of 'La Muse qui est la Grâce', namely the *enjambement* which embodies a reverential pause before some kind of revelation or regeneration; it is usually accompanied by *rejets* that are verbs of rejuvenation, coming, creation, and captures some of the rapt anticipation of the prayerful voice:

> . . . et qui pour le bien copier étalant devant lui
> l'Évangile à la première page
>   Recommence l'initiale d'or sur le diplôme de
> pourpre.
>
> ('La Maison fermée')
>
>   Comme sur un rouleau d'impression on voit par
> couches successives
>   Apparaître les parties éparses du dessin qui n'existe
> pas encore.
>
> ('La Muse qui est la Grâce')

In instances like these, the poet pauses to concentrate his energies, to will the happening to happen, so that the pause between the enjambing lines is a curious compound of awe expressed and faith exercised.

But this is not the only type. In 'L'Eau et l'Esprit', the four instances of *enjambement* involving 'l'eau' – e.g.:

> L'eau
> Toujours s'en vient retrouver l'eau,
> Composant une goutte unique

and

> . . . L'eau
> Odore l'eau, et moi je suis plus qu'elle-même
> liquide

– have a thematic-structural function, and an imitative one

also. The enjambing *contre-rejet* 'eau' is set against a 'stop-ped' (by *coupe*, caesura or line-ending) 'eau' in the following line; the water unconstrained seeks to combine itself with other, circumscribed water, the water above the firmament. So water is presented both as the impulse and the objective, a thrust towards infinity that finds fulfilment in finiteness, the drop both microcosmic and macrocosmic. Water is both the beginning and the end, that which seeks and that which resists.

Enjambement in Claudel's odes, then, presents two con-verse patterns: on the one hand, the transcendence of limita-tion by a *rejet* of genesis or dynamism, and on the other, the threat of, or desire for, expansion and limitlessness, over-come by the curbing, defining quality of the *rejet*. Nowhere do we see more clearly that these are two sides of the same coin than in 'La Maison fermée', where Claudel is anxious both to give his word power and versatility, and to make it a disseminator of God's 'mesure'; so we find 'parole' in the two enjambing positions, *rejet* and *contre-rejet*, in close prox-imity; as a *rejet* its irradiating power is increased by its capital letter:

> Faites que je sois entre les hommes comme une
> personne sans visage et ma
> Parole sur eux sans aucun son comme un semeur de
> silence, . . .

and as a *contre-rejet*, it is harnessed to a specific purpose by the following verb:

> Faites que je sois comme un semeur de solitude et
> que celui qui entend ma parole
> Rentre chez lui inquiet et lourd.

(b) *Endstopped*. The *verset* is that form of free verse which one could most logically expect to be consistently endstop-ped. But if we look into the work of Claudel, or Saint-John Perse, we shall find plenty of examples of intermittent *enjambement*. In fact, instances of completely endstopped

poems are difficult to come by, and those that do exist more
often than not have some traceable debt to the father of
endstopped free verse, Walt Whitman. The seven free-verse
poems in Maurice Maeterlinck's *Serres chaudes* (1889) are
consistently endstopped and Whitman's influence on his
work is well documented (see, for example, W. D. Halls,
1955, and P. Mansell Jones, 1951). In looking at these
poems, I do not wish so much to investigate the nature of
endstopped verse, as to show in what way terminal punctuation can itself become a resource for the free-verse poet.

   The punctuation at the end of Whitman's lines, whether it
be semi-colons or post-1881 commas, is invariably of the
same kind: it creates pause, but does not exert pressure on
us, is not an expressive code. Maeterlinck's end-of-line
punctuation, on the other hand, is varied and does not
articulate the lines syntactically as much as expressively. In
'Cloche à plongeur', for example, we meet the following
sets of lines:

> Essuyez vos désirs affaiblis de sueurs;
> Allez d'abord à ceux qui vont s'évanouir:
> Ils ont l'air de célébrer une fête nuptiale dans une
>   cave;

and

> Allez ensuite à ceux qui vont mourir.
> Ils arrivent comme des vierges qui ont fait une
>   longue promenade au soleil, un jour de jeûne;

One might expect the punctuation at the end of the two
'Allez' lines to be the same, since the syntax seems to be the
same. But this is not so. How do we account for the difference? Largely, I suppose, in terms of the ideas associated
with the punctuation-marks. In answer to the temporary
indisposition of 's'évanouir', Maeterlinck supplies a punctuation of survival, the punctuation that leads into explanation or exemplification without severing the thread of the
sentence. 'Mourir' demands a more definitive break; in the
specification which follows, the desires already have a separate, spectral existence.

Equally, even though Maeterlinck's exclamation-marks
often mean exclamation, particularly when they support
the explicit urgency of the imperative, they also often create
an implicit and special urgency for individual images, show
us that there is something hyperbolic in an idea, or account
punctuationally for an elliptical syntax. And so paramount
is this expressive punctuation that it often usurps the place
of grammatical punctuation, though not at the expense of
endstopping:

> Hôpital! Hôpital au bord du canal!
> Hôpital au mois de Juillet!
> On y fait du feu dans la salle!
> Tandis que les transatlantiques sifflent sur le canal!
>
> ('Hôpital')

Here the exclamation-mark at the end of the third line
interferes with the syntactic continuity of lines three and
four ('Inside . . . , while outside . . .'); one would normally
expect a comma. But there is a good reason for this; line
three is more potent a contrast with line two ('Even though
it is high summer outside, there is a fire inside') than with
line four; it belongs syntactically to line four perhaps, but
logically and emotively, its real function is to stand in relief
to line two. This view is supported by the self-sufficiency of
the fourth line, which is extraordinary, not as a contrast to
the third line, but in itself, in its juxtaposition of the ocean-
going steamers and the homely, stagnant canal. In these
four lines, one feels something of the range of the
exclamation-mark; in the first line it accompanies the
exclamation of invocation, in the second it conveys the
intensity of the heat and continues the invocation, in the
third it conveys the starkness of contrast and contradiction,
in the fourth the haunting uncanniness of an incongruous
image.

We find, therefore, in Maeterlinck, a variety of punctuation-
marks within the poem, and a variety in the use of individual
punctuation-marks, that we do not find in Whitman.
While Whitman uses his punctuation to comprehend and

make accessible, to safeguard by separation, the multiple splendours of a public world, every American's America, Maeterlinck's punctuation sets up a complex code of innuendo and thus of privacy. We find, too, that the light which plays on Maeterlinck's images has not the evenness of Whitman's light, that his mode of seeing explores the whole gamut between pure fancy and irrefutable vision, where Whitman's changes little; against Whitman's staple and uncomplicated 'I see', interspersed for modal variation, with the odd 'watch', 'behold' or 'examine', Maeterlinck switches, without warning, through a whole scale: 'on dirait', 'on a l'idée', 'on entrevoit', 'j'entrevois', 'je vois', 'il y a'.

Because both *enjambement* and endstopping are no longer, as in regular verse, devices affecting or modifying *more fundamental*, informing conventions, like the line or rhyme, they can establish *themselves* as conventions and become standard prosodic resources of free verse. It is obvious that to make a distinction between enjambed free verse and endstopped free verse is to make a meaningful distinction between different kinds – even though the two may coexist in the same poem. One would not think to make this distinction, or at least to make it as a *necessary* preamble to critical investigation, with regular verse; in regular verse, *enjambement* and endstopping are much more likely to be associated with a poem's general quality, *enjambement* being connected with technical sophistication, exhibitionism, or even decadence, while endstopping is regarded as primitivistic.

But this need to differentiate carefully between endstopping and *enjambement* has been made irrelevant in much free verse by the complete omission of punctuation. In unpunctuated verse, because we know that we shall only discover whether a line is endstopped or not retrospectively, by reading on, the line-ending itself ceases to be a place where we expend nervous energy, where we set up complex patterns of anticipation. In this kind of verse, *enjambement* and endstopping come into existence too late to matter:

Au cri poussé au dehors je sortis
Pour voir
Une femme se noyait
Une femme inconnue
Je lui tendis la main
Je la sauvai

(Reverdy, 'Allégresse')

The world puts itself together as best it can. The poet, it seems, knows no more than we do how things order, or did order, themselves, how events strung themselves together. Is 'sortis' sufficient action? Will 'voir' be transitive or intransitive? We can demonstrate uncertainty, but our interest in resolving it is academic, rather than being a kind of involvement. We, as readers, become the playthings of a poetry that looks to elude us, that settles us back into a receptive apathy. The line-endings are where we traditionally meet the poet, where he reveals a structure to us, gives us help by means of a convention and engages a special degree of attention. But here the line-ending is a shrug of the shoulders, a continual re-entry into a neutral zone from which almost anything may come forth; the line-ending is no proper preparation for the following line. It as though the poem were a series of afterthoughts, making the world strange precisely by putting things together without apparent intention.

The absence of punctuation may serve the interests of simultaneism, mystification, linguistic or imaginative anarchy, but most essentially it is a rejection of punctuation, with its assumptions about chronometric time and about the way to organise what is basically an unpredictable and never fully recoverable existence.

(iii) *Rhymed free verse*
    (a) *Rhyme.* Common to all *verslibristes*, to a greater or lesser degree, is a concern to reduce privilege in verse-structure and thus to even out the verse-surface, to make the potential effectiveness of all devices more equal. Inevitably

rhyme came in for some stern treatment. Kahn (1897) wished to mask the line-ending, not only by developing internal music (alliteration and assonance, internal rhyme) and by treating the internal *e atone* like the terminal one (feminine ending), but also by diminishing the degree of rhyme's homophony, by increasing the incidence of half-rhyme. His plan is for an unintentional-looking, 'natural' rhyme which is neither necessary to the overall structure nor the *culmination* of the line. He does not ask for the abandonment of rhyme, but does object that it can be too easily foreseen: 'D'ailleurs nous ne proscrivons pas la rime; nous la libérons, nous la réduisons parfois et volontiers à l'assonance; nous évitons le coup de cymbale à la fin du vers, trop prévu' (p. 33).

In his 'Reflections on Vers Libre' (1917), T. S. Eliot's comments on rhyme emerge from different assumptions – rhyme in English, as we have seen, has never been felt to be indispensable to verse's existence, but has seemed more like a grace-note – but move towards the same end as Kahn's. Eliot stands up for rhymeless verse, largely because rhyme's difficulty excuses too many sins. Rhyme, for Eliot, is the way that bad prose seeks to hide its badness by demanding to be tried in the ecclesiastical courts of poetry. But where he does allow rhyme, he has a much more positive and precise set of roles in mind. Eliot, like so many others, sees free verse as a shifting web of local effects, as adopting formal strenuousness only when it is appropriate to a particular purpose; the emphasis is on rhyme as a structuring, rather than structural, force: 'There are often passages in an unrhymed poem where rhyme is wanted for some special effect, for a sudden tightening-up, for a cumulative insistence, or for an abrupt change of mood' (p. 189). Eliot seems to conceive of an unrhymed verse in which rhyme is not regular enough to be an excuse, but comes into its own as a sparingly used dramatic asset.

Before examining some of the characteristics of rhyme in free verse, we need to remind ourselves of two things. First, although many free-verse poems are completely rhymed, we must mean by 'rhymed free verse', to be fair, free verse in which rhyme is a principal protagonist, but from which blank lines or half-rhymes are by no means excluded. 'Rhymed', in connection with free verse, must have relative, rather than absolute, value.

Secondly, we must remember that rhyme carries over into free verse some of its regular-verse functions. For example, rhyme is one of the prosodic ways that the poet can govern the intensity of accent and measure its variability; the accent on a rhyme tends to be stronger than accents at the end of unrhymed lines and within lines, and the poet can organise patterns of accent-intensity using the rhyme-accent as the *known* top of the scale. Rhyme is also the poet's way of re-absorbing us in what we have just read; rhyme entangles us in the poem, does not allow us to pass through it, and makes the reading of a poem a process of cumulative synthesis. And the pause connected with rhyme is idiosyncratic; it is compounded of many factors, constantly changing, but it is always a prosodic pause, a pause of *creative articulation* as well as a pause of definition, a pause of reaction (fulfilment, surprise, memory, relation) as well as a pause of anticipation and projection (which the pause of rhymeless *enjambement only* is). Finally, rhyme will always testify to a degree of self-awareness in the poet, which the *verslibriste*, toying with off-handness, rhetoric, sentimentality, needs in order to save himself from his own impulses; that rhyme itself, the instrument of self-awareness, may also be the target of that self-awareness is perhaps evidence of a common free-verse perversity: free verse feels it has to be seen to discredit devices upon which it, in fact, leans so heavily, and it often seeks to convince us that it is chasing regular verse's tail when it is really chasing its own.

In the following explorations, I would like to draw on English examples as well as French ones, as a way of coming back to the suggestion, if not demonstration, that the prosodic concerns of the two languages have become closely allied in free verse, that free verse is, in fact, an international prosody, or set of prosodies.

Often free verse is able to imply that rhymes are casual
extrapolations from ordinary speech, a *chance* emergence of
homophony which the variability of line-length alone
makes into rhyme. One feels that this is so, particularly
where rhymes are connected with *enjambement* in markedly
heterosyllabic free verse, as in Amy Lowell's 'Patterns'·

> And I sink in the shade
> Of a lime tree. For my passion
> Wars against the stiff brocade.
> The daffodils and squills
> Flutter in the breeze
> As they please.

In such instances, rhyme itself is the destroyer of privilege,
because free verse is able to suggest that all words are
rhymeable. With regular verse, it is natural, given the existence of rhyming dictionaries, to think that there are words
and rhyme-words, or to think that there are words and that
there are rhyming versions of those words. Because rhyming dictionaries and traditional ways of thinking about
rhyme concentrate our minds on *combinations of words,
rhyme-pairs*, we lose our sense of the wonderfully unassuming way that words can slip into a rhyme-role. What free
verse does by irregularising rhyme-structure is to bring our
attention back to the rhyme as a function of the line and as a
momentarily special case of everyday vocabulary, rather
than as a vocabulary on its own. Rhyme is thus a favour that
prose does poetry. One of the beauties of free verse is
precisely that the free-verse line can be both prose and
poetry, rhythmically and tonally *désinvolte*, unselfcon-
scious, and yet curiously involved in a concerted venture to
produce an aesthetically satisfying whole.

But obviously the shape of the line affects the way we
react to the rhyme at the end of it, and many free-verse
poems will use both the casual and the highly selfconscious
rhyme, the rhyme of free verse and the rhyme of regular
verse. And nowhere do we find the confrontation of
different rhyme-values so dramatically presented as in

the juxtaposition of a long-line rhyme and a short-line partner.

In the twelfth of Laforgue's *Derniers Vers* poems, we find the lines:

> Et que cela suffise . . .
> Et méprise sans envie
> Tout ce qui n'est pas cette vie de Vestale
> Provinciale,
> Et marche à jamais glacée,
> Les yeux baissés.

'Provinciale' is sheer verbal opportunism; the poet snatches a passing idea before more sedate partners like 'nuptiale' or 'virginale' have chance to set themselves up. 'Provinciale' as surely yanks these small-town girls back to their small town and confronts them with their prim pretensions, as 'Vestale' had connived at those pretensions and whisked the young girls into a realm of universal sanctity. The short line has an impudent personality which is bursting to check the longer line with a bold and witty correction. It is a form of associative virtuosity and fundamentally parasitic. In other words, the partner of 'Provinciale' is both rival and springboard, opponent and aid. Does 'Vestale' expressly set 'Provinciale' up and give it point, or is it undermined by it? Rhyme is irony's weapon and also irony's butt.

What we also find here is a play between the different natures of the rhymes. In the longer line, the rhyme is the culminating point of a rhythmic structure $((3+2)+3+3)$, semantically the most important word in the line, carefully put in position; the short line is itself the rhyme, rhyming as soon as thought of, born of an extremely unstable creative process, the reflex action; it is not quite the word surprised to find itself a rhyme, that we found in Lowell, but it belongs to the same opportunistic method, in Laforgue's case an aggressive opportunism, in Lowell's more nonchalant, but creating the same sense of the word *discovering itself* to be a rhyme. We might also notice in passing how, in another respect, Laforgue has diminished the fullness of

end-rhyme, by inserting surreptitious internal rhymes
('suffise/méprise', 'envie/vie').

Rhyme in free verse is essentially part of a total gamut
ranging from rhyme itself, through forms of half-rhyme,
repetition, internal rhyme to unrhymed lines; and the whole
gamut is continually available. We are here dealing with
predominantly rhymed verse, but we should perhaps consider the effect of the intermittent, single, unrhymed line in
rhymed verse, as an instance of the variety at the poet's
disposal.

I exemplify but two of the manifold functions of the
single unrhymed line. First, it can serve to introduce the
poem's subject with more emphasis, as in Ford Madox
Ford's 'The Starling':

> Suddenly,
> With a rush of wings flew down a company,
> A multitude, throng upon throng,
> Of starlings,
> Successive orchestras of song.

Here the unavoidable identification of the birds as starlings,
emerging from general collectives, and returning to collectives, commits the poet to self-study. The starlings might
simply have gone by as a multiplicity of birds, and perhaps
this is what the poet half wanted. The identification turns
out to be fateful; the starlings come to represent all
phenomena acutely and uniquely perceived, all impinge-
ments of a world demanding to be recognised and made
sense of. Because the poet cannot absorb the starlings into
the imagistic processes of the rhyme, he must treat his
encounter as decisive in the graphing of his life.

Secondly, the unrhymed line has a way of removing all
confidence and impetus from the predominantly rhymed
poem. The two unrhymed one-line stanzas which occur
towards the end of Apollinaire's 'Zone' –

> J'ai une pitié immense pour les coutures de son
> ventre

and

> J'humilie maintenant à une pauvre fille au rire hor-
> rible ma bouche

– are perhaps the nadir of his peregrination through Paris, are like spiritual impasses in which the contradictions of pity, desire, degradation, and contempt bring knowledge to a halt. The poem goes on to end in a 'zone' of aimlessness, apathy and discontinuity. These lines are in a sense acciden-tal, since they are what remains of a rhymed and a half-rhymed distich in the poem's first draft:

> Et j'ai une pitié immense pour son ventre
> C'est pour ne pas la vexer qu'avec dégoût j'y entre
>
> Et j'humilie à une pauvre fille au rire horrible ma
> bouche
> Je baise cette sorte de plaie chevelue et rouge

(see Michel Décaudin, 1965, p. 81). Whatever the reasons for the omission of the two accompanying lines, whether to avoid the charge of obscenity, or too direct a confession, the effect is beneficial. The meaning is not lost, and the sense of pointlessness and desolation is infinitely increased. The easy motion of the explanatory 'C'est' and of the coordinating 'Et's' disappears, to leave the 'Je' as the sole and labouring motor of actions difficult to connect and impossible to explain. The consecutive time expressed by 'Et' becomes the fragmented and artificial progress in time of 'mainten-ant', artificial because it has no bearing on any other tem-poral observation; it expresses surprise and suddenness more than anything else.

In treating the unrhymed line, we are already trespassing on the area of rhyme-scheme, of larger structural considera-tions. To what we have said about the way variability of line-length can affect the nature of a rhyme-partnership, we could add all that has already emerged in Chapter 4 about the possible relationships between rhyme-words. But in rhyme's relationship to the stanza, little that we have culled

from regular verse will help us understand free-verse practice.

(b) *Rhyme and the stanza.* The initial problem facing the
prosodist in this area is a problem of stance: do we best serve
the free-verse stanza by asking whether it exists or not, or
by asking how we define it, so as to distinguish it from the
regular-verse stanza? To help us answer this question, let us
listen for a moment to Donald Davie (1972–3):

> True free verse, as I have experienced it in the act of
> writing it, seems bound up with *improvisation*, with
> 'keeping it going now that it has started'. Writing it,
> you must not be interrupted and for long stretches
> you cannot afford to take a break. For this reason I
> think of free-verse composition as musical, whereas
> metrical composition lends itself to a steadily punc-
> tuated building up, block by block, architectural:
> metred verse can go into stanzas, free verse never
> can (pp. 17–18).

Despite the cogency of this view, our approach to rhymed
groups of free-verse lines is more likely to be governed by
humble considerations of sheer intellectual and mnemonic
capacity, that is, by the size of the groups. Length alone will
determine whether we regard a group of irregularly
rhymed lines as stichic (i.e. non-stanzaic, a continuous
sequence of lines) or stanzaic. But this distinction is an
important one, because it does fundamentally affect the way
we read the rhymes. If we read the group stichically, we
shall not look for the guidance of an overall scheme, but will
invent our own, or several schemes at once, as we go along;
returning to Davie's words, we may say of this kind of
group that as the poet improvises his poem, so the reader
improvises his reading. If we read the group stanzaically,
we shall feel the order of the rhymes as an immutable
sequence, arranging the lines for our profit, and it is to the
rhyme-scheme, rather than to our own fancy, that we shall
refer for help.

When a poem is homostanzaic, the uniformity of stanza creates forward momentum and perhaps a constant tonal background; the recurrent stanza is found to be a sufficient vehicle of expression for a subject, or attitude, that changes little, and indicates that the point of interest is not the subject itself, but the way it evolves as argument or narrative. Where a poem is heterostanzaic, each different stanza is a dramatic foreground, a different assault on the subject, struggling to complement, comment on, or supersede, other stanzas; each stanza has a unique, readily identifiable personality and presents a new, but obviously partial, point of view; the meaning of such a poem lies less in the way the subject unfolds than in the multiplicity of the subject's facets and the changing patterns of light that arise from their interaction.

Davie's words put in perspective a hesitation we may feel when coming to free-stanzaic poems. They should not permit us to forget that many free-verse poems are stanzaic beyond a doubt, written in quatrains, quintets, or whatever. And this fact alone should deter us from seeking new names for the free-verse stanza. A short discussion of problems of nomenclature took place at the colloquium on modern verse at Strasbourg (1967, ed. Parent); Monique Parent's plan for re-adopting the medieval term 'laisse' is unhelpful; not only is it too much connected with assonance, but it sounds, with its archaic ring, almost ironical; Henri Morier's desire to coin the term 'grappe' is equally indefensible; in the field of historically unsupported metaphor, one appropriate metaphor is as good as another and all are without authority; Jean Stefanini's suggestion seems the only reasonable one: 'Étant donné l'histoire de la strophe, je trouve normal que l'on reprenne le terme *strophe* en le réinterprétant' (p. 191).

One of the factors which plays some part in our desire or ability to treat the group of free-verse lines as a stanza or not, besides the group's mere size, is the distance between rhymes, or rhyme-interval. Is there a maximal distance between a rhyme-word and its partner beyond which no

rhyme is perceived, though it may strictly exist? If there
are rhymes in a group of lines and yet the scheme is too
far-flung to be assimilable, surely there is no stanza?
Part Three of Ford Madox Ford's 'Antwerp' poses the
problem:

1	For the white-limbed heroes of Hellas ride by upon their horses
2	For ever through our brains.
3	The heroes of Cressy ride by upon their stallions;
4	And battalions and battalions and battalions –
5	The Old Guard, the Young Guard, the men of Minden and of Waterloo,
6	Pass, for ever staunch,
7	Stand for ever true;
8	And the small man with the large paunch,
9	And the grey coat, and the large hat, and the hands behind the back,
10	Watches them pass
11	In our minds for ever . . .
12	But that clutter of sodden corses
13	On the sodden Belgian grass –
14	That is a strange new beauty.

This is a complete section of the poem, but is not, for that
reason, inevitably stichic; Part Six of the poem has three
stanzas, so retrospectively one might think of this passage as
a coincidence of stanza and part. The rhyme-scheme works
out as follows: *axbbcdcdxexaex* (where *x*=blank line);
remarkable is the ten-line interval between the *a* rhymes
'horses/corses' (though intervals of this length are to be
found in the nineteenth-century English irregular odes of
Patmore and Thompson).

   Free verse allows the poet not only to exploit rhyme-
schemes in the traditional way, it also allows him to exploit
interval-scale in relation to the mental strata of the reader.
By widening the gap between rhymes, the poet embeds
them, makes them rhyme, at a deeper level of conscious-

ness, subliminally even; 'horses/corses' works in the no
man's land between the remembered and the forgotten, the
rhyming and the non-rhyming. Ultimately we may catch
the connection, or rather the brutal contrast, between the
individualised, immaculate 'white-limbed heroes', proudly
mounted, and the anonymous mass of bodies almost indistinguishable from the rain-soaked soil on which they lie.
Perhaps, even, the rhyme, deep in our minds, expresses a
subconscious desire that the 'corses' should be trampled
underfoot, suppressed, by the horses, because we cannot
bear to admit the indiscriminateness of death or the death of
heroism. Conversely, the couplet 'stallions/battalions' happens at the front of the mind, as the power of recall momentarily oustrips the inner eye's ability to identify what is
recalled.

And with rhyme as it were on the point of evaporation,
the blank lines have a corresponding tendency to push, in
the reader's mind at least, in the other direction, towards
rhyme, so that both rhymed and unrhymed lines incline
towards a similar, ill-defined centre. It is likely, in our
example, that we shall connect the second and eleventh lines
as a distant rhyme, for though they do not homophonise,
they mean the same and contain, in a chiastic arrangement,
the same phrase 'for ever' (common also to the sixth and
seventh lines). One way of comprehending the diversity of
free verse is to assume that a prosody of variety or a variety
of prosodies inform the poem. Extensions of this attitude
might be: (i) to treat free verse as a *positive* prosody of
avoidance (of other prosodies), and (ii), as here, to treat free
verse as a prosody of fusion, or of the reduction of different
devices to non-differentiated states, so that variety is not
seen as a difference of kinds, but as difference on a scale of
similarities.

So far, the problem has been presented as one of alternatives – improvised or architectural, free-stichic or free-
stanzaic? But it is possible to have your cake and eat it, by
resorting to overflowing rhyme, that is, where a rhyme-
pair straddles two stanzas, so that the poetic fabric seems at

once seamed and seamless. This is a device to be found already in liberated regular verse irregularly rhymed, in the alexandrines of Georges Rodenbach's 'Le Voyage dans les yeux XVIII' (*Les Vies encloses*, 1896) for example. But the device is more at home in fully-fledged free verse, with its ever-changing momentum, its constant doubts about its own nature.

In Émile Verhaerenn' 'Une Statue' (*Les Villes tentaculaires*, 1895), we meet the lines:

> Il est volant comme une flamme,
> Ici, plus loin, au bout du monde,
> Qui le redoute et qui l'acclame.

> Il entraîne, pour qu'en son rêve ils se confondent,
> Dieu, son peuple, ses soldats ivres;
> Les astres même semblent suivre,
> Si bien que ceux
> Qui se liguent pour le maudire
> Restent béants: et son vertige emplit leurs yeux.

This is in fact a soldier's statue; there are three other statue poems in this collection. Overflowing rhyme lessens the stanzaic division without destroying it. The rhyme-word, in an overflowing rhyme, does not belong entirely either to its stanza or its rhyme-partner; put positively, it is bound to one stanza by its sense and to another by its sound. The rhyme ensures that the first stanza is 'kept in play' while the second is being read, so that the movement of the poem is accretive, that is to say, both progressive and simultaneous, simultaneous as dramatic interplay of stanzas, progressive as continuing improvisation. And once again rhyme slips away into a no man's land of perplexity. In which stanza does the rhyme rhyme? Or does it rhyme in neither stanza, but somewhere between or beyond the two? Or do these words rhyme at all? Do we hear them as blank lines in each stanza? When we say that free verse is a prosody of fusion, we also mean a prosody of uncertainty, an organisation of uncertainty into a wealth of very specific questions about very subtle differences.

(c) *Half-rhyme*. We must put from our minds any idea that assonance and consonance are easy ways out. Duhamel and Vildrac (1910) tell us, quite rightly, that: 'Le choix d'une assonance est plus difficile que celui d'une rime' (p. 47). It is obviously not as difficult to create a *rime pauvre* (bonté/attaché; say/pay) as it is to find words with homophonous vowels and dissonant flanking consonants (marche/regarde; have/sad); one must desire to rhyme and will oneself to antirhyme both at the same time. Full consonance, with dissimilar vowels and similar flanking consonants (vache/revêche; mad/mud), is even more demanding, and one can see that half-rhyme is a complicated enough concept to admit of different degrees of rhyming, just as full-rhyme does. Those analysts who have taken the classification of different kinds of assonance and consonance (*accords*) the furthest are Romains and Chennevière (1923) and, following in their footsteps, Jean Hytier (1923); Romains and Chennevière, for example, identify phenomena such as the 'accord renversé' (riche/chère, cor/varech) and the 'accord renversé imparfait' (sac/col, autre/troupe); and Hytier goes further still, cataloguing those *dissonances* which correspond to the *accords*, thus for instance, a 'dissonance double vocalique et consonantique' (César/moloch). It is not my intention, in this section, to explore these further reaches, first, because they belong to a 'new' verse which is essentially regular, 'le vers classique-moderne' (term coined by Hytier) – Romains and Chennevière have nothing good to say of free verse – and, secondly, because the phenomena classified take one, in my view, beyond the bounds of aural perceptibility; classification alone will not make types of highly subtle *accord* and *dissonance* audible realities, will not mean that the reader feels any *necessary* relationship between the words involved. Instead, I shall keep to the broad highway of assonance, as it appears in two examples from the work of Henri de Régnier.

First, the opening stanza of 'Odelette I':

Un petit roseau m'a suffi	5+3
Pour faire frémir l'herbe haute	5+3
Et tout le pré	4
Et les doux saules	4
Et le ruisseau qui chante aussi;	4+4
Un petit roseau m'a suffi	5+3
A faire chanter la forêt.	5+3

Here, the disconsonance of t and l in the half-rhyme 'haute/saules' embodies actual physical distance, as the poet wanders further afield and as natural objects lose their focus as the poet's enquiring eye takes in broader panoramas; the hard outline of t softens to l. The half-rhyme also backs up, or is backed up by, a conflict of *impair* and *pair* measures; the even sweep of the tetrasyllabic measures offers an altogether smoother and less complicated vision than the edgy and alert trisyllables and pentasyllables. All in all, the disconsonance that exists between 'haute' and 'saules' helps to prevent the reader from slipping into any lazy unification of vision; it introduces obstacles to ensure that the separate parts of the environment cannot be reduced to a common, one-plane order. Half-rhyme, by its disconsonance, encodes the recalcitrance of reality.

But equally, the disconsonance can suggest a process of attrition, an attrition of the assonant vowel, which remains the same, but in so many guises that it cannot really be trusted. In Régnier's 'Odelette IV' ('Si j'ai parlé'), in which a lover laments his lost love, half-rhyme may seem to be the measure of his self-delusion. The poet speaks to the echo of his love – the sounds of nature – and seeks the loved one's shadow, and these things are insubstantial not only because they are vestiges of the past, but because they are vestiges in the process of losing coherence and identity. In the first stanza, for example:

Si j'ai parlé
De mon amour, c'est à l'eau lente

Qui m'écoute quand je me penche
Sur elle; si j'ai parlé
De mon amour, c'est au vent
Qui rit et chuchote entre les branches;
Si j'ai parlé de mon amour, c'est à l'oiseau
Qui passe et chante
Avec le vent;
Si j'ai parlé,
C'est à l'écho

the natural phenomena that echo his love have something
elusive about them, seem to differ in their opinion of what it
is ('lente – penche – vent – branches – chante – vent') (the
half-rhymes in the second stanza are 'douce – bouche –
fraîche – cherche'); it refuses to be the absolute that the poet
perhaps wishes it to be. The half-rhymes taunt the poet, as
do the present tenses that govern the natural phenomena –
when the poet speaks directly of the loved one's graces in
the second stanza, he must use the peremptory and irremed-
iable past historic. The rhymes offer him views that have
something in common, and yet contain something discordant.

The poet's love loses its recognisability, not simply
because he is treating himself to an illusion, but because his
memory of the relationship is weakening. Half-rhyme
shows us that the images he attempts to reproduce, or hang
on to, are fading from his mind and losing their clarity.
Actually the assonant group of this first stanza presents
three perfectly acceptable rhyming pairs – 'lente/chante';
'penche/branches'; 'vent/vent'; the poet might be forgiven
for thinking that he had, after all, recaptured the sights and
sounds of love in all their pristine and unambiguous sharp-
ness. But this is an assonant group rather than three pairs of
rhymes, and not only because of the indications given by
other 'Odelettes' in this series, or by the second stanza of
this particular one. We cannot disregard one of the special
resources of free verse: its ability to use its variable rhythms
and line-lengths to distribute line-endings and to counter

more traditional ways of grouping lines; 'lente' and 'penche' are both parts of octosyllables, though their disconsonance is acknowledged in the dissimilarity of constituent measures (l.2: 4+4, l.3: 3+5), 'vent' and 'branches' both belong to *impair* lines (l.5: 4+3, l.6: 2+3+4), 'chante' and 'vent' are both parts of tetrasyllables. To safeguard itself, to disengage itself from rhymes which nevertheless in some sense exist, half-rhyme organises the rhythmical make-up of the stanza, uses a kind of regularity, namely parallelism, to establish its own irregularities. But at any rate, the possibility of rhyme has been allowed. The poet has been able to clutch at straws, to believe in the power of memory, before seeing that the rhyme-words are in fact a design of subtle indeterminacy.

Half-rhyme is appropriate to free verse precisely because it is an imperfect echo, an imperfect memory, existing on the very borderline between consciousness and unconsciousness. Few *verslibristes* would object to the notion that free verse deals with the psychic or instinctive self. We cannot explain, or relive, the imperfect memory, as we can the perfect memory or perfect rhyme; it is something which clicks in our mind, but obstinately refuses to surface, leaving us in a state of vague disquiet. We need hardly be conscious of a half-rhyme to be dogged by it. Like so many free-verse techniques, prosodic and acoustic, half-rhyme will strike us with an odd familiarity, as something pre-poetic and not fully and complacently articulated.

In regular verse, half-rhyme is a rival of rhyme and is considered in the perspective of rhyme, creating schemes like rhyme and so on. Half-rhyme fully gains its autonomy only in free verse, because rhyme is no longer the only point of reference; blank verse is as well. In free verse, half-rhyme represents as much the discovery of muted echoes in unrhymed lines as a fall from the grace of homophony. Half-rhyme holds the very fabric of free verse in its hands, because it exists at the very crossroads of euphony and cacophony, order and anarchy.

(d) *Terminal repetition*. Terminal repetition may challenge
us to make homonyms or puns of the words involved, and
thus encourage us to see them as the richest kind of rhyme.
Or we may think of repetition as an alternative to rhyme,
never embarrassing the poet or reader with overused combinations. Or we may think of it as a failed rhyme, or as a
prose rhyme, or as no rhyme at all. Repetition, like half-
rhyme, is extremely adaptable, finding its place almost
anywhere on the line between the perfectly rhymed and the
merely repeated; like half-rhyme, too, repetition is a useful
mediator between different free-verse prosodies within the
same poem.

   Terminal repetition may be a sign of imaginative lethargy,
or of laboured attitude. It may, however, be a courageous
obstinacy; we may admire a poet's ability to repeat himself against the odds. This is something of what we feel
in Richard Aldington's 'People'; the second stanza runs:

> You beat against me,
> Immense waves, filthy with refuse.
> I am the last upright of a smashed breakwater,
> But you shall not crush me
> Though you bury me in foaming slime
> And hiss your hatred about me.

Aldington hangs on grimly to 'me'. 'Me' is simply presented, imitatively, as 'the last upright of a smashed
breakwater', which is the line, and Aldington's intention
seems to be to maintain himself in the vulnerable final
position until he has the strength to turn the tables, to
reverse the order of 'you' and 'me' (or 'I'), which he has in
the final stanza:

> Yet I pierce through you

If 'me' is to retain its force as a last limit, it cannot rhyme
with anything other than itself. 'Me' must present itself as
an irreducible, that is, non-diversifiable entity. It repeats
itself to gain confidence, a task made more difficult by the

fact that that the free-verse line can subject it to pressures of varying intensity and duration. But the strange thing here is that 'me' is a feminine ending; the stress it receives is very slight if it can be called a stress; the real stresses are on the verbs ('crush', 'bury') and the prepositions ('against', 'about') rather than on the protagonist and antagonist – though we shall incline to stress 'you' in the fourth line of this stanza, and 'me' perhaps in the fifth line, so that we can find our way back to iambic; only in the line of reversal already quoted ('Yĕt Í pĭerce thrŏugh yóu') do the pronouns move into stressed positions. Our impression of the terminal 'me', then, is of someone weakened, but resilient.

Here repetition is repetition, marking non-eradication. If we wished to relate this instance to rhyme, we would probably have to call it an antirhyme, not because of any intention *not* to rhyme or any will to flout rhyme, but because the relationship between the homophones is 'non-musical', because the combination of like is not a method of complicating like, but a process of consolidation and reduction.

To find an example of repetition where words are homonyms rather than mere homophones, we should look to a poem like Pierre Louÿs's 'Glaucé':

> Son fin buste émerge de l'eau
> Comme un nénuphar chevelu d'or rouge
> Ses yeux sont comme deux flammes sur l'eau
> Vertes étoiles ses yeux doux d'Asie
> Mais sa bouche est un coquillage de pourpre
> Et sa chevelure est sur sa bouche
> Sa chevelure cramoisie.

'Eau', which appears in a terminal position five times in the poem – once in the plural – is a word looking not for a partner, but inexhaustibly into itself. Repetition here sets itself against the rhymes and half-rhymes; it is not a question of identity discovered in diversity, but of diversity growing out of identity. This is a poem of metamorphosis; the bathing Glaucé reflects, continually, the changing aquatic setting and the water in its turn absorbs the qualities of Glaucé – the water is both the constant, and the agent and subject of transformation, always and never the same.

Rhyme is essentially an activity of the civilised mind, journeying forward and abroad, indefatigably reorganising the relational framework of experience, taking positive pleasure in the disciplines of invention. Repetition is, at one pole, an extreme form of this civilised activity, that is, where it creates homonyms and puns, which are ostensibly a poverty, but in reality a wealth, which show man triumphing over the limitedness of the linguistic materials with which he works; under the poet's magic wand, single entities re-articulate themselves by a kind of internal combustion. At the other pole, repetition is a battle with an intransigent essential, a recovery of depth in singleness and simplicity; there is here a discovery that the barest words are ultimately euphemisms for mysteries. Terminal repetition has a special point in free verse, because free verse, setting repetition now against rhyme, now against blank lines, allows it to explore its full range, to oscillate between its poles.

(iv) *Conclusion*

This account of free verse has many shortcomings; it has not investigated to the full the function of internal rhyme or internal music generally; it has not explored the great variety of half-rhyme, or of repetition (initial and medial); it has not gone very deeply into punctuationless verse; it has omitted to consider the use of a variable margin in free verse, or different kinds of typography, or calligrammatic poetry, or concrete poetry; it has concentrated on the line-ending at the expense of the line-beginning; it has drawn its examples from a fairly limited field of poets. But we have before us sufficient material not only to provide a basis for further investigations and refinements, but to allow us to draw the following firm conclusions: that free-verse prosodies are manifold – many, one feels, have still to be charted – and manifold not simply in relation to different

poems, but in relation to the single poem; that traditional
methods of scansion can still take us a long way in the
description of the poem, will still provide us with a reliable
foundation on which to build a reading, but need to be
supplemented by other approaches (traditional scansion
often finds itself powerless in the face of the *e atone* and
problems of synaeresis and diaeresis, and is not a satisfactory instrument for dealing with long lines); that no scansional approach has any necessary priority in free verse –
with many poems, the right approach may remain to be
discovered; that any factor in a free-verse poem, not just
rhythm or rhyme or syllabism, but punctuation, repetition,
enjambement, phrase-length, phrase-number, and so on,
may be the source of its prosodic structure. But the most
important conclusion of all perhaps, given that a single
free-verse poem may be governed by several different prosodies, successively or concurrently, is that such a poem
may refer to any number of national versifications, indeed
can add up to a European prosodic compound. Some linguistic differences will never be eradicated – the French
sensitivity to the *e atone*, to the syllable generally, the exploitation of adjectival position, for example; the special considerations attaching to the monosyllable and to elision, in
English – but the newly developed prosodic elements we
have just mentioned (punctuation, repetition, and so on)
and the more radical ventures in typography and lay-out are
all, it can be argued, beyond the pale of national idiosyncrasy. Even in the more traditional areas, there have been
increasing signs of exchange; English free verse, with its
interest in cadence and phrase, has moved towards French
versification; and French free verse has moved towards
English versification in that it has envisaged a line which is
an almost accidental result of the stringing together of units
smaller than itself. Free verse has a fine way of making
devices – rhyme, rhymelessness, half-rhyme, the punctu-
ated and the unpunctuated, the stichic and the stanzaic –
coextensive; and yet we approach these devices most fruit-
fully if we bring with us an acute sense of their different

histories and of the differentiations which history has
wrought between them. However cosmopolitan verse has
become, or is becoming, its cosmopolitanism will only be
meaningful if we can enjoy it as a relationship of national-
isms.

APPENDIX

Combinations of vowels
These can only be approximate guidelines, not hard and fast rules.

The following combinations of vowels are usually counted as two syllables:

(1) ia (exc. *diable, effroyable* – note: just as -ay- in *pays* is two syllables, so are -oy-, -uy-, -ey-)
(2) iai
(3) iau
(4) iant, ient
(5) ien, pronounced yɑ̃, as in *audi-ence, consci-ence*
(6) ieux (paricularly in adjectives, but usually a synaeresis in nouns, e.g. *lieu, dieu*; the adverb *mieux* is also one syllable only)
(7) ion, ions (particularly in nouns, but a synaeresis in first-person plural verb-forms, except where the ending is preceded by two consonants, the second of which is an l or an r, e.g. *oubli-ons, cri-ons*)
(8) ius (in Latin names)
(9) oé, oè, oë
(10) oué, ouer, ouet (exc. *fouet, fouetter*)
(11) oui (exc. *oui* = yes)
(12) ué, uer

The following combinations of vowels are usually counted as one syllable:

(1) ien, pronounced yɛ̃, as in *bien, tien, viens* (but may be found as a diaeresis when it is an adjectival or substantival ending, e.g. *musici-en*; but see comments on this ending

in Chapter 1; in *ancien*, ien is either two syllables or
one)

(2) iè, ié, ier (particularly in nouns and adjectives, but dissyllabic in verbs and often dissyllabic in nouns after l or r, e.g.
boucli-er; other exceptions: *pi-été, inqui-et, soci-été; hier* may
be treated as either one syllable or two)

(3) ief (exc. *gri-ef*)

(4) iel (particularly in shorter words – *ciel, miel* – but a
diaeresis in longer words, as ending, e.g. *essenti-el, offici-el*)

(5) yeux

(6) oelle

(7) oi, oin

(8) ui, uir, uis, uit (exc. *ru-ine*)

REFERENCES & BIBLIOGRAPHY

Abernathy, Robert, 'Rhymes, Non-Rhymes and Antirhymes', *To Honor Roman Jakobson: Essays on the Occasion of his Seventieth Birthday*, vol. 1, The Hague, 1967

Banville, Théodore de, *Petit Traité de poésie française*, Paris, 1872

Berthon, H. E., *Specimens of Modern French Verse*, London, 1948 (1st ed. 1899)

Blum, Marcelle, *Le Thème symbolique dans le théâtre de Racine*, 2 vols., Paris, 1962–5

Bougnoux, Daniel, 'L'Éclat du signe', *Littérature*, No. 14, May 1974

Boulmier, Joseph, *Villanelles suivies de poésies en langage du XVᵉ siècle et précédées d'une notice historique et critique sur la villanelle avec une villanelle technique*, Paris, 1878

Champigny, Robert, *Le Genre poétique: essai*, Monte-Carlo, 1963

Chatman, Seymour, *A Theory of Meter*, The Hague, 1965

Chesters, Graham, *Some Functions of Sound-Repetition in 'Les Fleurs du Mal'*, Hull, 1975

Chomsky, Noam and Halle, Morris, *The Sound Pattern of English*, New York, 1968

Davie, Donald, 'Some Notes on Rhythm in Verse', *Agenda*, vol. 10 (4)-vol. 11(1), 1972–3

Décaudin, Michel, *Le Dossier d' 'Alcools'*, Geneva, 1965

Deguy, Michel, 'Encore une lecture des *Colchiques* ou: un poème de l'apophonie', *Poétique*, vol. 5, No. 20, 1974

Dobson, Austin, 'A Note on Some Foreign Forms of Verse', in *Latter Day Lyrics*, ed. Davenport Adams, London, 1878

Dorchain, A., *L'Art des vers*, Paris, 1933 (1st ed. 1905)

Duhamel, G. and Vildrac, C., *Notes sur la technique poétique*, Paris, 1925 (1st ed. 1910)

Eliot, T. S., 'Reflections on Vers Libre' (1st pub. in *New Statesman*, 3 March 1917), *To Criticize the Critic*, London, 1965

Elwert, Theodor, *Traité de versification française des origines à nos jours*, Paris, 1965

Fothergill, Roy, 'An Early Influence on the Poetry of Gray', *Revue de Littérature Comparée*, vol. 9, No. 3, 1929

Fowler, Roger, *The Languages of Literature: Some Linguistic Contributions to Criticism*, London, 1971

Gauthier, Michel, *Système euphonique et rythmique du vers français*, Paris, 1974

Gourmont, Rémy de, *Esthétique de la langue française*, Paris, 1955 (1st ed. 1899)

Grammont, Maurice, *Petit Traité de versification française*, Paris, 1965 (1st ed. 1908)

Guiraud, Pierre, *La Versification*, Paris, 1970

Halle, Morris, and Keyser, Samuel J., *English Stress: Its Form, its Growth, and its Role in Verse*, New York, 1971

Halliday, M. A. K., *A Course in Spoken English: Intonation*, London, 1970

Halls, W. D., 'Some Aspects of the Relationship between Maeterlinck and Anglo-American Literature', *Annales de la Fondation Maeterlinck*, vol. 1, 1955

Hamer, Enid, *The Metres of English Poetry*, London, 1969 (1st ed. 1930)

Harding, D. W., *Words into Rhythm: English Speech Rhythm in Verse and Prose*, Cambridge, 1976

Hough, Graham, 'Free Verse' (The Warton Lecture of the British Academy, London, 1957), *Image and Experience: Studies in a Literary Revolution*, London, 1960

Hytier, Jean, *Les Techniques modernes du vers français*, Paris, 1923

Jones, P. Mansell, 'Whitman and the Origins of the *Vers Libre*', *The Background of Modern French Poetry: Essays and Interviews*, Cambridge, 1968 (1st ed. 1951)

Kahn, Gustave, 'Préface sur le vers libre', *Premiers poèmes*, Paris, 1897

Kastner, L. E., *A History of French Versification*, Oxford, 1903

Lang, Andrew, 'Théodore de Banville', *Essays in Little*, London, 1891

Lanz, H., *The Physical Basis of Rime*, Stanford, Calif., 1931

Leakey, F. W., *Sound and Sense in French Poetry*, London, 1975

Leishman, J. B., *Themes and Variations in Shakespeare's Sonnets*, London, 1961

Lever, J. W., *The Elizabethan Love Sonnet*, London, 1956

Lowell, Amy, *Sword Blades and Poppy Seed*, London, 1914

'The Rhythms of Free Verse', *The Dial*, 17 January 1918

Lowes, J. L., *Convention and Revolt in Poetry*, London, 1938 (1st ed. 1919)

Malandain, Pierre, 'Chimères du rythme: Myrtho', *Romantisme*, vol. 1, Nos 1 and 2, 1971

Malof, Joseph, *A Manual of English Meters*, Bloomington, Ind., 1970

Maulnier, Thierry, *Introduction à la poésie française*, Paris, 1939

Mazaleyrat, Jean, 'Problèmes de scansion du vers libre: à propos d'un poème d'Apollinaire', in *Philologische Studien für Joseph M. Piel*, Heidelberg, 1969

Éléments de métrique française, Paris, 1974

Meschonnic, Henri (ed.), *Poétique du vers français*, Paris, 1974

Morier, Henri, *Le Rythme du vers libre symboliste et ses relations avec le sens*, 3 vols., Geneva, 1943–4

Dictionnaire de poétique et de rhétorique, Paris, 1975 (1st ed. 1961)

Nist, John, 'The Word-Group Cadence: Basis of English Metrics', *Linguistics*, vol. 6, June 1964

Pakosz, Maciej, 'Some Aspects of the Role of Intonation in English Versification', *Studia Anglica Posnaniensia*, vol. 5, 1973

Parent, Monique(ed.), *Le Vers français au 20ᵉ siècle*, Paris, 1967

Pendlebury, B. J., *The Art of the Rhyme*, London, 1971

Perloff, Marjorie, *Rhyme and Meaning in the Poetry of Yeats*, The Hague, 1970

Pound, Ezra(ed.), *Poetical Works of Lionel Johnson*, London, 1915

Pound, Ezra, 'A Retrospect' (1st pub. in *Pavannes and Divisions*, New York, 1918), *Literary Essays of Ezra Pound*, ed. T. S. Eliot, London, 1963 (1st ed. 1954)

Prévost, Jean, *Baudelaire*, Paris, 1964 (1st ed. 1953)

Rees, Garnet, *Baudelaire, Camus and Sartre*, Cardiff, 1976

Romains, J. and Chennevière, G., *Petit Traité de versification*, Paris, 1923

Spitzer, Leo, 'Interpretation of an Ode by Paul Claudel', *Linguistics and Literary History: Essays in Stylistics*, New York, 1962 (1st ed. 1948)

Starobinski, Jean, *Les Mots sous les mots: les anagrammes de Ferdinand de Saussure*, Paris, 1971

Thomas, L.-P., *Le Vers moderne: ses moyens d'expression, son esthétique*, Brussels, 1943

Trager, George L. and Smith, Henry Lee, 'An Outline of English Structure', *Studies in Linguistics, Occasional Papers*, vol. 3, Norman, Oklahoma, 1951

Walzer, P.-O., *La Poésie de Valéry*, Geneva, 1966 (1st ed. 1953)

Wimsatt, W. K., 'One Relation of Rhyme to Reason: Alexander Pope' (1st pub. in *Modern Language Quarterly*, vol. 5, No. 3, 1944), *The Verbal Icon*, New York, 1954

Further Select Bibliography

Allen, Charles, 'Cadenced Free Verse', *College English*, vol. 9, No. 4, 1948

Bernard, Suzanne, *Le Poème en prose de Baudelaire jusqu'à nos jours*, Paris, 1959

Beum, Robert, 'Syllabic Verse in English', *Prairie Schooner*, vol. 31, 1957

Broome, Peter and Chesters, Graham, *The Appreciation of Modern French Poetry 1850–1950*, Cambridge, 1976

Carmody, Francis, 'La Doctrine du vers libre de Gustave Kahn (juillet 1886–décembre 1888)', *Cahiers de l'Association Internationale des Études Françaises*, vol. 21, 1969

Cohen, Helen Louise (ed.), *Lyric Forms from France: Their History and Use*, New York, 1922

Cohen, Jean, *Structure du langage poétique*, Paris, 1966

Czerny, Zygmunt, 'Le Vers Libre français et son art structural', in *Poetics*, Warsaw, 1961

Delas, Daniel and Filliolet, Jacques, *Linguistique et poétique*, Paris, 1973

Deloffre, Frédéric, *Le Vers français*, Paris, 1969

Dujardin, Édouard, *Les Premiers Poètes du vers libre*, Paris, 1922

Elwert, Theodor, 'La Vogue des vers mêlés dans la poésie du XVIIᵉ siècle', *XVIIᵉ Siècle*, No. 88, 1970

Faure, Georges and Rossi, Mario, 'Le Rythme de l'alexandrin: analyse critique et contrôle expérimental d'après *Le Vers français* de Maurice Grammont', *Travaux de Linguistique et de Littérature* (Strasbourg), vol. 6(1), 1968

Françon, Marcel, 'La Pratique et la théorie du *rondeau* et du *rondel* chez Théodore de Banville', *Modern Language Notes*, vol. 52, No. 4, 1937

Fraser, G. S., *Metre, Rhyme and Free Verse*, London, 1970

Gross, Harvey, *Sound and Form in Modern Poetry: A Study of Prosody from Thomas Hardy to Robert Lowell*, Ann Arbor, Mich., 1964

Guiraud, Pierre, *Langage et versification d'après l'oeuvre de Paul Valéry*, Paris, 1953

    'L'Esthétique du vers français', *Essais de stylistique*, Paris, 1969

Hrushovski, Benjamin, 'On Free Rhythms in Modern Poetry', in *Style in Language*, ed. T. Sebeok, New York, 1960

Jakobson, Roman, 'Closing Statement: Linguistics and Poetics', in *Style in Language*, ed. T. Sebeok, New York, 1960

Jasinski, Max, *Histoire du sonnet en France*, Douai, 1903

Jost, François, 'Le Contexte européen du sonnet', *Zagadnienia Rodzajów Literackich*, vol. 13, 1 (24), 1970

Leech, Geoffrey, *A Linguistic Guide to English Poetry*, London, 1969

Le Hir, Yves, *Esthétique et structure du vers français*, Paris, 1956

Mazaleyrat, Jean, *Pour une étude rythmique du vers français moderne: notes bibliographiques*, Paris, 1963

    'Élan verbal et rythme ternaire dans l'alexandrin', *Le Français Moderne*, vol. 40, No. 4, 1972

Morvan, Jean-Baptiste, 'Psychanalyses de la rime', *Points et Contrepoints*, vol. 999, 1971

Nowottny, Winifred, *The Language Poets Use*, London, 1962

Robinson, J. K., 'Austin Dobson and the Rondeliers', *Modern Language Quarterly*, vol. 14, No. 4, 1953

Rudmose-Brown, T. B., *Étude comparée de la versification française et de la versification anglaise: l'alexandrin et le Blank Verse*, Grenoble, 1905

Scott, David H. T., *Sonnet Theory and Practice in Nineteenth-Century France: Sonnets on the Sonnet*, Hull, 1977

Souza, Robert de, *Du rythme en français*, Paris, 1912

Wesling, Donald, 'The Prosodies of Free Verse', in *Twentieth-Century Literature in Retrospect*, ed. Reuben Brower, Cambridge, Mass., 1971

Wexler, P. J., 'On the Grammetrics of the Classical Alexandrine', *Cahiers de Lexicologie*, vol. 4, No. 1, 1964

'Distich and Sentence in Corneille and Racine', in *Essays on Style and Language: Linguistic and Critical Approaches to Literary Style*, ed. Roger Fowler, London, 1966

Wimsatt, W. K. and Beardsley, Monroe C., 'The Concept of Meter: An Exercise in Abstraction', *Publications of the Modern Language Association of America*, vol. 74, 1959

Wimsatt, W. K. (ed.), *Versification: Major Language Types*, New York, 1972

INDEX

Poems and plays are itemised separately where the remarks about them are interpretative rather than purely analytical. The distinction is not always an easy one to make.